The Anatomy of Disillusion

Northwestern University
STUDIES IN *Phenomenology &*
Existential Philosophy

W. B. Macomber

The Anatomy of Disillusion

Martin Heidegger's Notion of Truth

NORTHWESTERN UNIVERSITY PRESS

Evanston 1967

W. B. Macomber is Assistant Professor of Philosophy in the University of California at Santa Barbara.

To Karl-Josef and Siegfried Frey

Contents

Foreword

THERE ARE THREE ASPECTS of the philosophy of Martin Heidegger, which we might call *phenomenology, ontology,* and *existentialism*. Heidegger's *phenomenology* is a new way of approaching experience, a new attitude toward explanation, or the attempt to evolve a new vocabulary to express the way in which man relates to things—in particular to undercut the Kantian dichotomy of subject and object. (Later this becomes a way of approaching great works of philosophy and a key to their ontological and existential exegesis.) Out of the phenomenology there then arises a doctrine of being, Heidegger's *ontology,* and a host of recommendations for being human, his *existentialism*. This corresponds roughly to the classical division of philosophy into logic, physics, and ethics. At least the comparison allows us to distinguish a method (phenomenology) from the doctrine which issues from it, and, within the doctrine, its purely contemplative dimension (ontology) from its practical import (existentialism). But this is as far as the analogy extends, for the divisions in Heidegger's thinking are not nearly so clear-cut as they are in the classical model. We find, for example, a continual communication between his ontology and his existentialism, his view of being and his view of what a man ought to be. It would be a great mistake to believe that Heidegger first comes to understand being and then, on this basis, decides what a man ought to be; if anything, the case is the other way around. We cannot *separate* the three aspects of Heidegger's thinking—so intimately are they woven together throughout his works—but for simplicity and clarity it is essential that we distinguish them.

In the present study I am concerned primarily with Heidegger's phenomenology. When I discuss ontological and existential questions, it is from this vantage point and within this context, and only in sufficient detail to keep the argument moving. It is my conviction that insufficient attention has been paid to Heidegger's new approach to experience and that, without a clear understanding of the approach, there can be no satisfactory discussion of the ontological and existential issues which it raises. From the bulk of secondary literature on Heidegger one gets the idea that his thinking (a) consists of a number of illuminating insights, bound loosely together by a method which lays great stock on wordplays and the arrangement of German roots into great fugal patterns, (b) stands substantially outside the tradition of academic philosophy, and (c) culminates in a mysticism which expresses itself by asserting that "nothing nothings" (*das Nichts nichtet*). It is this view which I want to displace, or at least to modify.

Being concerned primarily with Heidegger's phenomenology —his approach to experience—my study is meant to be introductory. It stops short of the questions which must figure prominently in any final assessment of Heidegger as a thinker: in ontology the relation of being (*Sein*), beings (*Seiendes*), and human being (*Dasein*), the temporality of being (*Being and Time*) and the historicity of thinking, the status of logic and metaphysics; in existentialism the significance of human being as being-unto-death, the revelatory power of love, boredom, and anxiety, and the distinction between authentic and inauthentic modes of being human. If I have not come to grips with these questions, which are really the central questions of Heidegger's philosophy, this is out of the conviction—or with the justification —that we need first to be in possession of a kind of fundamental ground plan of Heidegger's thinking as a whole before we can fruitfully discuss the most significant issues which it raises. It is this ground plan, in my estimation, which is presently lacking— at least in English—and which this study attempts to provide.

I have sought to portray Heidegger as a thoroughly systematic thinker. (In particular I have taken exception to the widely held view that there is a "turning," or reversal of position, from *Being and Time* to the later works.) This is partly because, as I believe, systematic presentation is especially valuable in an introductory work of this kind, partly because Heidegger's critique of logic and his own virulently anti-Cartesian method of exposition provide ample occasion for the mistaken view that Heidegger is himself illogical or unsystematic. The danger is that, in emphasizing the systematic side of Heidegger's thinking, I have turned him into an ideology. There is an ideological dimension to his thinking, certainly, but it may appear in this study in exaggerated form. In his masterful rendering of Mark Twain, Hal Holbrook has Huckleberry Finn say of his author, "He told the *truth*. Oh, he *stressed* some things, but mostly *he told the truth*." In surveying this study I find that I have stressed a few things so doggedly that it is doubtful whether, on the Finnian hypothesis, I can possibly have told the truth about Heidegger.

Most of all I stress the broken hammer of *Being and Time,* p. 69. This image, it seems to me, plays the same decisive role in Heidegger's thinking as billiard balls play in Hume's. Boredom, death, and contradiction, for example, all organize themselves easily around the model of the broken hammer. It may offset some of the ideological exaggeration of the present study to observe that Hume only introduces his billiard balls in order to teach us the rudiments of how to use the cue. In belaboring the broken hammer, my real aim is to portray as clearly as possible how, in my view, Heidegger uses his cue.

All quotations from Heidegger (and from Kant, Hegel, and Nietzsche as well) I have translated from the German. Where English translations are available, the reader who does not read German can compare the two renderings for their differences. Heidegger's own texts in German I have included in footnotes, and this has allowed me to feel considerably free in my translations. My first requirement is that the texts be readable; it must be possible to discuss—and even render—Heidegger in reasonably idiomatic English. All of Heidegger's works, and a number of other classic works, I refer to by abbreviations, the key to which can be found at the front of the bibliography. Numbers in parentheses immediately following references to the German text indicate page numbers in English translations, where these are available. I have omitted this only in the case of *Being and Time,* the English translation of which contains marginal references to the page numbers in the original edition. In order to keep the footnotes as uncluttered as possible, I have relegated publication data to the Bibliography at the end of the book.

I am very grateful to the Ford Motor Company of Canada and to the Alexander von Humboldt Foundation in Bad Godesberg for granting me fellowships which have made the writing of this book possible. I should also like to express my appreciation to Professors David Savan, Lawrence E. Lynch, and Emil Fackenheim of the University of Toronto, Professor Christian Gellinek of Yale

University, Professor Anne C. Bolgan of the University of Western Ontario, Mr. Sidney P. H. Robinson of Toronto, Miss Ann Adden and Messrs. Paul Friedrich and Alfred Hütt of the University of Munich, and Messrs. J. M. Freiermuth and Douglas Jones of the University of California at Santa Barbara for their help and encouragement. Finally, I am indebted to Professor Zygmunt Adamczewski of the University of Waterloo, Ontario, who read the manuscript for Northwestern University Press, and whose criticisms and suggestions led to many eleventh-hour revisions of the text. Every author deserves at least one reader like Professor Adamczewski.

W. B. MACOMBER

Santa Barbara, California
January, 1967

List of Abbreviations

WORKS BY HEIDEGGER

BH	*Brief über den "Humanismus"*
EH	*Erläuterungen zu Hölderlins Dichtung*
EM	*Einführung in die Metaphysik*
FD	*Die Frage nach dem Ding*
Gel	*Gelassenheit*
HH	*Hebel—der Hausfreund*
Ho	*Holzwege*
ID	*Identität und Differenz*
KM	*Kant und das Problem der Metaphysik*
KT	*Kants These über das Sein*
N I, II	*Nietzsche I, II*
PL	*Platons Lehre von der Wahrheit*
SG	*Der Satz vom Grund*
SZ	*Sein und Zeit*
US	*Unterwegs zur Sprache*
VA	*Vorträge und Aufsätze*
WD	*Was heisst Denken?*
WG	*Vom Wesen des Grundes*
WM	*Was ist Metaphysik?*
WP	*Was ist das—die Philosophie?*
WW	*Vom Wesen der Wahrheit*
ZS	*Zur Seinsfrage*

CLASSICAL WORKS

PLATO

Rep.	*Republic*

Soph.	*Sophist*
Tim.	*Timaeus*

ARISTOTLE

Cat.	*Categories*
De an.	*De anima*
Meta.	*Metaphysics*
Nic. Eth.	*Nicomachean Ethics*
Phys.	*Physics*
Rhet.	*Rhetoric*

DESCARTES

Disc.	*Discourse on Method*
Med.	*Meditations on First Philosophy*

KANT

A, B	*Critique of Pure Reason,* 1st and 2d Editions
GMS	*Foundation of a Metaphysic of Morals*

HEGEL

PG	*Phenomenology of Spirit*

NIETZSCHE

ASZ	*Thus Spake Zarathustra*
FW	*The Joyous Science*
WzM	*The Will to Power*

The Anatomy of Disillusion

1 / The Phenomenon of Truth: Correspondence

1. The Paradox

IT IS PARADOXICAL THAT, whereas philosophy is regarded as a search for truth, few philosophers have inquired deeply into the question of what truth is. Aristotle, for example, treats the question only cursorily in Books VI and IX of the *Metaphysics*,[1] while Kant does not come to consider the nature of truth until after he has determined the structure of human understanding and the irreducible data with which it has to deal.[2] Yet Aristotle puts the matter very succinctly. "It belongs to the same sort of thinking," he says, "to show *what it is* and *that it is*."[3] It should then "belong to the same sort of thinking" to prove that something is true and to show wherein its truth consists, or what truth is.

Plato raises this problem in the *Meno*. Meno asks, "And how will you inquire, Socrates, into that which you do not know? What will you put forward as the subject of inquiry? And if you find what you want, how will you ever know that it is the thing which you did not know?"[4] How can the philosopher search for truth until he has determined what it means for something to be true? Yet Meno's demand hardly seems reasonable. Clearly the philosopher cannot provide a notion of truth at the outset of his inquiry, for truth can only manifest itself in and through particular,

1. *Meta.* 1027b17–28a5, 1051b33–52a12.
2. B 113–16. Kant's discussion of truth occurs for the first time in the Second Edition of the *Critique of Pure Reason* and is omitted in Norman Kemp Smith's abridgment in the Modern Library series.
3. *Meta.* 1025b18 (italics added).
4. *Meno* 80.

concrete *truths*. We can hardly form any notion of poetry until we have encountered a number of poems. No more can the philosopher decide what truth is prior to reaching any conclusion about what is true. We are all familiar with those professional educators who spend so much time elaborating a theory of pedagogy that they never get down to the immediate business of teaching. So Socrates, after recasting the objection in even stronger form, berates Meno for introducing a "tiresome objection" which can only lead to "intellectual indolence," and proceeds straightway to the matter at hand, leaving aside the question of what truth is until he has first established something of what is true.

The difficulty is not that philosophers often fail to consider the nature of truth at the outset of their inquiry but that they sometimes fail to consider it at all. Descartes is the best example of such omission. His little work *The Search for Truth* presents a summary recapitulation of Cartesian method, but nowhere does it raise the question, as one might expect from the title, of what truth is. On the contrary, Descartes argues here that there are certain notions like whiteness, thought, doubt, existence, and selfhood which are so simple in themselves that any investigation of what they *mean* can only lead to obfuscation and confusion.[5] Among such notions, which are to be accorded asylum from analysis, Descartes implicitly includes truth. He thus places truth beyond the pale of philosophical investigation in a work entitled *The Search for Truth*.

In refusing to make truth a subject of analysis, Descartes assumes that his working notion of it is essentially that of common sense. The criterion of its validity is the only one available to common sense: it is immediate self-evidence, what "everybody knows." We may not all agree on what is true, but we all agree on what truth is. This attitude is familiar to us from the Platonic dialogues as the one which Socrates invariably attacks. Yet we ought not to be too hard on Descartes, for there is a special difficulty implicit in the notion of truth which seems to be insuperable. In order to recognize a notion of truth as true, we have already to know what it means to be true. In seeking to elaborate such a notion, therefore, we are really involved in an infinite regress, since any notion of truth presupposes some prior notion to account for *its* truth. Hence any notion of truth which claims to be *true* cannot at the same time claim to be ultimate. This is the confusion against which Descartes warns. It explains why Kant calls the question of truth "the old and celebrated question by

5. *The Search after Truth,* ed. Haldane and Ross, I, 324–25.

which one thinks to drive the logician into a corner." [6] "By which *one thinks . . . ,*" because Kant is himself, among many other things, a logician.

Despite such objections, a doctrine of truth plays a central role in the philosophy of Martin Heidegger. The question of truth is a constant concern of Heidegger's—there is hardly a book or essay of his in which it does not arise—and we have only to compare this concern with the peripheral treatment which truth receives, at least explicitly, in Aristotle or Kant to realize how specifically Heideggerian the question is.

It is common knowledge that Heidegger is no logician. [7] Yet he recognizes the paradox entailed in any attempt to elaborate a notion of truth: he sees that, in the strict sense, the question of truth is an impossible question. In the opening paragraphs of his essay *On the Essence of Truth* (1943) he asks, "Does not the extravagance of such a question bring to light the groundlessness of all philosophy?" And he adds, "No one can fail to recognize the solid grounds on which such considerations are based. No one may overlook their crucial seriousness." [8] But he raises the question nonetheless. Our first task is to see *how* he approaches such a question and *why*. Both considerations focus upon his "phenomenological" approach to truth—at least in his sense of the term—and it is important that one understand what phenomenological inquiry is, how it proceeds, and what it claims to accomplish. In particular Heidegger conceives the aim and method of phenomenology in a very different sense from Edmund Husserl, with whom the term is most often associated.

2. The Phenomenological Approach

THERE IS ONE WAY OUT of the immediate difficulty that any notion of truth presupposes some prior notion to account for its truth. This is the recognition of a fundamental distinction between *the* truth and *a* truth, between truth itself (*veritas*) and

---

6. A 57, B 82. Quoted by Heidegger SZ 215.

7. Heidegger's early writings, however, are almost all concerned with a philosophical justification of logic. In his doctoral dissertation, *The Doctrine of the Judgment in Psychologism: A Critical-Positive Contribution to Logic* (1914), he defends the purity of logic (*die eine reine Logik*) against what he regards as the attempt by Wundt, Maier, Lipps, and Brentano to reduce logic to psychology.

8. "Bringt die Verstiegenheit solchen Fragens nicht das Bodenlose aller Philosophie an den Tag? . . . . Niemand wird sich der einleuchtenden Sicherheit dieser Bedenken entziehen. Keiner darf den drängenden Ernst dieser Bedenken leichthin missachten" (*WW* 5 [319–20]).

anything which is true (*verum*). We find no difficulty with the assertion that the essence of a tree—that which makes a tree what it is—is not itself a tree. Similarly, taking truth as the essence of anything which is true, we can maintain that truth itself is not true. Such a distinction serves as the fulcrum of Heidegger's thinking. He insists that we recognize that being (*Sein*) is not *a* being (*Seiendes*) nor any aspect of beings generally, and that we cannot explain beings simply by tracing their origin back to some other being or aspect of beings. Plato warns us not to "tell stories about being," and Heidegger quotes him in the opening paragraphs of his first major work, *Being and Time* (1926).

> The being of any being "is" not itself a being. The first step toward a philosophical understanding of the problem of being is to avoid *mython tina diēgeisthai*—"telling stories"—i.e., not to determine the origin of any being by tracing it back to another being, as though being itself could possibly be *a* being.[9]

Heidegger draws a similar distinction between truth and anything which is true. We cannot explain truth by tracing it back to some touchstone which is absolutely or indubitably true. In this sense his notion of truth does not itself purport to be true, nor to be grounded in any eternal, unshakable truth (*verum*).

There is another sense, more important to our present purpose, in which Heidegger seeks to circumvent the paradox implicit in the question of truth. At the outset of his discussion he is not concerned with devising his own notion of truth but only with examining the implications of a historical notion with which he is confronted: the notion that truth consists in the correspondence of the mind with the object of its knowledge. He calls this the "phenomenon of truth."[10] Heidegger is not willing to admit that this is what truth *is*, but he insists that this is what it has *appeared to be*. He argues that it has dominated the entire history of philosophy. This notion provides the subject matter of his phenomenological investigation. He asks what it means, what it presupposes, and how it comes about. And the question of truth in

9. "Das Sein des Seienden 'ist' nicht selbst ein Seiendes. Der erste philosophische Schritt im Verständnis des Seinsproblems besteht darin, nicht *mython tina diēgeisthai*, 'keine Geschichte erzählen,' d.h. Seiendes als Seiendes nicht durch Ruckführung auf ein anderes Seiendes in seiner Herkunft zu bestimmen, gleich als hätte Sein den Charakter eines möglichen Seienden" (SZ 6). The reference is to *Soph.* 242c. For the distinction between *Sein* and *Seiendes* see below, p. 19.

10. SZ 213–14.

this sense is a different matter from the question of truth as such.

By examining the implications of the traditional notion, however, Heidegger seeks to arrive at a comprehensive and original notion of what truth is. Although the historical phenomenon provides him with an approach to the question, the question itself remains an impossible one. Here again Heidegger appeals to history. He must find in the Western philosophical and cultural tradition the justification for posing such a question: the phenomenon of truth which dominates our tradition must be shown to lead inescapably to such a question. Heidegger speaks of the "unattainable inescapable" (*das unzugängliche Unumgängliche*).[11] The phenomenon of truth must reveal its own *logos*. This is what Heidegger understands by a *phenomenological* notion of truth.

Heidegger represents the traditional notion of truth as leading to a more original and comprehensive notion—the one which he himself advances—in two ways, which we might call *logical* and *existential*. The *logical* argument seeks to show that the traditional notion presupposes a prior notion which analysis can reveal, even though it tends to conceal its own presupposition.[12] The *existential* argument portrays the history of Western thought—and of Western life—as leading to a series of crises which eventually become so acute that we are driven to undertake such analysis, even though it entails an impossible question.[13] In this portrayal Western man is driven by his own history to confront the "unattainable" but "inescapable." These two sides of the relationship between the traditional notion of truth and the phenomenological notion reflect the most fundamental division in Heidegger's thought, or what he calls the "two parts" of his philosophy. The logical derivation forms the subject matter of the following two sections of this chapter, though its elucidation will continue to occupy us in Chapters 2 and 3. Chapter 4 sketches the broad outline of Heidegger's philosophy of history, which constitutes the existential derivation.

The "first part" of Heidegger's philosophy is to be found in *Being and Time* (1926). Here Heidegger seeks to portray the immediacy of human experience, which he claims that philosophers have traditionally falsified in their accounts. So formative is the influence of tradition, he holds, that we are scarcely aware of *what* our immediate experience is *like*. It is only with the greatest

11. VA 66.
12. SZ 223–25.
13. WW 23 (346); BH 75 (281); EM 27–38 (35–50).

difficulty that phenomenological investigation can win its way back to such immediacy.[14] The later works, beginning with *Kant and the Problem of Metaphysics* (1929), consist chiefly of studies in the history of philosophy. Here Heidegger is concerned with the reflection of man's experience in his most significant thinking, which he sees as characterized by inner conflict. The most controversial question of Heideggerian interpretation is whether these "two parts" hold together, whether Heidegger does not completely reverse his position in the later writings, abandoning the original intuition of *Being and Time* altogether.[15] The phenomena under investigation have changed, a concern for the immediate experience of the concrete individual is replaced by a cosmic concern for history, the vocabulary is altered beyond all recognition, and there are statements in the later works which contradict *Being and Time*. The young Husserlian appears to have matured into an old Hegelian. Still it is clear that the two parts of Heidegger's philosophy are meant to hang together—especially when we consider that it is the conflict in man's thinking which drives him back to an encounter with his immediate experience—and it is my contention that they do. Through all the changes of emphasis, I will maintain, Heidegger's aim and method always remain the same. I hope to show that the two parts of his philosophy are actually unthinkable *except* in conjunction.

The first part of Heidegger's philosophy is essentially original; the second owes much to Hegel, the Hegel of *The Phenomenology of Spirit*. In the *Phenomenology* Hegel does not begin with any hypothesis of his own about what is true but simply examines historical positions, which he approaches as "phenomena" genuinely expressing human experience as it appears.[16] The dialectic which Hegel employs is fundamentally the same as Plato's, only by his time, Hegel maintains, philosophical positions have become fixed and exhaust all possibilities of thought. Heidegger begins his discussion of truth in both *Being and Time* and the essay *On the Essence of Truth* by approaching the traditional notion of truth as a phenomenon, which he similarly regards as fixed.[17] For Hegel such phenomena lead necessarily to truth, but to the truth *of appearance*, the truth *of history*, which does not exclude error and

14. SZ 22, 35–37.
15. See, for example, Karl Löwith, *Heidegger, Denker in dürftiger Zeit,* pp. 20–21, 37–41. Löwith holds for a decisive break in Heidegger's thinking, and his view has found wide acceptance.
16. PG 70–71 (139–40).
17. SZ 214–17; WW 6–9 (321–26).

illusion but embraces them as moments of its own life.[18] For Heidegger, too, the phenomenon of truth, though it is illusory, leads necessarily to recognition of truth itself, but of this truth error and illusion again constitute an integral part.[19] Hegel argues that we attain to truth when all possibilities of thought are exhausted and seen in their necessary sequence and order.[20] Heidegger argues that we attain to truth *after* the possibilities of traditional thinking have been exhausted and we are brought to confront the source of our tradition in a dimension of human experience which precedes such thinking.[21] Accordingly, in Heidegger's view, the approach of truth ought to be heralded by a crisis in thinking.

In fact Heidegger holds that the status of any science can be judged by the extent to which it is capable of experiencing a crisis in its fundamental concepts.[22] In this century almost all the special sciences have undergone such a crisis, from subatomic physics to depth psychology. Heidegger's aim is to precipitate an equally fundamental crisis in philosophical speculation. For him this means "renewing the question of the sense of being," [23] which he sees as having fallen into disregard in the course of the history of philosophy, and posing the impossible question of truth. When we begin to question not only what is true but what truth is— when truth itself becomes "questionable"—the crisis has arrived. Heidegger regards speculation as a dangerous undertaking, involving the same element of risk in philosophy as on the stock market. Where his own speculation is concerned, his severest critics tend to agree. Yet Heidegger claims that he is not creating the crisis in thinking but only recognizing its existence. The crisis really begins, he argues, with *The Phenomenology of Spirit* and its "self-completing skepticism." [24] It is the product of a tradition which culminates in the philosophy of Hegel and in the scientific and technological organization of life in the twentieth century.[25] With Hegel and twentieth-century science and technology the traditional and common sense notion of truth has run its course and destroyed itself, precipitating a crisis in thinking and driving

18. *PG* 30 (94–95), 34 (98–99), 39 (105–6).
19. *WW* 21–23 (344–47).
20. *PG* 11–12 (69–70), 23–24 (85–86), 39 (105–6).
21. *WW* 19 (340–41); *Ho* 104.
22. *SZ* 9.
23. "Die Frage nach dem Sinn von Sein" (*SZ* 1, 3 [22–25]).
24. *PG* 67 (136).
25. *VA* 72–73; *EM* 34 (44–45); *Ho* 137–38; *BH* 88 (287). See below, pp. 178–84.

us to a more original confrontation of truth, even at the cost of raising an impossible question.

But this is one of the last steps of Heidegger's thinking, which, like Hegel's, circles back into its starting point.[26] It is with the first step, with his portrayal and analysis of the phenomenon of truth represented by common sense and the Western philosophical tradition, that we must begin.

3. Common Sense and Tradition

IF WE CANNOT ASK STRAIGHTWAY what truth is, we can at least ask what it has appeared to be, how the term is commonly used and understood. It is by analyzing our common-sense notion of truth that Heidegger attempts to discover its essence. In this sense his approach remains fundamentally the same as that of Plato and Hegel. Truth, he begins, evidently refers to whatever it is which makes anything true *to be* true.[27] Like any universal, we take truth to be the property or characteristic which all true things have in common.[28] The question is: what is a truth, a "true thing" (*verum*)?

We use the word "true" to describe things and people. We call a person true if we regard him as faithful, steadfast, or reliable. We speak of a "true friend" and of lovers' being "true to each other"; we swear into our juries twelve "good men and true"; we sign our letters "yours truly." This sense of the word ordinarily implies approbation, but not always. Some people can be relied on to behave badly, and when they do we think of them as "running true to form." There is a slight shift of emphasis when we say that something is "truly a pleasure" or describe a man as a "true Democrat" or a "true academic." Here "true" is synonymous with "genuine," and we call a thing true in this sense when it is what it appears to be. We do not think of a short story as being "untrue," as we do a falsified news account, because it does not purport to be factual: there is all the difference in the world between play money and counterfeit. Again the term generally conveys ap-

26. Heidegger regards circular thinking as inescapable in philosophy: the only question is how comprehensive the circle is. See SZ 78, 152–53, 314–15.

27. WW 6 (321).

28. Heidegger ultimately rejects this notion of essence. What applies equally to a class of things (*gleich gültig*) he regards as "indifferent" (*gleichgültig*), and essence cannot be indifferent in this way. See, for example, Ho 38–39 (675–76); WW 25 (350). But he nevertheless employs the notion as a hermeneutic device in introducing his discussion in the essay *On the Essence of Truth*.

proval, but not necessarily, for the Republican may be the first to recognize the marks of a "true Democrat." That there is no fundamental difference between these two senses of the word can be seen in expressions like "true love" and a "true leader." Both are steadfast and dependable, but only in this way do they succeed in being what they appear to be, or ought to be. This is why such expressions generally convey praise, but not always: because we use the word to indicate that a thing is either what it appears to be or what it ought to be. The latter case implies praise, but not the former. So there is only one fundamental sense of the word "true" as it describes things and people, because both are dependable only if they are what they appear to be and ought to be.

But this use of the word "true" applied to things and people strikes us as being merely metaphorical, much as though we were to talk of a man as being "crooked" or of a situation as "confused." A lawyer or a historian or a reporter can give us a *true* account of the facts; Newton provides an explanation of planetary motion which is *truer* than Ptolemy's; dictatorial regimes invariably suppress the *truth*. This is the strict and literal sense in which the word "true" is employed. In all its activities—in its theories, descriptions, calculations, and assessments, as well as its everyday opinions and most trivial judgments—the mind seeks to reflect the world, the facts, or whatever it confronts, and to the extent that it does so accurately we call its judgment *true*. Our thinking is true if it corresponds with reality, agrees with the facts, or portrays a situation as it really is. Truth, we want to insist, is properly in the mind, not outside it—a property of human judgments, not of human beings or of things—and its essential characteristic is *accuracy*. Strictly speaking, the true is the correct as this applies to our thinking, and it is only by a sort of metaphorical extension that we come to apply the term in our everyday speech to people and things.

Here, then, are two quite different senses in which the word "true" is used. It is used in a strict and literal sense when the mind corresponds with things as they really are, and in a metaphorical sense when a thing corresponds with our notion of what it is or ought to be. Heidegger calls these two senses the truth of judgment (*Satzwahrheit*) and the truth of things (*Sachwahrheit*).[29] In the one case the mind agrees with reality, in the other reality with the mind. In either case, though, truth consists in agreeing (*Stimmen*). The verdict of common sense is that truth is

29. WW 7 (322–23).

correspondence (*Übereinstimmung*). Heidegger, however, challenges this verdict of common sense. He denies that the one sense of the word is literal while the other is only metaphorical, that the two senses are really distinct, with no more than a formal affinity between them, and that such a notion is self-evident and can be taken for granted.

We cannot say that truth applies properly to human judgments and is extended to describe people and things only in a loose metaphorical sense, for the truth of things is more fundamental than the truth of judgment, which is derived from it as a special case. We call a man a "true friend" or a "true leader" because he measures up to our expectations of what a friend or leader ought to be. But the human mind in its judgments must also measure up to our expectations of it. We may call a judgment true in the first instance because it reflects the facts accurately, but in the final analysis this is because, by doing so, it fulfills our notion of what a judgment ought to be. A judgment which is correct and accurate is the sort of judgment we value, and we value it because it is steadfast and dependable, like a true friend. It is not difficult to see how the notion of dependability can be extended to human judgments as correctness or accuracy; it is much more difficult to see how correctness or accuracy can describe lovers, even in a loose metaphorical sense.

What appears to be only common sense, Heidegger argues, is really the product of a great historical tradition, the same tradition which has taught us to see objects in three-dimensional, rectilinear space, to regard ourselves as souls inhabiting bodies, to distinguish our inner, subjective experience from outer, objective events, and to conceive our relations to the things of the world in the same way that we conceive their relations among themselves. "What is 'natural,'" he says, "is not in the least 'natural' in the sense of being self-evident to every man, no matter who he might be or when he might live. The 'natural' is always historical." [30] It is our tradition, Heidegger suggests, which has given us the notion of common sense in the first place, and he regards the common-sense view of truth and its traditional philosophical conception as two sides of the same coin.

Heidegger sees a single notion of truth underlying the entire history of Western philosophy: the correspondence of intellect and thing, or the agreement of the mind with the object of its

---

30. "Was 'natürlich' sei, ist ganz und gar *nicht* 'natürlich,' d.h. hier: selbstverständlich für jeden beliebigen je existierenden Menschen. Das 'Natürliche' ist immer geschichtlich" (*FD* 30).

knowledge (*adaequatio intellectus et rei*).[31] The definition is medieval in origin, but in his numerous historical studies Heidegger attempts to show that Greek thinking, especially Plato, prepared the way for such a conception, and that modern thought—even in Kant, Hegel, and Nietzsche—reflects a series of covert variations on the same theme.[32] The two essential characteristics which Heidegger attributes to this notion of truth are (1) that truth is primarily in the mind and (2) that it consists in the correspondence of a judgment with its object, the judgment combining subject and predicate in the same way that a thing and its property are combined in nature.[33] So Aristotle says, "Falsity and truth are not in things . . . but in thought. . . . [T]he true judgment affirms where the subject and predicate really are combined and denies where they are separated." [34] And Kant says, "Truth and illusion are not in the object insofar as it is perceived but in the judgment of the object insofar as it is thought." [35]

The term "true" has traditionally been employed to refer primarily to the truth of judgment, but the philosophers of the Middle Ages, who gave the notion its classic formulation, recognized that the truth of judgment must be grounded in the truth of things. This could mean that man, who decides what he chooses to mean by any term, is ultimately the "measure of all things." The survey office decides what constitutes true gold, historians pass on the qualifications of a true leader. Must scientists and epistemologists determine the requirements of a true judgment? Certainly not for the medieval philosophers, who conceived the formula quite differently when they applied it to the truth of things. In the truth of judgment it is the human intellect which corresponds with the thing known. But in the truth of things it is not the finite intellect of man with which things must correspond but the infinite intellect of God their creator. For medieval thought all things are creatures, and they are true insofar as they are in harmony with the divine scheme of creation, thus realizing their creatureliness and fulfilling a divine ideal. The human intellect is also a creature and fulfills *its* ideal by corresponding with the thing which it knows. Things and the human intellect are essentially directed toward each other in the unity of the divine plan of creation, and both are true insofar as they fulfill ideals

31. *SZ* 214–15; *WW* 7 (322–23).
32. *PL* 44–46 (266–67). See also *SZ* 21–26; *EM* 143–44 (187–89).
33. *SZ* 214.
34. *Meta.* 1027b20–26.
35. B 350.

which are united in the mind of God. According to this conception, to be true is to fit into the order of creation.

By the dawn of modern thought this conception of truth has become so integral a part of the philosophical tradition that, while its theological foundation is discarded, the conception itself is not even questioned. The rationality or ultimate order of the world must simply be presupposed. Kant asks how it is possible for things and the human intellect to correspond, but he does not question that they *do* correspond and that truth consists in such correspondence. "The definition of truth as the agreement of knowledge with its object," he says, "is here granted and presupposed." [36] The notion of truth as the agreement of intellect and thing has come to be regarded as self-evident; the decisive role which a doctrine of creation played in its evolution is forgotten. "The formula for the essence of truth," Heidegger says, "thus . . . attains a universal validity which is immediately apparent to every man." [37] This, as we have seen, is just how Descartes regards it.

It is considered equally self-evident that truth has an opposite, that there is such a thing as error or falsity; but since these are located outside truth, they are looked upon as irrelevant to a consideration of the nature of truth itself. They constitute a special problem: the "problem of error." This view, too, Heidegger attacks. Like Freud he insists that we have not taken error and illusion sufficiently seriously. Truth and untruth are inseparably conjoined, in his view, and an understanding of untruth even provides the "decisive step" toward a genuine notion of truth. [38]

So deeply is this conception of truth rooted in common sense and tradition that it is only with the greatest difficulty that the question of truth can be reawakened at all. Kant wants to renew the foundations of Western thinking with his Copernican Revolution, but in the end he only argues that, while empirical knowledge must correspond with its object, such knowledge is only possible because, in a deeper sense, things correspond with the structure of the human mind. Such a doctrine does not alter the framework within which thinking occurs. Just as, from a Marxian point of view, any bourgeois revolution only transfers power within the established framework of society, leaving the structure itself untouched, so Kant's Copernican Revolution, in Heidegger's

36. B 82.
37. "So gewinnt die Formel für das Wesen der Wahrheit . . . ihre für jedermann sogleich einsichtige Gemeingültigkeit" (WW 9 [325]).
38. WW 17 (338).

view, only provides new variables for the traditional formula without in any way altering the formula itself. "Kant's basic ontological orientation, despite all the differences consequent upon a new way of putting the question, remains [essentially] Greek." [39]

This is a greatly oversimplified version of the history of the doctrine of truth, but it may at least provide the necessary background for a discussion of Heidegger's own notion.[40] What is important is that Heidegger introduces his notion with a critique of what he regards as a dominant theme of the Western philosophical tradition. His immediate aim, as we have said, is to penetrate a given notion rather than to formulate a new one. He approaches the question by asking what a doctrine of correspondence presupposes. In defining truth as the correspondence of a judgment with a thing, we assume that we know what a judgment is, what a thing is, and what it means for the two to correspond. "Do we know this?" Heidegger asks.[41]

4. Analysis of the Traditional Notion of Truth

THE DEFINITION OF TRUTH as a relation of correspondence does not tell us very much. For while correspondence necessarily implies relation, not every relation is one of correspondence. A sign is essentially related to, but does not correspond with, the thing which it signifies: the arrow saying "Exit" does not "correspond" with the revolving doors. Again, while every truth may consist in a certain correspondence, not every correspondence is an instance of truth. Two silver dollars correspond in appearance and purchasing power, but this is not what we mean by truth. We need to know what sort of relation can obtain between the human mind and a thing, or how it is possible for a judgment to "correspond with" its object. By pursuing this question Heidegger seeks to discover the origin of the traditional notion of truth and to penetrate its original meaning. This is the first sense in which he understands the question "what is truth?": how is the traditional notion of truth possible? Having put the question in this way, he can ask, "What is to preclude the propriety of this question?" [42]

In asking for the conditions of the possibility of the traditional

39. ". . . *Kants* ontologische Grundorientierung [bleibt]—bei allen Unterschieden eines neuen Fragens—die griechische" (*SZ* 26).
40. Chapter 4 takes up the matter in greater detail.
41. *WW* 9–11 (325–28). See also *SZ* 154–60 (for judgment); *Ho* 12–21 (653–62); *FD* 34–37 (for the thing).
42. "Was soll die Rechtmässigkeit dieser Frage verwehren?" (*SZ* 216).

notion of truth, Heidegger is employing terminology and following a method which remind us of Kant. Kant begins by asking how
the sciences of geometry and pure mechanics are possible: what
is the necessary presupposition of scientific knowledge? Heidegger asks how *any* correspondence between mind and thing is
possible, whether scientific or not: what does any such relation
presuppose? This is what he understands by the essence (*Wesen*)
of a thing: "the ground of the inner possibility of what is familiar
and generally thought to be known." [43]

Every relation presupposes some *totality* within which it is
possible for its two terms to relate. The relation of magistrate and
subject presupposes government; the relation of two objects in
juxtaposition presupposes space; the relation of premise and conclusion presupposes the structure of an argument or proof. What
is the totality within which the relation of a mind and a thing is
possible? A relation of correspondence further presupposes some
respect in which the two terms agree, as two silver dollars correspond *in* appearance and $16 - 6 = 10$ *in* quantity. In what respect can we say that a mind and a thing correspond? Heidegger
demands a *context* and a *focus* as conditions of the possibility of
correspondence between the mind and any thing. [44]

It is easy to see how two physical objects or two ideal representations like numbers correspond. It is much more difficult to see
how an ideal representation can correspond with a physical object. For this we must inquire into the mode of being of such
correspondence, which is neither physical nor ideal, and this carries us into the realm of ontology. But Heidegger does not leap
straightway into ontology. He first examines a hypothetical example of a true proposition to find out wherein its truth can possibly
consist.

Whatever it may be, truth is what we attempt to establish in
the process of verification. Heidegger asks what is going on when
verification takes place. Let us assume that the judgment "The
picture on the wall is crooked" is made by someone with his back
to the wall. The judgment is then verified by turning toward the
wall and perceiving the picture. What does such verification reveal about the picture, the judgment, and the relation between the
two? What does it *prove*? It does not prove a correspondence
between one picture on the wall and another in the mind. For the

43. ". . . der Grund der inneren Möglichkeit dessen, was zunächst und
im allgemeinen als bekannt zugestanden wird" (*WW* 13 [331]).
44. SZ 215–16; WW 10 (326–27).

judgment does not consist in a picture of the picture. It relates directly to the picture on the wall, and any explanation which interposes anything between it and the real picture is misleading. There is only *one* picture, both on the wall and in judgment. So verification does not prove a correspondence between two pictures. It rather establishes that the judgment has disclosed the real being as it is, permitting the picture on the wall to manifest its identity. Thus Parmenides says, "It is one and the same thing which can be thought and which can be." [45]

Heidegger insists on the immediate presence of judgment to its object. In another context he says, "In 'merely knowing' the constitution of any being, in 'simply representing' it in my imagination, in 'just thinking' about it, I am no less directly *with* the things of the outer world than when I originally experience them." [46] It is this immediate presence of the judgment to things which a notion of correspondence tends to conceal. And yet apart from such immediate presence it is difficult to see how any judgment could be verified. [47]

The judgment, Heidegger is here arguing, does not originally describe, portray, or reflect things; it *renders them accessible.* [48] The point becomes clearer when the example is not so primitive. What corresponds with what when I say that Andrew is angry, or that American foreign policy took on a new direction after World War II, or that there is no system of mathematics for which there is not at least one insoluble problem? Such judgments bring us into the immediate presence of things—genuinely and fruitfully if they are true, confusingly if they are not—and such immediate presence is then a necessary condition of their verification. But this is obscured by a notion of correspondence, with its implication of duality.

The being of the judgment is not essentially *descriptive* but *revelatory.* What verification proves is not the accuracy of description but the genuineness of revelation. Any notion of the judgment which emphasizes its descriptive character presupposes, and yet tends to conceal, its original revelatory character. So truth

45. Frag. 5 (Diels). Quoted by Heidegger *SZ* 212; *EM* 104 (136).
46. "Im 'blossen' Wissen um einen Seinszusammenhang des Seienden, im 'nur' Vorstellen seiner, im 'lediglich' daran 'denken' bin ich nicht weniger beim Seienden draussen in der Welt als bei einem *originären* Erfassen" (*SZ* 62). See also *SZ* 60–62, 136–37, 204–8; *Ho* 55 (689–90).
47. When this immediate presence *is* recognized, the question is rather how any judgment can be *false.*
48. *SZ* 218–21. See also *SZ* 154–55.

consists not in the correspondence of an ideal representation with its original but in the activity of discovery which first renders things accessible, bringing us into their immediate presence.

What sort of being *is* this which essentially discovers, renders accessible, brings into immediate presence? It cannot have any determinate character of its own, because its being is to reveal other beings in their determinate character. In Heidegger's terminology it cannot be primarily *a* being (*Seiendes*) but being itself (*Sein*). He characterizes it as "being toward . . ." (*Sein zum*). "Verification is only possible insofar as the knowledge which is asserted and verified has the ontological sense of a discovering 'being toward' real beings themselves." [49]

The idea that the mind, if it is to comprehend things in their determinate character, cannot have any determinate character of its own is not new. We find it in Aristotle's *De anima.*

> Since everything is a possible object of thought, mind, in order . . . to know, must be pure of all admixture, for the presence of what is alien to its nature [would be] a hindrance and a block; it follows that it . . . can have no nature of its own, other than that of having a certain capacity. Thus that in the soul which is called mind . . . is, before it thinks, not actually any real thing.[50]

It is not in the position but in its implications that Heidegger differs from Aristotle. Aristotle has not taken the difference between the mind and its object sufficiently seriously, or has not expressed the difference in sufficiently radical terms. His philosophical vocabulary comes from the realm of things and objects —from the *Categories*, the *Physics,* and the *Metaphysics*—and is carried over into the *De anima* to be applied negatively and by way of analogy. What kind of un-thing (or no-thing) is Aristotle's mind? It is difficult to see how it could correspond with any (real) thing. So Descartes, who conceives truth more explicitly as correspondence, forsakes Aristotle's negative notion of mind and describes it as *res cogitans.*[51] Here the fundamental difference between the mind and its object, *res cogitans* and *res extensa,* has disappeared: both are things.

For Heidegger the difference between the mind and a thing—or rather between human being and the beings which it

49. "[Die Bewährung] ist nur so möglich, dass das aussagende und sich bewährende Erkennen seinem ontologischen Sinne nach ein *entdeckendes Sein zum* realen Seienden selbst ist" (*SZ* 218).

50. *De an.* 429a18–24.

51. *Med.* II, 205–6; VI, 254. Descartes' "rational soul" is further "joined and united" with the body (*Disc.* V, p. 149).

encounters—is crucial to philosophical explanation, and it is this difference upon which his critique of the notion of truth as correspondence is based. The judgment is not primarily *a* being, and neither is human being, of which it is a characteristic attitude. To distinguish human being from all *things*—all other beings (*Seiendes*)—and to preserve its affinity to being itself, Heidegger calls it *Dasein,* "being there." The distinction between being (*Sein*), human being (*Dasein*), and all other beings (*Seiendes*) has already been elaborated by the time Heidegger comes to consider the nature of truth in *Being and Time* and provides the background against which his notion appears as more than an empty formula.[52] I shall take it up in the following chapter, prior to considering the doctrine itself in Chapter 3.

Truth cannot be conceived as a relation of correspondence

52. The distinction between *Sein* and *Seiendes* is what Heidegger calls the "ontological difference" (*SG* 15; *ID* 46 [43]), and its clarification is virtually the final goal of his thinking. It is roughly the Latin distinction between *esse* and *ens.* I have chosen the simplest and most malleable English usage in speaking of "being" (*Sein*) and "beings" or "a being" or "any being" (*Seiendes*). (One exception to this rule is *das Seiende im Ganzen,* which I occasionally render "being in its totality," though generally "the totality of beings," meaning the same thing in both cases.)

There seems little reason to have recourse to unusual expressions like Macquarrie and Robinson's "entities" or Manheim's "essents" or to unwieldy circumlocutions like Langan's "things-that-are" or Brock's "what-is." On the other hand, to capitalize "being" smacks of *fin de siècle* British idealism, with its Spirit and Matter and Truth. If the majuscule is employed at all, it ought to be reserved for Heidegger's later use of the word, when, as J. L. de Azavedo points out, it comes to take on the characteristics of a personal absolute (*Philosophisches Jahrbuch,* LX [1950], 165), and especially to cases in which Heidegger writes *Seyn* (e.g., *WW* 26 [350]).

Between being and beings there are two other Heideggerian expressions: "beingness" (*Seiendheit*) and "the totality of beings" (*das Seiende im Ganzen*). Beingness I take to mean whatever makes any determinate and intelligible being determinate and intelligible. It appears to be convertible with "the being of any being" (*das Sein des Seienden*), which, in turn, must be sharply distinguished from "being itself" (*das Sein selbst*). *Das Seiende im Ganzen* means both "being(s) *as* a whole" and "(any) being *within* the whole," i.e., any being seen within the total context of beings as the basis of its determinate character and intelligibility. Occasionally this leads me to substitute "being in its totality" or "the totality of being" for "the totality of beings," but these expressions should be taken as equivalent, remaining within the realm of the concrete, particular, determinate, and intelligible—if only as its limit—and thus referring to *Seiendes* rather than to *Sein.*

Neither *Seiendheit* nor *das Seiende im Ganzen*—nor even *das Sein des Seienden*—can be identified with *Sein,* Heidegger argues, although we have traditionally blurred the distinction (*WW* 25 [350]; *WM* 44 [382]), and it is the aim of "fundamental ontology" (*Fundamentalontologie*) to re-establish "the difference." This entails recognizing the radical difference which separates human being (*Dasein*) from all other beings (*Seiendes*). See *SZ* 13; *WM* 19–21 (217–19), 44 (382); *BH* 109–10 (297–98); *KM* 207–21 (239–55); *WW* 25 (350).

between two *beings*, ideal and real, subject and object, or whatever. Such truth, we have argued, could not be verified. It is difficult to see how it could be binding on human thought and behavior.[53] But most of all a relation of correspondence is impossible between two beings which have nothing in common. As long as truth is conceived as a relation between beings, correspondence is impossible, and as soon as it is conceived in any other way, the notion becomes inappropriate. This is the substance of Heidegger's direct critique of the notion of truth as correspondence.

5. The Search for the Presupposition

THE HISTORY OF PHILOSOPHY can be read as a constant search for the presuppositions which underlie human experience. It is these presuppositions, rather than the experience which they make possible, which the philosopher calls reality or truth in the highest degree. Aristotle expresses this attitude with admirable clarity in Book II of the *Metaphysics*.

> Now we do not know a truth without its cause; and a thing has a quality in a higher degree than other things if in virtue of it the similar quality belongs to the other things as well. For example, fire is the hottest of things, for it is the cause of the heat of all other things. So that which causes derivative truths to be true is *most true*.[54]

Plato is thinking in this vein when he calls his eternal and immutable ideas "more real" and "more true" than the fleeting things of this world, for they are the source of the transient being and limited intelligibility which such things possess.[55] In the central books of the *Metaphysics* Aristotle calls the form of a thing, taken without its matter, "primary substance"—substance in the highest degree or in the truest sense—because it makes any *corporeal* substance what it is.[56] Plato asks: what is the necessary presupposition of human virtue? Or more generally: what makes estimable qualities possible, in man and in all other things as well? Aristotle asks: what is the necessary presupposition of movement or change in the world, and especially of movement or change which we can understand? The aspect of experience which is regarded as fundamental has changed, but in both cases the search is for the necessary presupposition of experience. And

53. WW 10–12 (327–30).
54. *Meta.* 993b23–27 (italics added).
55. *Rep.* 514–15.
56. *Meta.* 1032b1–14, 1037a28–29, 1041b25–28.

when this presupposition is found, it is regarded as supremely real, more real than anything *within* experience, which it makes possible.

Kant undertakes fundamentally the same sort of search in his three *Critiques*. Only Kant's concern is not so much with changeable things as with man's knowledge—especially his exact, scientific knowledge—of such things, and not so much with human virtues as with the binding or obligatory character which virtue possesses. The goal of Kant's philosophical endeavor is to express the ultimate presuppositions of scientific knowledge, moral conduct, and religious belief, which he regards as man's three most fundamental and characteristically human activities. At the end of the *Critique of Pure Reason* he formulates the ultimate object of philosophical—and human—concern in three questions: "What can I know? What ought I to do? What may I hope?" [57] How is it possible for man to know anything about the world with absolute certainty, to make responsible decisions in a world governed (as he must assume) by deterministic, scientific law, and to believe in a transcendent reality (God) which shatters his powers of understanding? The unity of these three questions Kant sees as providing a philosophical doctrine of man, and so he later summarizes them in one final question, "What is man?" [58] It is in the structure of human being that Kant finds the supreme condition of experience. This is the "cause" of truth and so, in Aristotle's sense, "most true."

Hegel follows Kant's direction—being concerned not directly with the world but with man's experience of the world—only he widens the scope of the inquiry to include all conscious or cognitive aspects of experience, many of which, he insists, cannot be dealt with adequately within the framework of Kant's three fundamental questions, e.g., economic competition, political organization, historical development, artistic creativity, and philosophical reflection itself. Hegel is in search of the most fundamental presupposition of all conscious experience—not simply scientific, moral, and religious experience—and this he finds in a total context of intelligibility which makes knowledge and action possible.

All knowledge and action—in fact all conscious experience—implies a context of intelligibility. A word takes on determinate meaning only when it is seen in the context of a sentence, and in order to understand a sentence properly we must locate it in the context of a paragraph. This is why meaning can

57. A 804–5, B 832–33.
58. *Werke* (ed. Cassirer), VIII, 343.

be completely distorted when a statement is taken out of context—which does not mean that it is understood apart from any context but rather that it is taken out of the context in which it belongs and put into some *other* context. Even pictures can lie when they are taken out of context in this way. And what is true of words and pictures is true of all our experience. Andrew flushes. What does this mean? Is he angry? Or embarrassed? To answer this question I must consult the situation in which the event occurred. So in his search for the source of meaning in human experience, Hegel pursues the ultimate context in which such experience takes place. This is what he calls the "absolute." [59]

There are, of course, many different contexts in which knowledge and activity occur, and Hegel insists that we recognize and accept this plurality.[60] We cannot reduce the necessary presuppositions of one sort of knowledge or activity to that of another. The physicist, for example, must assume a given order of things in the world, while the politician must assume that man has the power to alter the given order. This is to say that the physicist and the politician think and act on the basis of different presuppositions appropriate to different contexts. The jurist, the psychologist, and the moralist all regard the same human action from fundamentally different points of view—in different contexts—and they change roles to their cost. Hegel accepts such a plurality of presuppositions and contexts as irreducible, but he is convinced that he can show that there is a necessary order in which all such presuppositions are related to one another. There is a context of contexts, and this is the intelligible order which emerges out of human history and the Western philosophical tradition.[61]

No isolated proposition can adequately express the basis of truth, Hegel argues; no single presupposition or point of view can provide a context wide enough to embrace it.[62] But there is an order implicit in all the propositions and presuppositions which have made the attempt, and this is the basis of their intelligibility, just as the order of language is the basis of the meaning of all individual words. It is this order which Hegel calls truth (or the absolute). "The true," he says, "is the whole." [63] The context of facts and events, he insists, is the real source of their meaning and significance, not the facts and events themselves. Both action

59. *PG* 21 (81–82).
60. *Philosophy of Right,* Addition to Preface (Knox trans.), pp. 224–25.
61. *PG* 26–28 (89–91), 31 (95), 44–45 (111–13).
62. *PG* 23 (85), 30–31 (94–95), 49–50 (118–19).
63. *PG* 21 (82–83).

and knowledge presuppose intelligibility, and intelligibility presupposes some total context, which must therefore be regarded as the ultimate source of meaning in our experience.

Heidegger attempts to extend the scope of inquiry still further. He asks for the presupposition of all human experience whatever, whether significant or banal, whether conscious or not. Heidegger is concerned with habitual activities like shaving and typing, with conventional behavior like idle chitchat, and with what we regard as "subjective feelings" like boredom and anxiety. Such activities are specifically human—if man is the only being who thinks or lives in cities, he is also the only one to shave—and yet they have escaped Hegel's investigation no less than Kant's. Kant has recognized only the peaks of human experience, while Hegel has included the foothills; but between the peaks and the foothills there are valleys. What makes *them* possible? The necessary presupposition of the valleys of human experience, which he regards as also that of its peaks, Heidegger calls truth.

Hegel anticipates Heidegger's criticism of the notion of truth as correspondence. He argues that truth is not to be found in any thing or proposition but in a total context of intelligibility from which all things and propositions draw their meaning and significance. Heidegger finds a further presupposition of the truth of any thing or proposition in what he calls man's "openness to beings," which makes such a thing as a total context possible.[64] Such openness, he argues, is consequent upon human decision: decision is the origin of the context which, as Hegel recognized, makes individual things accessible and individual judgments intelligible.[65] A landscape, for example, provides a very different context of intelligibility for a farmer, an architect, and a military tactician. The divergent viewpoints of the psychologist, the moralist, and the jurist are dictated by their different concerns. And this is the crucial point in Heidegger's doctrine of truth: *if some human decision is the basis of all intelligibility, that decision cannot itself be intelligible.*[66] It is in this sense that I have said that his notion of truth does not itself purport to be true.

Hegel opposes the notion of correspondence, but he does not reject it out of hand. On the contrary, he assumes it as a working hypothesis and allows it to destroy itself as, one after another, all propositions purporting to be true (i.e., to correspond with a given

64. *SZ* 221; *WW* 11–12 (328–30).
65. *Ho* 55–56 (689–91); *SZ* 297–300.
66. *SZ* 76, 134. Hegel's "absolute" is reflected in Heidegger's "world," which is the principal theme of the following chapter.

object) prove to be inadequate and have to be replaced.[67] Only out of this movement of mind emerges the order of propositions—or the order of experience—which Hegel himself holds to be truth. Such truth does not stand over and above all untruth; it is rather the truth *of such untrue* (i.e., in themselves inadequate) *propositions*, or of all one-sided (in themselves misleading) human experiences. Heidegger, too, does not simply reject the notion of correspondence or seek to replace it with one of his own. With Hegel he holds that the traditional notion must contain a nucleus of truth and lead of itself to its own *logos*. He therefore begins his discussion of truth with an analysis of the traditional notion and advances his own notion, in the first instance, not as a presupposition of all human experience (cognitive or noncognitive, significant or banal) but as a presupposition *of the traditional notion*.

We have seen Heidegger's claim that the truth of a judgment consists not in its correspondence with an object but in its discovery of a being. Correspondence is only possible because a being has been discovered, taking its place within the intelligible context of an area of openness, as a landscape does when it becomes the scene of a military campaign or housing project, as planets do when they are represented in a field of gravitational forces, as the oversight does when Freud puts it into a new context. The judgment about the picture permits it to reveal itself as hanging *either* straight *or* crooked. So correspondence presupposes discovery, which it nevertheless tends to conceal. The openness of beings is traditionally taken for granted. At best it is explained through a "light of nature" (*lumen naturale*) in which things become intelligible. But light (*Licht*) presupposes openness (*Lichtung*), and such openness, if it is the source of meaning in our experience, cannot simply be taken for granted.[68]

Judgment is one way in which man discovers beings, but it is not the only way, nor even the original way. Man discovers beings not only through his theoretical and practical judgments but through his pragmatic conduct prior to all judgment—in the course of simply "muddling through." [69] The judgment expresses what something is, but the fact that we can be concerned with what something is indicates that we have already encountered it, have already drawn it into the context of life. So the judgment may be one seat of truth, but it is not the only one, nor even the

67. PG 39 (105), 67–69 (135–37).
68. SZ 133, 147, 170, 350–51; Ho 41–44 (677–80); BH 75–77 (281–82), 83 (285), 100–101 (293); HD, 18, 55, VA 247.
69. SZ 69.

original one.[70] "The judgment is not the primary locus of truth. . . . On the contrary, truth in the most original sense is the locus of judgment." [71]

The judgment is true insofar as it discovers; things are true insofar as they are discovered and acquire a discovering power of their own. (Heidegger thus retains the distinction between the truth of judgment and the truth of things.) But true in the deepest sense—in Aristotle's sense—is the being of man, on whom all discovery depends, whose very being it is to discover.[72] The essential character of man, whose being it is to discover other beings, Heidegger wants to convey in the name *Dasein,* "being there." As essentially discovering, Dasein is always "in the truth," in openness.[73] And truth, which consists in openness, depends upon the being of Dasein. So Heidegger affirms, *"There can be truth only insofar as and so long as Dasein exists."* [74]

In his search for the presupposition of the traditional notion of truth—and beyond this of all human experience—Heidegger, like Kant, is thus brought to confront the being of man. For truth, as the discovery prior to all context, from which in turn judgments draw their meaning and hence the possibility of corresponding with an object, depends upon human presence. Such a doctrine appears relativistic in the extreme, but before drawing this conclusion we should wait until we see something of Heidegger's doctrine of man (in itself a misleading expression), which I shall take up in the following chapter. In passing we may observe that he is strongly opposed to what he regards as the anthropological (or anthropocentric) tendency of modern philosophy in Kant, Schelling, Hegel, Nietzsche, and Marx.[75]

The being of man, in Heidegger's view, has also been taken in large measure for granted. Man is a being with one unique characteristic: an animal endowed with reason, the power of making judgments (*animal rationale*).[76] Man may occupy a position at the pinnacle of creation, the topmost branch of the Porphyrian tree,

70. SZ 32–34, 153–60, 218–89, 223–26; WW 11–12 (329); WG 11–15; N II 74.
71. "Nicht die Aussage ist der primäre 'Ort' der Wahrheit, sondern *umgekehrt.* . . . Die ursprünglichste 'Wahrheit' ist der 'Ort' der Aussage" (SZ 226).
72. SZ 220–21.
73. SZ 221.
74. *"Wahrheit gibt es nur, sofern und solange Dasein ist"* (SZ 226).
75. PL 49–50 (268–69); Ho 84–86; VA 86–87; KM 185–97 (212–26).
76. SZ 48, 165; PL 49–50 (268–69); BH 64–68 (276–78); BM 108 (141–42); WD 66, 95–96; VA 72–73, 91, 177; SG 147, 210–11; WM 9 (209); ID 24 (23); N II 26.

endowed with the power of comprehending the whole of creation—a little higher than the ape, a little lower than the angel—he still remains *a* being, like the ape and the angel alike.
Such a view of man implicitly underlies a doctrine of truth as
correspondence between *beings*. To make truth relative to such a
being would certainly be to fall into relativism. A crane could just
as easily define truth in relation to cranes. But this is a view of
man which Heidegger strenuously combats.

We have now seen the broad outline of Heidegger's objection
to tradition and common sense. He refuses to accept any view of
truth as correspondence (*adaequatio*), as the property of judgments made by a rational animal (*animal rationale*), or as occur-
ring in an area of openness which can be presupposed (*lumen
naturale*). These three doctrines belong together, for truth becomes a relation between beings, of which man is one, and it is
the light of nature which spans the gap between him and the
object of his knowledge. Heidegger regards all three as perennial
human illusions, but he does not dismiss them, any more than
Freud dismisses the illusions of his patients. He looks instead for
their presuppositions, studying them for clues to the truth which,
in the first instance, they tend to conceal.

Having seen something of Heidegger's critique of tradition, we
now know what we need to know before his own notion of truth
can make sense. Since he objects to a light of nature which is
intelligible per se, insisting that light presupposes openness, we
must see what he means by openness and how it comes about.
Here we must look for the context and the focus which he insists
are required for a relation of correspondence. Since he objects to
the traditional conception of man as *animal rationale*, we need to
know what he understands by *Dasein* and how the two notions
differ. Here we must see how, if not through knowledge, Dasein
originally encounters things, drawing them into the area of openness which judgment presupposes. And since, most of all, he is
opposed to any notion of truth as a relation between *beings,* we
must clarify his distinction between being (*Sein*)—or at least
human being (*Dasein*)—and particular beings (*Seiendes*). The
most important question is how truth can depend upon the being
of Dasein, that all too fallible being we call man.

2 / The Background of Truth: Man's Being-in-the-World

1. Discovery and Dasein's Being-in-the-World

KNOWLEDGE, ACCORDING TO PLATO, is recollection. This is his way of expressing the fact that we can never discover a first moment of knowledge. For we can only come to know something in terms of something else which we already know. All knowledge presupposes some prior "knowledge" or familiarity. And what is true of knowledge is true of all our conscious experience: we always experience things—even the utterly incomprehensible—within a framework which has been sketched out by our previous experience. This problem has occupied philosophers throughout history, but none more directly than Plato and Kant. The point on which Heidegger takes exception to the tradition which unites Plato and Kant is whether the source of knowledge is to be understood in terms proper to knowledge itself, whether we can represent the original after the model of the recollection.

Plato recognizes various kinds or degrees of knowledge—my knowledge that the sun is shining, the geometer's knowledge of the properties of triangles, the wise man's knowledge of life—and it is an oversimplification to lump all these indiscriminately together under a single heading. Nor can all these sorts of knowledge be expressed in propositions. The knowledge of the wise man is ineffable, and so is my knowledge of what a starched collar feels like on a hot summer day. We may think of these two forms of knowledge as being too exalted and too humble to find an appropriate place in human discourse. There are various kinds of knowledge, of which only some—those roughly at the middle of a scale running from the lowliest to the most exalted—can adequately be expressed in propositions. This is a conviction shared by almost all the philosophers of the Western tradition, and we do not do it justice when we characterize the traditional notion of truth simply as the truth of knowledge and identify knowledge with the judgment.

But on two points we find a unanimity in tradition which tends to justify this oversimplification. The scale of knowledge is usually regarded as continuous from the familiar out of which it arises (my knowledge of the collar) to the ineffable which it is finally brought to confront (the wise man's knowledge of the good), and at the middle of this scale is to be found the sort of knowledge which can be expressed in propositions. The scale is extended both ways from the middle, which provides the model for the interpretation of every form of experience. In formulating a doctrine of categories, for example, both Aristotle and Kant arrive at the structure of things by analyzing the structure of propositions.[1] Human thinking thus takes its direction from the proposition; other forms of experience are understood as prepropositional or postpropositional. Knowledge becomes the focal point of experience and the judgment the focal point of knowledge. There is thus considerable justification for Heidegger's attributing to tradition a notion of truth as the correspondence of the judgment with its object. The question, as he sees it, is this: "Has man borrowed the structure of the proposition from the structure of things, or has he read the structure of the proposition *into* things?"[2]

Whatever the answer to this question, Heidegger presses to know how it is possible. We have argued that the possibility of judgment presupposes a prior activity of discovery, creating an area of openness in which it is possible for an object to manifest itself as it is. It is of this original activity, setting the scene for knowledge, that knowledge itself, in Plato's terms, is a recollection. But against tradition Heidegger insists that we cannot assume that it is continuous with knowledge, that the original is of the same fundamental structure as the recollection.[3] To call it

1. *Cat.* 1a1–2a3; A 69, B 94 ff.
2. "Hat der Mensch den Bau des Satzes am Bau des Dinges abgelesen, oder hat er den Bau des Satzes in die Dinge hineinverlegt?" (*FD* 35). Compare *Ho* 13 (654–55); *EM* 142–43 (186–87); *N II* 78.
3. *WG* 13; *SZ* 148–60; *FD* 139–40.

precognitive or prepropositional or intuitive knowledge is really to beg the question. Heidegger sees a fundamental discontinuity—a break—between our immediate experience and the knowledge to which it gives rise. To portray this break is the principal aim of this chapter. In order to be known, Heidegger argues, a thing must first be accessible to judgment. The question is: how, if not through knowledge, are things originally discovered, in order to be accessible to judgment? And what does such discovery presuppose?

Discovery presupposes first a being which, itself essentially open, discovers other beings by drawing them into its openness. This being is Dasein. Heidegger does not equate the openness of Dasein, however, with *consciousness,* which he regards as a development within openness.[4] Discovery presupposes further that the discovered being belongs to a context or organized whole within which it is accessible to discovery. This context or organized whole Heidegger calls the world (*Welt*). Discovery presupposes finally that the context of the discovered being belongs to the being of the discovering being, that the world belongs to the being of Dasein.[5]

Dasein can discover beings only because it "has a world," because the world, as a condition of the encounter of any particular being *within* the world, belongs to the essential structure of its being. Attempts to explain the world apart from its essential reference to Dasein have invariably failed. The world is not merely the sum of all the beings encountered within it—houses, trees, men, mountains, and so on—for we always encounter these things as having a specific place *in* the world; we cannot apprehend it through them. The same is true of categories like substance and nature, which are also encountered within the world and are only meaningful in relation to it. As a condition of the discovery of things and categories, the world must be distinct from them and prior to them in its being and encounter.[6]

Heidegger is here arguing about the world in the way in which Kant argues about space and time in the Transcendental Aesthetic. We must have a primordial experience of space and time, Kant insists, before we can experience any concrete being as spatiotemporal. Kant also recognizes the eternally prior character of the world in granting it the status of a transcendental idea.

4. WM 16 (214–15); SZ 207–8.
5. SZ 63–69; WG 24–44.
6. SZ 63–64; Ho 33–34 (671–72); BH 100–101 (293).

Only Kant approaches the world theoretically and looks upon it as the ultimate context of knowledge.[7] Such a context itself requires a context. Heidegger approaches the world pragmatically and understands it as the ultimate context of human life, embracing every form of human activity, of which knowledge is only one.

Heidegger asks us to understand the world and Dasein as reciprocal notions. If its nature is to discover beings, Dasein cannot be a being substantially distinct from the world, one which only *happens to be* in the world as its locus. Insofar as Dasein is essentially discovering, its being can only be understood as being *in-the-world*. So Heidegger concludes, " 'World' in the ontological sense is not a determination of that being which Dasein essentially *is not* but a characteristic of Dasein itself."[8] Heidegger defines Dasein as "being-in-the-world" (*In-der-Welt-sein*); all other beings he calls simply "innerworldly" (*innerweltlich*).[9]

Worldliness originally permits Dasein to encounter things and so is a necessary condition of all human experience as well as of the traditional notion of truth as correspondence. But it is a condition which is prior to knowledge, and one which the traditional notion of truth, cast in terms of knowledge, overlooks. We must now see what Heidegger's ontological sense of the world is, how it makes discovery possible, and in what way it belongs to the being of Dasein. Since the world and Dasein are reciprocal notions, their meaning can only be elaborated in conjunction: we cannot define and describe them adequately one at a time. Heidegger addresses himself first to their relation as this is expressed in the preposition "in." In what sense, he asks, can we say that Dasein is "in" the world?

Dasein is "there" (*da*), "with it." Its being Heidegger characterizes in a preliminary way as care or concern (*Sorge*).[10] This is what he understands by a being's being "there": to care or to be concerned. Dasein is concerned with being, and in the first instance with its own being, with what it is to become or what is to become of it. This is Heidegger's initial definition:

7. A 334, B 391. Kant calls the world the "concept of appearance in its totality" (*Inbegriff aller Erscheinungen*). In his terminology appearance (*Erscheinung*) refers primarily to the subject matter of scientific theory. See SZ 321; WG 27–35; FD 100.

8. " 'Welt' ist ontologisch keine Bestimmung *des* Seienden, das wesenhaft das Dasein *nicht* ist, sondern ein Charakter des Daseins selbst" (SZ 64).

9. SZ 52–59.

10. SZ 56–57, 191–92, 196, 200, 316–18.

Dasein is not simply a being which presents itself along with others. It rather has the unique ontic characteristic that, in its very being, it is concerned with its being.[11]

In its very being this being relates to its being. As a being of this kind it is entrusted to its own being.[12]

This concern for being—in the first instance its own—sets Dasein apart from every other being, which simply is what it is without being concerned for what it is or is to become. It is only by virtue of this essential concern, as Heidegger elaborates the notion, that Dasein can relate to other beings or even to itself. Heidegger wishes to make a concerned attitude fundamental to all human activities, including the most detached and disinterested speculative inquiry. The definition has a peculiar status: it is not incontestable, but in contesting it we exhibit the concern which we wish to deny.[13]

In essence Dasein is not a particular being (*Seiendes*) but a relation to being itself (*Sein*). It is not primarily a *what. What* is the primary characteristic of all the beings discovered within the world, but it does not apply to the being whose being consists in the activity of discovery itself. It rather applies specifically to that being which Dasein *is not.* Of course Dasein is also a particular being, also a *what*, for it too is encountered in the world alongside purely innerworldly beings, but it is not essentially this. Dasein is rather a *way* of being than a being, and all its characteristics as a being are grounded in the direct relation in which it stands to being, primarily its own. "Where this being is concerned, all being

11. "Das Dasein ist ein Seiendes, das nicht nur unter anderem Seienden vorkommt. Es ist vielmehr dadurch ontisch ausgezeichnet, dass es diesem Seienden in seinem Sein *um* dieses Sein selbst geht" (*SZ* 12).

12. "Im Sein dieses Seienden verhält sich dieses selbst zu seinem Sein. Als Seiendes dieses Seins ist es seinem eigenen Sein überantwortet" (*SZ* 41–42).

13. Julius Kraft's article in *Philosophy and Phenomenological Research,* I (1940–41), 339–65, is a particularly striking case in point. Referring to the "vacuum of long-winded Heideggerian declamations" (p. 349) and to Heidegger's "trivial analytic propositions" (p. 351) and affirming that he is "no friend to metaphysical horror stories" (p. 354), Kraft launches a verbal barrage against the suggestion that an attitude of concern underlies all man's speculative activities. "In fact, in entertaining, in asking, in considering, one cares for the object of the entertaining, the asking, etc.! The philosophical bearing of this seemingly subordinated hermeneutic device is great enough! With its help we may hope to solve the 'problem of knowledge.' . . . Unfortunately logic . . . has to insist on showing that the caring being-in-the-world is a considering being-in-the-world which does not become a kind of care by being called so, but remains an intellectual faculty" (p. 352). One is most of all struck by the author's punctuation.

this or that is primarily *being*. Hence the title 'Dasein' . . . does not express its *what*, like table, house, or tree, but simply *being*." [14] Dasein is not so much a particular being as a possibility of being (*Seinkönnen*) which offers itself for realization: "it must become itself by realizing its being as properly its own." [15] All this is implied in concern, the essence of "being there." [16]

There are two essential attributes of Dasein which reflect its being as concern: (*a*) existence (*Existenz*) and (*b*) "mineness" (*Jemeinigkeit*). (*a*) Concern is both a relation *to being* and an obligation *to be*. The two are combined in Heidegger's expression "being-to" (or "being-toward"): *Zu-sein*. "The 'essence' of this being consists in its being-to," [17] i.e., in its unique relation to being and its having to be. The being to which Dasein relates in striving to realize itself Heidegger calls existence, using the term in the etymological sense of "standing out" or "rising above" and often emphasizing this sense by writing *Ek-sistenz*.[18] The word is meant to point up the fact that, in all its distinctively human activities and attitudes—knowing, loving, planning, worrying, and so on— Dasein is always outside itself, beyond itself, in advance of itself as *a* being. (*b*) The existence of Dasein, the being with which it is concerned, is in the first instance always its own—"mine"—and this characteristic Heidegger calls "mineness." [19] Wherever there is human being—wherever being is "there"—there is a unique focal point of events and situations, a unique possibility of realization, and this is conveyed in the expression "mine." We should note in passing that Heidegger gives mineness ontological priority over the "I" or ego.[20]

Dasein is neither particular nor universal, neither concrete nor abstract, for such categories apply properly to the beings which Dasein encounters in the world—*this* shoe or *any* shoe, red and redness, Socrates and manhood—and Heidegger objects to

---

14. "Alles So-sein dieses Seienden ist primär Sein. Daher drückt der Titel 'Dasein' . . . nicht sein Was aus, wie Tisch, Haus, Baum, sondern das Sein" (*SZ* 42).

15. ". . . es [hat] je sein Sein als seiniges zu sein . . ." (*SZ* 12).

16. *SZ* 191–92, 284, 322; *WG* 37; *EH* 34.

17. "Das 'Wesen' dieses Seienden liegt in seinem Zu-sein" (*SZ* 42). As we have already seen, it is with the notion of being-toward (in the judgment) that Heidegger introduces his notion of truth (*SZ* 218).

18. *SZ* 12; *WW* 14–15 (333–37); *WM* 14–16 (213–15); *BH* 66–71 (277–79).

19. *SZ* 42–43; *EM* 22 (28–29).

20. On the derivative character of the self see *SZ* 316–23; *WM* 15–16 (214–15), 35 (370); *BH* 101 (293); *Ho* 96–97; *WG*, 19–20, 37–38, 44; *EM* 110 (143–44).

the attempt to interpret human being according to categories derived from the world of things.[21] Dasein can perhaps best be understood as spanning this dichotomy: mineness is analogous to the concrete and particular, which existence transcends without thereby becoming abstract or universal. (The same ambivalence can be seen in the combination of *da* and *Sein*.) The relation of being, existence, and mineness admittedly poses a difficult problem: in what way and to what extent am I essentially concerned with what is to become of me, of man, and of being itself, both in man and in all other things? How do these three concerns reflect the unity of human being? The question remains an open one. Without attempting to deal with it adequately, we may at least observe that it is being itself which distinguishes this particular, existent dollar from the abstract concept "dollar." Thus, for St. Thomas Aquinas, *esse*—not matter—serves as the ultimate principle of individuation. Similarly, for Heidegger, existence and mineness penetrate each other to the core, being united in the notion of concern as the being of a being which relates essentially to being as a possibility uniquely its own. It is with reference to this being that the world must be understood.

Dasein's concern with being requires that beings be open to it; its world is the specific form which the openness of beings assumes for it. Dasein is first concerned with the things of the world, and only through the world can it relate to, or assume an attitude toward, its own being. "Selfhood requires a world, which in turn is essentially Dasein-oriented." [22] The world provides an open area of encounter which is indispensable to the being of Dasein as concern. So Dasein *must* be in the world. But in what way is Dasein "in" the world? Not in the sense in which a chair is in the room or a suit of clothes in the closet: Dasein and the world are not related spatially, one "within" the other. Unlike innerworldly beings, Dasein is in the world in the sense of being "with" it through its concern, through its in-volvement with the world, the things of the world, and its own being-in-the-world.[23] Dasein is in the world in the sense in which the broker is *in* stocks and bonds.

Dasein's being-in-the-world is the basis of its constant contact with innerworldly beings, which cannot be explained simply through spatial proximity or contiguity. For one being to contact

21. *SZ* 44–50.
22. "Zur Selbstheit gehört Welt; diese ist wesenhaft daseinsbezogen" (*WG* 37).
23. *SZ* 53–57; *HH* 16–18; *WD* 143.

or encounter another, it must be open to the encounter and have a world in which contact is possible—innerworldly beings do not contact or encounter one another. Since the world makes possible the encounter of any innerworldly being, we must be able to discover it in such an encounter. And this brings us back to the question with which we began: how does Dasein originally encounter things? What is its original relation to things which comes to be expressed in the traditional notion of truth as correspondence?

2. Dasein's Original Encounter with Things

DASEIN, AS WE HAVE ARGUED, does not originally encounter things through knowledge. For knowledge—Plato's recollection—requires that its object has already been encountered.[24] Dasein's being as concern (*Sorge*) manifests itself immediately and necessarily in various activities of the care and management of things (*Besorgen*), and it is in such activities, prior to knowledge, that Dasein originally encounters things. When knowledge comes to stand for Dasein's original relation to the world, man and the world come to be regarded as two distinct entities, and their mutual relation poses an insoluble problem: the subject-object dichotomy.[25] "Being-in-the-world is not simply a relation of subject and object, but that which originally makes such a relation possible. . . ."[26]

Seeking to avoid any construction, Heidegger portrays Dasein in its most ordinary manifestation, as it reveals itself first and foremost in the routine of its daily existence (*Alltäglichkeit*).[27] Kant begins the *Critique of Pure Reason* by watching a scientist peering through the lens of his microscope. Heidegger begins by considering man—perhaps Kant's scientist—shaving, answering the doorbell, shifting his newspaper from one hand to the other in order to get out money for the bus.

At the outset of the analysis it is especially important that Dasein not be interpreted in any particular mode of existing but revealed in

24. See *Ho* 133; *SZ* 62, 76; *N II* 74.
25. *SZ* 59–62, 132, 176, 208, 366, 388; *BH* 101 (293); *VA* 258–59; *Ho* 268; *SG* 99; *ZS* 28; *FD* 21; *ID* 23–24 (22–23).
26. "Das In-der-Welt-sein ist aber nicht erst die Beziehung zwischen Subjekt und Objekt, sondern das, was eine solche Beziehung zuvor schon ermöglicht . . ." (*KM* 212 [243]).
27. *SZ* 41–45, 126–30, 370–72; *KM* 211–15 (242–47).

the indifferent way in which it exists in the first instance and for the most part.[28]

Here Dasein reveals itself immersed in the countless preoccupations of daily life, involved in the incessant managerial activities which reflect its essence as concern. Such activity is inescapable. Even in the most disinterested, purely speculative inquiry we are involved in the investigation, preoccupied with the proof or argument, concerned with illuminating a problem or verifying a theory. Practical activity should not be regarded as a form of applied theory—though this is the way it has frequently been represented by philosophers, whose chief concern is for theory—for it is the *immediate* way in which Dasein exists and the *original* way in which it encounters things. It is theory which is derivative.[29] Dasein is immediately and constantly in the world encountering innerworldly being through its careful activities, from watching the pot to proving the theorem. This is the immediate and unavoidable way of "being there." And yet because it is so close—like the glasses on our nose—it has been continually overlooked.

And because its routine daily existence constitutes the immediate ontic character of [Dasein], it has been and is continually bypassed in explanation. What is ontically the first and [most] familiar is ontologically the most distant, unknown, and continually overlooked in its ontological significance.[30]

A notion of truth as correspondence overlooks—and even tends to obscure—the original way in which Dasein relates to things.[31]

Dasein is immediately in the world through its incessant and unavoidable preoccupation with the care and management of things: handling and using them, shaping and fashioning them, processing and consuming them, investigating and organizing and planning them. Such activities situate Dasein in the midst of things. But the being of Dasein is always uniquely its own, so that

28. "Das Dasein soll im Ausgang der Analyse gerade nicht in der Differenz eines bestimmten Existierens interpretiert, sondern in seinem indifferenten Zunächst und Zumeist aufgedeckt werden" (*SZ* 43).

29. *SZ* 59, 61, 69, 149, 202, 324, 356–64; *BH* 54–55 (271–72).

30. "Und weil nun die durchschnittliche Alltäglichkeit das ontisch Zunächst dieses Seienden ausmacht, wurde sie und wird sie immer wieder in der Explikation des Daseins *übersprungen*. Das ontisch Nächste und Bekannte ist das ontologisch Fernste, Unerkannte und in seiner ontologischen Bedeutung ständig Übersehene" (*SZ* 43).

31. *SZ* 59, 225.

Dasein exists immediately not in the world (*Welt*) but in its own world or environment (*Umwelt*).[32] It is therefore to its environment that we must look for Dasein's initial encounter with things.

Things first manifest themselves as they are useful or available to human design, as instruments and materials of work (*Zeug*).[33] We do not first encounter things and then see them in relation to some possible use. Usefulness is not a fortunate veneer of things which man is able to turn to his own purpose: it is only *insofar as they are instrumental* that things first manifest themselves at all. This is the phenomenological justification of teleology, the doctrine that everything exists for some purpose, which the philosophers of the Enlightenment were so intent on discrediting. The instrumental character of beings as they are originally encountered Heidegger calls "available being" or "being at hand" (*Zuhandensein*), and he maintains that this is the reality of things as they are originally encountered. " 'Being at hand' is the ontological-categorial determination of a being as it is 'in itself.' "[34] At the dawn of Western thought the Greeks recognized this in naming things *pragmata* or "workables."[35]

Not the *thing* but the *instrument* is immediately given.[36] This observation is crucial. For the thing offers no resistance to being transformed, as it invariably is, into an object of knowledge. Things first manifest themselves (as the word "mani-fest" itself suggests) not to the speculative eye but to the careful hand. Since Dasein originally encounters things in their instrumentality, we must now probe the being of the instrument.

There is no such thing as a single, independent instrument, *an* instrument per se. Every instrument is part of a complex and involves an intrinsic reference to other instruments, its significance deriving from the manifold of references which go to make up the complex. A lamp is only a lamp in conjunction with a desk and chair, and all belong together to a totality which includes pen, paper and ink, books and bookshelves, carpet, fireplace, doors and windows—the complete organization of a study. The study is not simply the sum of the things which go to make it up. It is presupposed by every object within it: if it were not for *it*, they would not

32. SZ 66–67.
33. SZ 66–71; Ho 17–24.
34. "Zuhandenheit ist die ontologisch-kategoriale Bestimmung von Seiendem, wie es 'an sich' ist" (SZ 71, where the sentence is italicized for emphasis).
35. SZ 68.
36. Heidegger contrasts the thing, the instrument, and the work of art in Ho 10–28 (652–67).

be there. An instrumental totality is the condition of the possibility of any individual instrument. The room is prior to its furnishings.

These "things" do not first occur by themselves and then go to make up a room as a collection of objects. What we first encounter—although it is not explicitly comprehended—is the room itself, and this in turn not as a space between four walls in a geometric sense, but as a place to live. It is on this basis that its organization manifests itself and within this context that the "individual" instrument occurs. An instrumental totality is always discovered *prior to* the individual instrument.[37]

Because the instrument depends upon an instrumental complex for its being as an instrument—because the lamp can only be a lamp in the context of a study—Dasein must permit the individual instrument to be instrumental, and so *to be*. It does this by drawing it into the instrumental totality which organizes itself around some project (*Entwurf*).[38] Dasein *lets* the instrument *be* by using it within the context specified by its project. This is the first appearance of the notion of "letting be" (*sein lassen*), which continually recurs in Heidegger's thinking and plays an especially important role in his doctrine of truth.[39] We should note that it does not appear here in contrast to manipulation but as its necessary complement.

Because the instrument depends for its instrumentality upon the complex of which it is a part, Dasein must apprehend the complex prior to the instrument itself. Every instrument has a proper place and function, and if Dasein is to let the instrument be, it must first know something of the totality on which its place and function depend. We must have some notion of a study before we can make use of a lamp or desk. So Dasein must relate to its environment prior to relating to any individual thing within it.

This prior awareness of its environment which Dasein must have before it can encounter any individual instrument is not the result of knowledge—at least not of any theoretical knowledge.

37. "Diese 'Dinge' zeigen sich nie zunächst für sich, um dann als Summe von Realem ein Zimmer auszufüllen. Das Nächstbegegnende, obzwar nicht thematisch Erfasste, ist das Zimmer, und dieses wiederum nicht als das 'Zwischen den vier Wänden' in einem geometrischen räumlichen Sinne—sondern als Wohnzeug. Aus ihm heraus zeigt sich die 'Einrichtung,' in dieser das jeweilige 'einzelne' Zeug. *Vor* diesem ist je schon eine Zeugganzheit entdeckt" (*SZ* 68–69). See also *SZ* 352–53.

38. *SZ* 145–48, 221; *KM* 210–12 (240–44); *WG* 39; *ID* 23 (22); *FD* 171–72.

39. *SZ* 84–85; *WW* 14 (333); *Ho* 20 (660–61), 54–55 (688–90).

Dasein's practical activities do not result from the application of knowledge but provide the setting out of which knowledge arises. Its original encounter with things, however, need not on this account be regarded as "blind." Practical activity has its own sort of vision, quite distinct from that of theory: the vision (*Sicht*) of prudence (*Umsicht*), or what we might call pro-vision.[40]

Dasein does not take explicit cognizance of its environment in the course of its immediate activity. The environment consists in a manifold of reference (*Verweisungsmannigfaltigkeit*) which determines what can be done; in proceeding to work, Dasein submits to these references without explicitly recognizing them. Nor does Dasein take explicit notice of the very instrument it is using, which has been fashioned so as to require a minimum of attention, allowing complete preoccupation with the work at hand. I switch on the light, pull up a chair to my desk, light a cigarette, reach for paper and insert it into the typewriter, and all the while I am thinking of what I am going to write, paying no attention to the organization of the study which makes this activity possible. If, when I begin to write, I should become conscious of the keys of my typewriter, I am almost certain to make a mistake. Dasein's original encounter with its world and the instrumental beings which go to make it up is not a *conscious* encounter, nor do the beings which it encounters thereby manifest their *explicit* presence. (This is why, as we have said, Heidegger's "openness" cannot be equated with consciousness.) In the course of its immediate activity Dasein does not explicitly discover either the instrumental totality or the individual instrument. Together these render possible Dasein's preoccupation with the work at hand, but precisely because it is preoccupied, Dasein does not—and cannot—take explicit account of them.

A dilemma thus arises concerning Dasein's explicit comprehension of the things by which it is surrounded. For the being of the instrument does not reveal itself to detached contemplation. We cannot grasp the nature of the hammer by *contemplating* it, for it is not there to be contemplated. If we wish to understand the hammer, we must seize it—grasp it in the literal sense—*hammer* with it. Only then will it reveal its being—never to pure contemplation. And yet, while we cannot discover the being of an instrument by contemplating it, neither do we discover it, in the first instance, by *using* it. For as soon as we seize the hammer we become immersed in the work which it is meant to perform, and our attention is drawn away from the hammer itself to the end

40. *SZ* 69, 79, 146–50, 357–60, 412.

which it serves. The more immediate and intimate the relation of instrument and use—the more functional or instrumental the instrument—the more it realizes its (instrumental) being, and yet the less it manifests its presence.[41] If I am conscious of the shoe I am wearing, it is not a proper fit; if I am aware of the hammer at work, it is not a good hammer; if my typewriter obtrudes upon my attention, it is not functioning as it should. It is the nature of the instrument to withdraw from explicit consideration in order to be properly instrumental. "It is the peculiar characteristic of that which is immediately at hand to withdraw in its being at hand precisely in order to be properly at hand." [42] It is for this reason that the being of the instrument is distorted if it is regarded as an object.

The instrument is essentially *inconspicuous*. Its inconspicuous character is not merely a negative determination, designating in a general way what it *is not,* but belongs to its nature as an instrument.[43] Here the negative appears for the first time in Heidegger's thinking, and we should observe that its character is not purely logical. It manifests itself in things and not as a device of the mind for classifying things. This theme recurs constantly in a variety of forms, but always expressing the same motif: that there is negation in human experience as it is lived which is only subsequently reflected in human thinking.

Dasein's immediate concern is not with the instrument but with the work which it is meant to perform. It is the work and not the instrument which is immediately "at hand." And so it is to the work that we must look in search of Dasein's world. There are three ways in which the work manifests the totality within which things are encountered and so serves as the unifying principle of Dasein's world.

1. While it is the end which the instrument serves (*Wozu*), the work is itself a means to some further end and so manifests a referential totality of ends and means. The hammer, nails, and wood are *for* the construction of a desk, but the desk is *for* study or administration, which in turn are for some further purpose. In

---

41. This runs counter to an age-old identification of reality (efficacy) and manifest presence (intelligibility). The Platonic *eidos*, for example, is a principle both of being and of visibility; the supreme form, the form of the good, is like the sun, which both sustains things in being with its heat and renders them visible with its light (*Rep.* 509b). See below, pp. 151–52.

42. "Das Eigentümliche des zunächst Zuhandenen ist es, in seiner Zuhandenheit sich gleichsam zurückzuziehen, um gerade eigentlich zuhanden zu sein" (*SZ* 69).

43. *SZ* 75–76.

this way the references implicit in the work project as far into the future as human purpose extends.

2. The work is not only *for* something but involves the use *of* something for something and so requires materials (*Woraus*). If these materials are produced or processed, as is most often the case, we are referred to further materials and ultimately to material which lends itself to our purpose prior to all production or processing. In this way there emanates from the work a hierarchy of materials reaching down into what we call "nature," the nature of the natural product. Shoes are made from leather, leather is processed from the skins of animals, and animals are the product of animal husbandry. But animals are also found wild in nature. Though natural, such beings are nevertheless instrumental—substantially the same as the "products" of animal husbandry—and this is how they are originally encountered.

Nature first reveals itself not in contrast to the artifact but as that which is useful prior to all processing. We do not first encounter a natural being and then discover that there is something we can do with it, that it fits somehow into our plans and designs. It is only in relation to some possible use or insofar as it fits in with our designs that we first encounter it at all. So the references implicit in the work sink their roots into the fecundity of the earth. "The forest is timberland, the rock formation a quarry, the river is waterpower, the wind is 'wind in the sails.'" [44] In recognizing no more fundamental distinction between things than whether they are natural or artificial, philosophers have falsified immediate experience. There is no clear line to be drawn between the horse and the diesel engine, rock, brick, and cement, the orange and the loaf of bread.

We should add that Heidegger's category of being at hand is to be understood negatively as well as positively. It applies equally to that *with* which and to that *about* which something must be done. Frost, drought, and darkness are also first encountered pragmatically, in relation to human purpose.

3. The work embodies, finally, a reference to the being which it is meant to serve, to Dasein (*Worumwillen*).[45] In its functional being the instrument adapts itself to the human hand. The hammer, the switch, the street, the windmill, the calculator, and the factory are all tailor-made to the measure of man's being. "The work is cut to the contour of [man's] body; he is 'there' as the work

44. "Der Wald ist Forst, der Berg Steinbruch, der Fluss Wasserkraft, der Wind ist Wind 'in den Segeln'" (*SZ* 70).
45. *SZ* 84–87, 143–46, 191–93.

takes shape." [46] The references implicit in the work thus open out to include Dasein itself.

This is the way in which Heidegger accounts for Dasein's original encounter with others. We discover our fellow men as they are involved in the project of our own lives, as beings with whom, about whom, or for whom something can or must be done. An aspect of Dasein's being as concern (*Sorge*) is a sense of social responsibility (*Fürsorge*). The vision of prudence (*Umsicht*) Heidegger extends to include consideration (*Nachsicht*) and respect (*Rücksicht*) for others: Dasein not only cares *for* things; it also cares *about* others.[47] We do not initially encounter other human beings as we do things, as means to ends, but as coproprietors of the things which go to make up our world. We first encounter others in the watch and the calendar, in the trodden path, the loaf of bread which serves a family, the mail delivery before lunch, and the grooved seats of wooden chairs. This is not an altogether satisfactory account, and Martin Buber takes Heidegger to task for it.[48] Like many other philosophers, however—Buber himself is the most notable exception—Heidegger is concerned first and foremost with an explanation of Dasein's relation to *things*, and when he comes to consider relations between men he finds them embodied in things and mediated by them. The suggestion that we originally encounter our fellow men in the field of our own concern, without thereby reducing them to the status of means, may nevertheless provide the basis of a more satisfactory account of this question.[49]

In Heidegger's analysis of immediate experience, Dasein's work is the focal point of a complex of *instruments, materials,* and *proprietors* which leads out of the subjective private environment into the objective public world. The world is the one all-embracing workshop in which all individual workshops eventually merge. The watch and the calendar involve the whole solar system

46. "Das Werk wird ihm auf den Leib zugeschnitten, er 'ist' im Entstehen des Werkes mit dabei" (*SZ* 70–71).

47. *SZ* 121–23, 262–64, 297–98.

48. Martin Buber, *The Problem of Man* in *Werke*, I, 366–68.

49. The existence of others gains increased importance in Heidegger's thinking from *Being and Time* (1926) to *Vom Wesen des Grundes* (1929). In the later work Heidegger defines the being of Dasein as "being with . . . beings on hand, being together with . . . the being of others, and being toward . . . itself" ["das Sein bei . . . Vorhandenem, das Mitsein mit . . . dem Dasein Anderer und Sein zu . . . ihm selbst," *WG* 43]. This reference to others is absent in *Being and Time*, where the being of Dasein is defined simply as "being-already-in-advance-of-oneself-in (the world) as being-with (the beings encountered there)" ["sich-vorweg-schon-sein-in-(der-Welt-) als Sein-bei (innerweltlich begegnendem Seienden)," *SZ* 192, 249].

in human design, and the street, the river, the dike, the market place, legal tender, a standard of weights and measures, and the army all bring Dasein out of its individual environment into a shared world, the limits of which extend to the outermost reaches of human experience.[50]

The world in Heidegger's sense is not the name of a place or a term signifying some imaginative totality of things. It is more a generic notion than a name and refers to the field in which human activity takes place. If he speaks of *the* world, it is not, like Kant, as a theoretical postulate, but as the necessary implication of Dasein's most immediate daily preoccupations. We rise gradually from *The World of Washington Irving* through the world of sport and the world of finance, beyond even the world of Dr. Einstein, to a single world which includes all these. This is the sense, Heidegger suggests, in which the Church Fathers used the word *mundus*, the world of "the world, the flesh, and the devil." [51]

We have seen that the study allows a lamp to be what it is and that Dasein manifests an implicit comprehension of the study in relating to the lamp. The workshop is prior to any individual instrument within it, and the worker must have an implicit comprehension of it before he can relate to any of the instruments which go to make it up. Heidegger traces the implications of this argument outward from the workshop through the environment to the world. Taking the study as our model, we must conclude that it is the world which allows any innerworldly being to be what it is, and Dasein must have an implicit comprehension of the world in order to relate to any innerworldly being.[52] This is the way we should understand the primordial, preontological understanding of being (*Seinsverständnis*) which Heidegger attributes to Dasein.[53]

Analysis of Dasein's most common activities has led us necessarily to a consideration of the totality of beings, but only as they are available to human design. It has not yet revealed beings in their simple presence, nor has it involved any conceptual or theoretical knowledge. This is because beings do not originally manifest themselves in their simple presence and because knowledge is a derivative form of the encounter of any being. "[Knowledge] first

50. SZ 71; WG 36–39; Ho 33–38 (671–76); BH 100–101 (293).

51. WG 24–26. For Heidegger's recapitulation of the history of the notion of the world see WG 24–36.

52. Since this implicit comprehension of the world makes experience possible, it cannot itself be the result of experience, and this is why Heidegger insists that it be regarded as belonging to the being of Dasein.

53. SZ 12–13, 85–87, 147, 200–201; EM 63 (83–84); SG 146–47; KM 204–8 (233–38).

presses forward over what is available to human design to lay bare what is *then* merely present." [54]

The world has thus far been implied in all Dasein's activities, but it has not yet manifested its explicit presence. On the contrary, its presence has remained necessarily implicit. The individual instrument and the workshop both withdraw before the aim or product envisaged in the work. This product is then regarded as a means toward the implementation of some further project, and the whole dialectic of the instrument repeats itself, with instrumental beings withdrawing successively from our attention ad infinitum. Under these conditions the wonder is that anything appears at all. In the course of his immediate practical activities *homo faber* is not aware of himself at work, nor of the particular instrument with which he is working, nor of the workshop which allows the work to proceed. Dasein, the innerworldly being, and the world all remain implicit in their presence. The subject-object dichotomy as the model of man's cognitive relation to things has not yet emerged. Dasein's being expresses itself in the project, and its project carries it away from the present into an indeterminate and illusive future. "Lost in the world of instruments, the self must forget itself in order to be capable of really addressing itself to a task and manipulating something." [55] The immediate character of human life, according to this description, is *preoccupation* and *distraction*.

How then does man first become aware of the present? How do things first manifest themselves in what we have called their simple presence? In contrast to being in its instrumentality—being "at hand" (*Zuhandensein*)—Heidegger calls the explicit manifestation of being as it is simply present being "on hand" (*Vorhandensein*).[56] Such being is the proper object of knowledge, and from it the notion of truth as correspondence

---

54. "Dieses [viz., das Erkennen] dringt erst *über* das im Besorgen Zuhandene zur Freilegung des nur noch Vorhandenen vor" (SZ 71). (Italics altered in translation.)

55. "Um an die Zeugwelt 'verloren' 'wirklich' zu Werke gehen und hantieren zu können, muss sich das Selbst vergessen" (SZ 354).

56. SZ 73–75, 157–58. We should not confuse this distinction with the traditional distinction between the natural being and the artifact, as Werner Brock does when he says, "These things, when they are there by nature, are termed 'vorhanden' . . . and when they are made by men, such as utensils, they are termed 'zuhanden' " (*Existence and Being*, p. 28). Nature too, as we have seen, is first encountered insofar as it figures in human design (SZ 70). Heidegger opposes the traditional distinction between the natural being and the artifact (Ho 17–21 [658–61]). His two categories do not indicate "two different kinds of beings," as Brock suggests (*op. cit.*, pp. 44–45), but two different *ways* in which any being figures in human experience.

arises. Being must first manifest itself as "on hand" in Heidegger's sense before there is anything with which our thinking can "correspond." But Heidegger argues that this is not the way in which beings are originally encountered, that it is a derivative manifestation of being in life which must be seen in the living context out of which it emerges.[57] The question is: how does the instrument, which is not an object, come to reveal itself as an object? How is man called back out of the distraction which necessarily results from his work to an immediate awareness of things in the present? In short, how does speculation arise out of life?

3. The Moment of Truth

WE HAVE SEEN MAN IMMERSED in the instrumental complex necessary to his work, in a practical design sketched out by some fundamental project. And because he is immersed in it, he cannot see the design. Then suddenly the instrument with which he is working breaks down or wears out or otherwise reveals itself as defective—it will no longer do the work. It thereby obtrudes on our awareness and reveals itself for the first time as a thing or object, something which is merely "on hand" and in the way, an *ob-jectum* in the literal sense. Being at hand has suddenly become being under foot. The hammer breaks, the carburetor is out of gas, the typewriter ribbon wears out. And suddenly we can no longer manipulate such beings as instruments. We now see them—we *cannot help* seeing them—as mere things.[58]

A broken instrument or deficient material not only reveals itself. For its instrumentality consists in its relation to other instruments, all of which together go to make up the complex in which alone any instrument can function. The broken instrument thus reveals, in addition to itself, all the other instruments, which are now useless without it, and the structure of the complex of which they are a part. The broken hammer reveals the boards and nails, which are now simply *there,* and the organization of the shop, in which it is now impossible for the work to proceed. The dry carburetor reveals the automobile, the character of the highway, other cars as possible sources of assistance, and the possible distance to the nearest filling station. The worn-out typewriter

57. Henceforth I shall sometimes use the word "life" as a shorthand expression for being-in-the-world.

58. *SZ* 73–74, 81, 354–55; *Ho* 19–20 (659–61). For Heidegger's sense of the "thing" in contrast to the "mere thing" see *Ho* 10–21 (652–61); *VA* 151–58, 163–81; *US* 21–30.

ribbon reveals the entire study, which has now become a *factum brutum,* a thing divested of its practical significance which calls attention to itself and everything within it. There they all are for the first time: on hand, under foot, merely present.

Only when it thus confronts an impasse and is unable to proceed with its work is Dasein called back out of its preoccupation to an explicit awareness of the present. In the broken instrument it now recognizes what the individual instrument is, how it relates to other instruments, where it belongs in the complex, and what end its specific function serves. With the broken instrument the workshop first appears, opening out upon the environment and the world. And now for the first time Dasein becomes explicitly aware of itself, being forced to confront itself in the question, "What do I do now?" (This is why, in Heidegger's view, Dasein must take precedence over selfhood.) All the references implicit in the work—*necessarily* implicit as long as work was in progress—now become explicit. And only now do beings manifest themselves in their simple presence, as the proper objects of theoretical knowledge.

This revelation of the defective instrument is a vanishing moment. Only for a moment is the broken tool merely present, revealing itself and the complex of which it is a part. For it at once becomes material for repair and so once again instrumental. If the tool is broken, it must be repaired; if materials are deficient, they must be processed and improved; if a thing is worn out *beyond* repair, it is at least to be got out of the way. So the broken instrument, which for a moment is simply on hand, is drawn into a new project and once more becomes available to human design, withdrawing once again from awareness. The revelation of the defective instrument can only be fleeting and transitory.[59]

In this fleeting moment, however, the referential structure of the workshop is broken, there occurs what Heidegger calls a rupture of reference, and Dasein stumbles upon a void which forces it to become aware of the world in a way which was not possible so long as work was in progress. This is Dasein's original confrontation with nothingness, and it is out of this confrontation that Heidegger sees truth arise.[60] The vicious circle of Dasein's

59. SZ 73.
60. In the passage which I am here recounting (SZ 74–75) Heidegger does not actually speak of "nothing" (*das Nichts*). He refers to a "rupture of reference" (*Störung der Verweisung*) and a "break in the referential context" (*Bruch der Verweisungszusammenhänge*) and has prudence "stumble upon a void" (*stösst ins Leere*). I make this the focal point of my interpretation of Heidegger's thinking in order to make sense of the notion of

practical activity is broken—broken, observe, from without—and the preoccupation which characterizes such activity is overcome. A "gap" appears in the environment, and through this gap Dasein first attains the awareness which is an indispensable condition of truth. Subject and object, intellect and thing, here emerge out of a living context which cannot properly be characterized in terms of subject and object or as a relation of intellect and thing. This is the openness of being which Heidegger argues is presupposed by the traditional notion of truth and by all human experience.

There is one other way in which Heidegger sees truth emerge as forcefully and inescapably as it does with the broken instrument. This is in the *work of art*. The relation of the work of art to truth is the theme of the first essay of *Holzwege*, "The Origin of the Work of Art" (1957 [1936]). This is a curious juxtaposition: the broken instrument and the work of art. What have a pair of worn-out shoes to do with a painting by van Gogh or a leaky roof with the ceiling of the Sistine Chapel?

We have seen that Heidegger objects to the fundamental distinction between the artifact and the natural being. Both, he argues, are initially approached insofar as they are useful, and whether a thing's usefulness is the result of human production is of secondary importance. He likewise objects to the man-made instrument and the work of art being lumped together in the category of the artifact. Leather for shoes has more in common with steel for automobiles than it has with a dwarfed tree in a Japanese garden, and a sonnet has more in common with the dwarfed tree than it has with a treatise in physiology or a note to the milkman.[61]

Heidegger objects to any aesthetic explanation which puts exclusive or primary emphasis on the *form* of the work of art.[62] Form takes precedence over matter in the being of the instrument. The distinction derives from the realm of instruments and always entails the priority of form, for it is through its form that a thing is adapted to a particular function, as the ax is to cutting by virtue of

---

"nothing," which has been the subject of so much controversy. It is true that Heidegger himself refers to this stage of his inquiry (*WG* 36, n. 55) as being "of subordinate importance in relation to the ultimate goal" of his thinking ("im Ganzen und auf das leitende Ziel hin angesehen von untergeordneter Bedeutung"). As a hermeneutic device it nevertheless appears to me indispensable. In the final analysis it is of subordinate importance because Heidegger leads our thinking away from things and their fragility.

61. *Ho* 13–21 (654–61).
62. *Ho* 17–19 (657–60).

its sharp edge and the length of its handle. The material out of which an instrument is made is of secondary importance: the axhead may be made out of anything which provides a sharp enough edge, its handle out of whatever will bear the strain of chopping.[63] When the instrument is used—thus realizing, in Aristotle's classic formula, its being as an instrument—its matter is taken up into its form or function; the heavy intransigence of steel and wood is transformed into the pure activity of cutting. If Heidegger suggests that the instrument disappears in its function, he is thinking primarily of its matter. Similarly in the treatise on physiology and the note to the milkman, if they are well written, the words become the transparent medium for the communication of a message. If we are conscious of the words themselves, the writing is defective.

But the work of art is not an instrument—it is neither a means to the attainment of pleasure nor the medium for the communication of a message—and it cannot be explained properly in terms appropriate to the instrument, the distinction of matter and form. If we use such terms, we find that their relation is reversed. Where, in the instrument, matter is subordinate to form and absorbed in it when the instrument is performing its function, the form of a work of art is meant to body forth and call attention to the material out of which it is made. The wooden handle of the ax disappears in the activity of cutting and the words of my note to the milkman in conveying information. But a great woodcut *manifests* the wood out of which it is carved, saying in effect: look at what wood can be. And the sonnet reveals its words, which here appear as something more than a means of communication. If we are aware of the leather of a shoe, it is not a good shoe; but if we are *not* aware of the marble of a statue, the colors of a painting, or the sounds of a symphony, we have failed to encounter them as works of art.

The better or more suitable material is, the more it vanishes without resistance in the instrumental being of the instrument. With the temple, however, it is just the opposite: it does not allow its materials to disappear but brings them forth for the first time in the openness of a world which it itself exhibits. Granite now comes to be solid and enduring and so really granite; metals gleam, colors radiate, tones resound, the word is spoken and heard. All this comes about precisely insofar as the work of art returns to the weight and density of stone, to the tough suppleness of wood, and the gleaming strength of bronze,

63. *Meta.* 1036a30–b8.

to the highlights and shadings of color, tonal harmonies, and the power of the word to name.[64]

Aristotle does not recognize the gulf which separates the work of art from the instrument when he suggests that a statue of Hermes is "out of bronze" in the same way as a brazen disk.[65] The instrument is essentially inconspicuous, but the work of art must draw attention to itself, and to its matter as much as to its form. The work of art is not so much "out of bronze" as it reaches down "into bronze" to allow it to body forth. This is what Heidegger understands by beauty (*das Schöne*). He traces the German word to its root in the verb "to shine" (*scheinen*)—the root, incidentally, of the word for illusion or deceptive appearance (*Schein*) as well.[66]

The instrument always fits into some given context of human design, but the work of art creates a context of its own, which always transcends our given designs in some sense.[67] To do this it must draw us out of the familiar context of our everyday world. Drawing us out of our familiar context and drawing our attention to matter as the merely present—to sounds, colors, words, stone, and metals—are really two sides of the same coin. Both appear to have become more difficult in the course of history, and this may be why contemporary composers have discarded classic harmony for the diatonic scale and why contemporary novelists like Joyce, Faulkner, and Virginia Woolf often refuse to narrate events in the traditional way.

For all their differences the broken instrument and the work of art both call us back from the future into the present, manifest the material out of which they are made in a way that cannot be overlooked, and break through the familiar, self-evident context of our daily lives. It is really not so surprising that modern art is widely regarded as a broken instrument and that many artists

64. "Der Stoff ist umso besser und geeigneter, je widerstandsloser er im Zeugsein des Zeuges untergeht. Das Tempel-Werk dagenen lässt, indem es eine Welt aufstellt, den Stoff nicht verschwinden, sondern allererst hervorkommen und zwar im Offenen der Welt des Werkes: der Fels kommt zum Tragen und Ruhen und wird so erst Fels; die Metalle kommen zum Blitzen und Schimmern, die Farben zum Leuchten, der Ton zum Klingen, das Wort zum Sagen. All dieses kommt hervor, indem das Werk sich zurückstellt in das Massige und Schwere des Steins, in das Feste und Biegsame des Holzes, in die Härte und den Glanz des Erzes, in das Leuchten und Dunkeln der Farbe, in den Klang des Tones und in die Nennkraft des Wortes" (*Ho* 35 [672–73]).
65. *Phys.* 191a8–13.
66. *Ho* 44 (680); *EM* 100–101 (131–32); *N I* 130; *WD* 8.
67. *Ho* 31 (669), 59 (693), 62 (695); *EH* 62, 97–98.

from the Dada movement onward have even welcomed the identification.

This has been a long digression on a theme to which we
cannot do justice, but it is important because, like Heidegger in
Being and Time, we have been hammering away at an abstraction—the instrumentality of beings as Dasein originally encounters them—so that the end effect is a rather gross exaggeration.
We have talked of things disappearing, and obviously they do not
disappear. We may be less explicitly aware of them most of the
time than the traditional philosophical portrayal of experience
would suggest, but this does not mean that they disappear altogether. Our discussion has been potentially misleading in concentrating on one aspect of things and tending to confuse it with the
things themselves. Things do not vanish, but the first aspect they
present to man is their vanishing aspect. Is it not reasonable to
suggest that none of the instruments we encounter is a perfect
instrument and that every instrument therefore entails a certain
appearance as the index of its imperfection? This is Heidegger's
position up to a point, but it is not altogether satisfactory, being
still cast in terms of our one initial abstraction. We answer better
for Heidegger when we say that things are beautiful, and if this is
not an aspect of things to which man initially relates, it is still one
which is never wholly absent, even in the hubbub of the market
place and the traffic of Main Street. Beauty and instrumentality—shining forth and vanishing—are poles of human experience,
and if Heidegger accords phenomenological priority to the instrumental, it is because he conceives the beautiful in relation to
wonder and wonder as a phenomenon which occurs only when the
familiar is divested of its familiarity. We will return to this theme
in section 5. In the meantime it is important to minimize the
exaggeration which results from our exclusive concern with the
instrumentality of things by placing it alongside its counterpart,
their beauty.

In *Being and Time* Heidegger is primarily concerned with
truth at what we might call its lowest level. In revealing the
process by which human awareness arises out of human activity
he takes as his model activities which immediately concern
things. His frame of reference is economic: *homo faber* related to
ens utile. But his argument should be understood in a wider sense.
For the sequence of activity, breakdown, and awareness is applicable at every level of human experience: economic, social, psychological, scientific, and metaphysical. Pragmatic *breakdown*
is repeated in psychological *disillusion* and in theoretical

contradiction. This is why Heidegger claims that the status of any science is to be judged by the extent to which it is capable of experiencing a crisis in its fundamental concepts. The event which Heidegger here describes should not be understood exclusively in a pragmatic, psychological, or metaphysical sense, for it is not meant to be any one of these but to reveal the tenuous thread of coherence which unites them all.[68]

Once again we should recall Aristotle. In the opening paragraphs of Book III of the *Metaphysics* Aristotle confronts the dilemma with which we introduced our discussion: where can thinking make a start and how is it to find guidance or direction? Confronting an inexhaustible variety of things about which we might think, and being in possession of no reliable criterion to guide our thinking, how are we to proceed? We must look for the difficulty or impasse, Aristotle asserts, for a "knot in the object"—a contradiction—and think about *this*. When we resolve one contradiction or break through one impasse, another immediately presents itself, and we must think about it until we resolve it and again break through. We have only to follow the difficulties in this way, resolving successive contradictions, and reality will unfold before us—and, what is more, *it* then determines the direction of our thinking.

For those who wish to get clear of difficulties it is advantageous to discuss the difficulties well; for the subsequent free play of thought implies the solution of the previous difficulties, and it is not possible to untie a knot of which one does not know. But the difficulty of our thinking points to a "knot" in the object; for in so far as our thought is in difficulties, it is in like case with those who are bound; for in either case it is impossible to go forward. Hence one should have surveyed all the difficulties beforehand . . . because people who inquire without first stating the difficulties are like those who do not know where they have to go; besides, a man does not otherwise know even whether he has at any given time found what he is looking for or not. . . .[69]

Plato speaks in a similar vein in the *Republic* when he sees, as one of the greatest benefits of vision, the fact that it drives man to reflect by exposing him to the contradictions of the sensible world and so lifts him out of his immediate experience into a higher realm of contemplation.[70] Both Plato and Aristotle here recognize the origin of awareness in a kind of breakdown, but both talk in a

68. See SZ 45–50.
69. *Meta.* 995a26–b1.
70. *Rep.* 523b–524d.

theoretical context and conceive the difficulty from which thinking receives its impetus and direction as a difficulty *of thought*. It
is indeed a difficulty which impels us to reflect, Heidegger argues,
but not originally a *cognitive* difficulty. He traces the origin of
truth or awareness not to any breakdown of thinking—though
this later plays a decisive role—but to a breakdown in life, out of
which thinking emerges and of which theoretical contradiction is
a special case.

4. Nothing and the Source of Knowledge

IN SEARCHING FOR the presupposition of the traditional notion of truth, Heidegger traces back knowledge to its
origin in human life, out of which it necessarily arises. Knowledge
has forgotten its source in life, as the traditional notion of truth
witnesses. Beginning with Plato and Aristotle it has come to regard itself as grounded in itself—it has started on the way to
becoming absolute. In view of the way in which Heidegger describes the living situation out of which knowledge arises, it is not
surprising that this should be the case.

(*a*) Knowledge requires first a certain familiarity with its
object and an intelligible context in which the object is encountered. Such a context Heidegger calls the world, and he argues that
its structure is not created by knowledge but sketched out by Dasein's practical activities prior to knowledge. (*b*) Knowledge requires further a relation of subject and object. But such a relation
cannot be assumed as given, for Dasein does not relate immediately
to things as a subject to an object. This may be the way in which
the scientist relates to the microbe under his microscope, but it is
not the way in which the rider relates to the horse under his saddle.
(*c*) Knowledge requires finally a certain distance, the distance
necessary to objectivity and vision, and such dis-[s]tance—we
must emphasize the negative sense of the word—comes about
only when there is a disturbance of equilibrium, a breakdown in
Dasein's activities in which things withdraw, paradoxically, to
become explicitly *present* for the first time.[71] These presuppositions of knowledge Heidegger insists cannot be taken for granted,
and in *Being and Time* he attempts to show how they emerge out
of a living situation which is not characterized by knowledge.

The description culminated in a breakdown of Dasein's

71. Heidegger emphasizes the paradox of "distance" in this sense by
writing *Ent-fernung*. The nuance, however, is different. See *SZ* 105–8; *ID*
61–62 (56–57).

activity which first reveals the world and all the beings which go to make it up, recalling man out of his preoccupation to an awareness of his position in the midst of beings. This is the original manifestation of beings in their simple presence as possible objects of knowledge. But it requires a withdrawal of instrumentality in a rupture of referential structure which we have called, after Helmut Kuhn, an encounter with nothingness. What is important is that this withdrawal and the revelation to which it gives rise—the emergence of openness—occur "from without." They are not possible apart from Dasein's activity in organizing instruments, but neither are they, like knowledge, Dasein's own achievement—quite the contrary.

"Nothing" (*das Nichts*) is the central theme of the essay *What Is Metaphysics?* (1930), where the subject of investigation is not human experience at its lowest level but at one of its highest, the level at which knowledge attains its most exact and objective expression in science. Heidegger finds "nothing" at the heart of science as he has at the heart of human existence in its most common manifestation. From a quite different starting point he arrives at the same conclusion.

Science Heidegger regards as a special way of relating to beings resulting from a "freely chosen attitude of human existence" (*frei gewählte Haltung der menschlichen Existenz*)[72]—whence its almost total absence in the history of the Orient. The distinguishing feature of this attitude is that it gives the being which is the object of its inquiry the last word.[73] This is Francis Bacon's contribution to the methodology of science: insisting that observation be the final arbiter of all scientific questions. Science involves a far-reaching subjection to beings, but one which is ultimately limited. In scientific questions beings have the last word, but it is the scientist who puts the question and forces nature to answer—in Kant's analogy, like a judge examining a witness. Scientific research cannot proceed without a hypothesis, which observation must then confirm or reject. This aspect of science, which Bacon overlooks, is first emphasized by Hobbes. Scientific research proceeds where man puts questions to which nature can—and indeed must—give clear and specific answers (yes or no); no other type of question can claim to be scientific. It

72. WM 25 (357). See also VA 62.
73. Heidegger himself speaks of "the first and last word" (*WM* 25 [357]), but he goes on immediately to insist on the necessity of a scientific breakthrough (*Einbruch*) into the totality of things. This occurs through the hypothesis, which it seems reasonable to call the "first word."

follows that science is concerned solely with particular, determinate beings, for only such beings are capable of giving the clear and specific answers which scientific questions demand.[74] With "nothing," which is wholly indeterminate, science has nothing whatever to do.

Yet when we attempt to define science and to say what distinguishes it from other human activities, we cannot avoid referring to nothing. We say that it is concerned with determinate beings *and nothing else* and that it requires specific answers *and no other.* The scientific judgment takes the form "*x* is *y* and nothing else" or "*x* and *y* are related in this way and no other" or "if *x*, then *y* and under no other condition." This reference to nothing is specifically characteristic of the scientific judgment, which necessarily excludes others of the same order in a way which is not true of nonscientific judgments (e.g., literary, philosophical, religious). Although science has nothing to do with nothing, it cannot be defined without recourse to nothing. Heidegger asks, "What sort of ambivalent creature are we faced with here?"[75]

No one would deny that scientific inquiry requires a determinate object and that, for a thing to be determinate, it must be set off from other things by a negative, a *not* or *non-*. Spinoza's dictum is well known: *omnis determinatio est negatio.* But negation is one thing and Heidegger's "nothing" another. To say that science requires negation is not to say that it depends upon nothing in the way in which Heidegger suggests. So Heidegger pits nothing against the negation implicit in all strict, scientific judgments. His claim is that the *negatio* on which all determination and intelligibility depend does not have its origin in knowledge, in the negative judgment, but in human life as it precedes and transcends knowledge. The question is: is nothing a special case of negation or negation a special case of nothing? Heidegger's answer is already clear: "It is our claim that nothing is more original than the *not* and negation."[76]

First we must determine what this nothing is which we are asked to weigh against negation. But we cannot ask what nothing is, for the question treats it as though it were *something*.[77] Nothing cannot be thought, for all thought is about something: thinking of nothing is simply not thinking. Logic rules out the

74. *WM* 24–26 (355–58). See also *EM* 19–20 (25–26); *Ho* 71–77.
75. "Welch zwiespältiges Wesen enthüllt sich da?" (*WM* 27 [359]).
76. "Wir behaupten: das Nichts ist ursprünglicher als das Nicht und die Verneinung" (*WM* 28 [361]).
77. *WM* 27–28 (360); *EM* 18–19 (23–24); *N II* 51–52.

possibility of the question of nothing. But Heidegger challenges its competence to pass final judgment in such a question.[78] Certainly negation must submit to the rules of logic, and nothing is traditionally regarded as an instance of negation: as non-being, the negation of being in its totality (*das Seiende im Ganzen*). This is the way Descartes regards it, for example.[79] But being can only be negated in its totality if it can be thought in its totality, and this is not possible. So this is not what Heidegger means by nothing.

Though we may not be able to represent being in its totality, we are nevertheless situated in the midst of beings and confront them *in the context of* being in its totality.[80] In its daily preoccupations as well as in its scientific judgments Dasein may seem to attach itself exclusively to this or that being or area of beings, but its being-in-the-world still implicitly comprehends all beings in a tenuous unity on which its thinking and action depend. In *Being and Time* we became aware of this totality in the breakdown of the instrument. In *What Is Metaphysics?* Heidegger speaks of such a confrontation in boredom, an experience in which all things become superfluous and everything and everyone, the self included, are united in a singular indifference. Similarly in love, the encounter of a being who means more to us than all things. Love and boredom situate us consciously in the midst of being in its totality. They reveal being in its totality, but not nothing. Is there a mood which reveals no particular being, not even being in its totality, but nothing?

Heidegger claims that anxiety (*Angst*) is such a mood. Anxiety must be distinguished from fear (*Furcht*), which is always fear *of* something more or less determinate. Fear binds the fearful to some particular object or situation and robs him of his powers of apprehension. Anxiety has no particular object and rather

78. Heidegger's objection to traditional logic is that it is oriented exclusively toward things. "That even traditional logic proves to be incapable of dealing with such phenomena is not surprising when we consider that it is rooted in an ontology of beings-on-hand, and a crude one at that" ("Dass auch die traditionelle Logik angesichts dieser Phänomene versagt, kann nicht verwundern, wenn bedacht wird, dass sie ihr Fundament in einer überdies noch rohen Ontologie des Vorhandenen hat" [SZ 129]). For Heidegger's critique of logic see SZ 158–60, 165–66; WM 47–50 (387–90); BH 55 (271–72), 98–99 (292–93); EM 91–94 (119–22); WD 99–101; Ho 287; ID 53–56 (49–52).

79. Descartes equates being and perfection. As an imperfect being man is "a something intermediate between God and nothingness, that is to say, placed between sovereign Being and not-being"; he "participates in nothingness, i.e., in not-being" (*Med.* IV, ed. Kemp Smith, p. 233).

80. WW 18–19 (338–40); WM 30–31 (363–64).

heightens our powers of apprehension. In anxiety all things become strange—we do not know why. They seem to slide away, only in sliding away they turn toward us, revealing a new, uncanny visage. There remains nothing to hold on to. The individual personality slips away along with all other things, and only pure "being there" remains.

> We are suspended in anxiety. More precisely, anxiety brings us into suspension by allowing being in its totality to slip away. . . . Only pure Dasein, pure "being there," remains in the trembling vibration of such suspension, in which there is nothing on which to hold fast: it alone is still there. [In this way] anxiety reveals nothing.[81]

The language here is metaphorical and so requires some interpretation. What is it about anxiety to which Heidegger ascribes the power to reveal nothing? What distinguishes it from boredom and love, which reveal being in its totality but not nothing? Of anxiety Heidegger says that "only pure 'being there' remains." What remains in boredom and love? We can only suggest that boredom and love both entail a point of view—the point of view from which being is affirmed or denied—that both are essentially centrifugal movements which never completely sever the bond to the self or ego. They are also *what*-oriented, however all-embracing this orientation may be. In boredom, for example, all things are lumped together in a single indifferent *what*. In anxiety, on the other hand, Dasein transcends the point of view and the self to which it is tied and relates exclusively to the *that* of things. It is as though Heidegger were describing a kind of existential *epochē*.[82] We may conclude that boredom and love extend to the outermost limits of the subject-object dichotomy but that anxiety goes beyond—or undercuts—the dichotomy, which the argument of *Being and Time* has shown no reason for regarding as absolute. Such an interpretation is supported by the context in which the discussion occurs, for it is in science that the subject-

81. "Die Angst offenbart das Nichts. Wir 'schweben' in Angst. Deutlicher: die Angst lässt uns schweben, weil sie das Seiende im Ganzen zum Entgleiten bringt. . . . Nur das reine Da-sein in der Durchschütterung dieses Schwebens, darin es sich an nichts halten kann, ist noch da" (*WM* 32 [363–64]). (In my translation I have put the first sentence last because it represents a sort of conclusion.)

82. Actually the notion of an existential *epochē* is absurd in Husserl's sense of the term, and it marks the gulf which separates Heidegger from the founder of phenomenology. Husserl's ideal, with the *epochē*, is of a kind of detached vision, purified of all concern, all "positing." For Heidegger this is an impossible ideal, since vision is rooted in concern. Heidegger adopts a great deal of his terminology from Husserl, but he completely transforms its significance.

object dichotomy—the clear-cut distinction between the scientist and his subject matter—finds its consummate expression.

We must transcend the subject-object dichotomy in order to encounter it as a problem, as we do in philosophy, or in order to manipulate and control it, as we do in science. This transcendence Heidegger calls a "projection into nothing" (*Sichhinein-halten in das Nichts*),[83] and he argues that it is encountered directly—if rarely—in a mood, anxiety.[84] "Nothing" in this sense is not the contrary of any being in particular or of beings in general, and in being projected into it we do not go beyond them into another world or into utter irreality but come for the first time into their presence. Such projection into nothing is fundamental to every human project, including science. Science thus presupposes an experience which we can never have through thinking but only in a mood.

Anxiety is the final distillation of care, the essence of being *there*.[85] It is care divested of its attachment to any particular being, to the self on the one hand and to the *what* of things on the other. In the second half of *Being and Time* Heidegger portrays anxiety as a dimension of Dasein's care which is no longer care for things but goes beyond things to the limit of human experience in the anticipation of death. Death is the broken instrument par excellence, and the revelation which it entails is not fleeting or transitory: it is fundamental to our experience of being as such in the way in which the broken instrument is fundamental to our experience of particular beings in their autonomy and otherness (resistance). The experience of being as such Heidegger thus sees as inseparable from the experience of one's own being-to-an-end (*Sein zum Ende*), one's being-to-death (*Sein zum Tode*).[86] It is this concern for being as such which he argues science presupposes, even though it can never be encountered in thought, much less scientific thought. This is the projection into nothing which anxiety reveals.

83. *WM* 35 (370), 41 (379); *Ho* 321.
84. *WM* 31–36 (365–71); *SZ* 186–91, 251, 265–66, 276–77, 342–43; *KM* 214 (246).
85. *SZ* 182; *KM* 215 (247).
86. *SZ* 234, 240–52, 260–66, 384; *EM* 121 (158); *VA* 177, 256; *SG* 186–87; *US* 215. In *Being and Time* the experience of being-unto-death reveals Dasein's most proper possibility of being. "As the end of Dasein, death is its most proper possibility, one which is not referred to anything beyond itself, indefinite because it is certain, and irretrievable" ("Der Tod als Ende des Daseins ist die eigenste, unbezügliche, gewisse und als solche unbestimmte, unüberholbare Möglichkeit des Daseins" [*SZ* 258–59, in italics]). In the later works it reveals being as such. For Heidegger these two are inseparable.

Dasein's projection into nothing is reflected in the experience of the finitude of its own being in the midst of being in its totality.[87] Such an experience is fundamental to science in three ways. The experience of being in its totality provides the context for our specific knowledge of being *as such and such*. The experience of nothing adds the sharp edge of intelligibility, as we understand what it means *to be* (this or that) against the background of what it means *not to be*. And because it severs the ties which bind Dasein to itself and to the *what* of things, the experience is the source of the detached attitude which we must bring to science. Heidegger's nothing thus plays much the same role in human experience as the Platonic idea.[88]

The fact that nothing is encountered only in a mood renders it inaccessible to logic. It is nevertheless a condition of the manifestation of beings as such, whether to Dasein's prudent concern in its practical activities in the world or to its dispassionate concern in the pursuit of scientific inquiry. If mood and its revelation inevitably elude the vision of logic and science, it is because it is the source out of which they arise. So Heidegger calls mood the primordial event of Dasein (*das Grundgeschehen unseres Daseins*), the genesis of our "being there." [89] We will take up this theme again in the following chapter.

We can now return to the question of the relative priority of negation and nothing. If nothing is responsible for the openness of beings, it must be prior to negation and the activity of understanding which it makes possible. Understanding does not create the *not* out of itself and insert it between things for the purpose of distinguishing and contrasting them. Science does not create its own pigeonholes—this is a Hobbesian exaggeration. Understanding only negates that which manifests itself as negatable. Nothing is not grounded in negation as a specific instance of the *not;* negation is rather one form of negative conduct, or one way of relating to nothing.[90]

The nothing of which Heidegger speaks in *What Is Metaphysics?* is encountered in human experience as its limit—and its source—not one which is postulated outside experience as the opposite of the totality of beings. The notion of nothing which underlies the classic formula *ex nihilo nihil fit* is an imaginary nothing which reflects the unwarranted intrusion of logic into the

87. WG 47–54; KM 197–222 (226–55).
88. See below, pp. 151–52.
89. WM 31 (364); KM 214–15 (246–47).
90. WM 36–37 (372–73); BH 112–13 (298–99).

living experience out of which it arises. The nothing which we encounter in mood is the source out of which beings first present themselves in their explicit presence, and this can best be expressed by reversing the classic formula: *ex nihilo omne ens qua ens fit.*[91]

Heidegger's nothing is not a *nihil negativum*—an imaginary nothing or the reification of a logical function—but the source of knowledge and its object which is not itself a possible object of knowledge. It is like Aristotle's *nous,* which can have "no nature of its own," a no-thing. If we recall the essentially negative character of the instrument as in-conspicuous, nothing here appears, in Hegelian terms, as the "negation of a negation." It is constitutive of the pure presence in which any being can *be* and manifest itself as a being, as such and such. It is like space and time in the *Critique of Pure Reason,* which are not themselves sensible (or given) but allow things to be sensible, which are not themselves "present" or manifest but go to constitute the presence in which it is possible for things to manifest or "present" themselves. Kant himself must have something like this in mind when he calls space and time "categories of nothing (*Nichts*)." [92] In fact Heidegger's nothing has much in common with Kant's thing-in-itself, only with the decisive difference that it is not primarily a logical postulate and is not conceived of as beyond time; on the contrary, it is inextricably bound up with time. And while it is unknowable, Heidegger's nothing is directly encountered in the anticipation of death and in our awareness of things in the "light" of our impending and inevitable death, i.e., in the mood of anxiety.

What Heidegger opposes with his notion of nothing is the view of transcendence in which man exists beyond time in order to comprehend temporal phenomena—Plato's world of ideas. He regards this as an imaginary transcendence which complements the imaginary nothing of logic. His claim is that an experience of the limit, *but no more,* is presupposed by all experience within the limit: the hammer need only break in order to manifest itself. The experience of the limit is the anticipation of death in the mood of anxiety. Conflict over Heidegger's philosophy tends to center in one way or another upon this point.

Only a being characterized by care and capable of experiencing anxiety can encounter the nothing of which Heidegger speaks,

91. WM 38–40 (375–77). See also Ho 104; BH 112–14 (298–99); EM 19–25 (24–32).
92. A 291, B 347. See below, pp. 161, 164–65.

and only such a being can understand and pursue science. "Both 'theory' and 'practice' are ontological possibilities of a being whose being must be determined as care." [93] Science as an attitude of subjection toward beings can emerge only out of a primordial attitude of concern for being. Knowledge is possible only for a being characterized primarily by a passionate involvement with itself, its kind, and the things of the world. And such a being must have nothing at its very heart—it must be radically finite.

This view of science may seem far removed from the empirical reality of scientific research. It is what Heidegger calls the "existential concept of science." [94] And yet in contrast to the two classic positions of Bacon and Hobbes it does justice to both the active and passive dimensions of science, both to the sense in which science, in depending on a hypothesis of man's devising, is essentially a human product, and to the sense in which the scientist must subordinate himself to the way in which things manifest themselves. Against the realist claim that man can simply read off the intelligibility of nature, it insists that man must "break into" the presence of beings. Against the idealist claim that man introduces the *not* of intelligibility into things, it insists that the negation of human judgment must be traced back to an origin which precedes and transcends the theoretical point of view and the *ratio* of *animal rationale*.

Heidegger's view of science brings theory and practice closer together than ever before. "Thinking does not first become action when it is applied or when it produces a [tangible] effect. Thinking acts in the very process of thinking." [95] It provides an ontological explanation for the fact that two scientists can dispute the most abstruse scientific question with the heat and fervor which usually characterize political argument. For however much scientific research, like human action, may seem to attach itself to this or that being in particular—the behavior of a subatomic particle or the evolution of a biological organ or the mutation of a verb in Old French—it always relates implicitly to human experience as a whole, and in every scientific development human being itself is

93. " 'Theorie' und 'Praxis' sind Seinsmöglichkeiten eines Seienden, dessen Sein als Sorge bestimmt werden muss" (*SZ* 193).
94. *SZ* 357.
95. "Das Denken wird nicht erst dadurch zur Aktion, dass von ihm eine Wirkung ausgeht oder dass es angewendet wird. Das Denken handelt, indem es denkt" (*BH* 53 [271]). See also *SZ* 300–301, 357–58; *BH* 53–55 (271–72), 111 (298), 115 (300), 117 (301); *WM* 50 (390); *N* I 177–78, 381–82.

at stake. Since Aristotle we have drawn too sharp a distinction between these two ways of "being there," a distinction which culminates in Kant's first two *Critiques* and the dilemma which they pose in relation to each other.

Heidegger portrays knowledge in two ways: the one positive, the other negative. We have seen knowledge arise in *Being and Time* when the innerworldly being is divested of its instrumentality and is "then"—at least temporarily—"merely present" (*nur noch vorhanden*). Against this background Heidegger describes knowledge in some passages as the last—and highest—way in which Dasein can manifest its concern for a thing, "now merely lingering by" it (*nur-noch-verweilen-bei* . . .) to dwell on its being and allow it to reveal itself as it is.[96] It is the one way of relating to things which remains when all other ways have been exhausted and human activity is divested of every trace of manipulation. Such knowledge represents the final distillation of man's being as concern, purified of all pragmatic considerations. More often, however, Heidegger sees in "pure theory" a covert drive toward control, a concealed effort to bring beings *out of* their mere presence and back into human design as reliable components of manipulation.[97] The distinction is a valuable one, but it is not clear why Heidegger regards scientific theory as almost invariably representative of the latter attitude,[98] reserving the former primarily to the poet.

Aristotle seems to recognize pure theory as the final distillation of practical activity in Book I of the *Metaphysics*. "Hence when all such inventions were already established, the sciences which do not aim at giving pleasure or at the necessities of life were discovered, and first in the places where men first began to have leisure." [99] The question is whether such a statement should be accorded metaphysical or purely sociological significance.

Heidegger rejects all conceptions of knowledge which are formed on the basis of an analogy with *vision*.[100] In vision more

96. *SZ* 61–62; *BH* 53–58 (270–73); *WM* 48–50 (388–91); *VA* 68–70; *HH* 21–22, 27–28.
97. *SZ* 61–62; *WM* 43 (381), 48 (388); *Ho* 80; *BH* 58–60 (273–74); *VA* 33–36, 58–63; *SG* 167–70, 173–74, 194–203; *EM* 48 (62–63); *HH* 30–31; *US* 263–64.
98. *VA* 63 (133–34); *US* 179.
99. *Meta.* 981b20–22.
100. *SZ* 147; *PL* 35–36 (262); *BM* 48 (63); *VA* 252; *Ho* 318–22. "Vision is divested of its priority in knowledge. With this being-on-hand loses the ontological priority which corresponds to the noetic priority of pure contemplation" (Otto Pöggeler, *Der Denkweg Martin Heideggers*, p. 44).

than any other sense man dissociates himself from his world, and when knowledge comes to be regarded as absolute or underived, its nature is invariably expressed in visual terms: Plato's *eidos* and *idea,* Descartes' "clear and distinct idea," Hume's "representations," Kant's *Anschauung* and *Vorstellungen,* Husserl's *Wesensschau.* More fundamental than the knowledge of the eye, Heidegger insists, is that of the hand. This can be seen in our language—even when knowledge is conceived primarily in relation to the eye—in a host of words like "concept," "comprehension," "grasp," "manifest," "premise," "proposition," and "distinction." Heidegger wants to reverse the order of theory and action, vision and preoccupation, the eye and the hand. "Every work of the hand abides in thinking. For this reason thinking is the simplest, and hence the most difficult, handiwork of man, if . . . it is genuinely to come to fruition." [101]

The argument of *What Is Metaphysics?* is not clear unless it is read against the background of *Being and Time.* It is a favorite target of critics who accuse Heidegger of reifying nothing or of simple obscurantism in claiming that an experience of nothing is the source of all knowledge. But to make nothing the source out of which "things" emerge is hardly to reify it, and the notion is not so obscure if we associate it with the broken hammer of *Being and Time.* (In using the term "nothing" in this way, Heidegger can even invoke the precedent of Kant, who is often considered obscure but is rarely accused of being obscurantist.) The trouble is that *What Is Metaphysics?* takes up where the argument of *Being and Time*—as we have traced it thus far—leaves off. *Being and Time* portrays the initial manifestation of beings and the source of human awareness; *What Is Metaphysics?* relates intelligibility (the determinateness of any determinate object of knowledge) to the same source.[102] In both works we find the same persistent themes: the finitude of human being, the derivative character of knowledge, and a notion of truth as beyond human disposing, a dynamic notion which conceives truth as an event, and one which

101. "Alles Werk der Hand beruht im Denken. Darum ist das Denken selbst das einfachste und deshalb schwerste Hand-Werk des Menschen, wenn es . . . eigens vollbracht sein möchte" (*WD* 51).

102. Jean Wahl presents a mirror-image of Heidegger's argument when he says, "We do not believe that the fact of casting doubt on understanding leads necessarily to the affirmation of nothing, as *What Is Metaphysics?* maintains" (*Revue de métaphysique et de morale,* LXI [1956], 129). Heidegger argues quite the reverse: *from* the affirmation of nothing *to* a position which casts doubt on understanding.

occurs, so to speak, from without. It is this event which we must continue to pursue.

5. The World and the Earth

WE ARE IN SEARCH of the most fundamental presupposition of all human experience, but more immediately of the traditional notion of truth as the truth of knowledge. The world provides knowledge with the familiar context which it requires. But the world is not the only presupposition of knowledge. We have spoken of an event in which the context is broken and things are divested of their familiarity. Such an event implies a reference to a second principle, which we must now portray.

There are three aspects of the world which we must recall.

1. The world is not the mere sum of innerworldly beings. For the innerworldly being is essentially instrumental, and yet it is only when it is divested of its instrumentality—or innerworldliness—that the world itself appears. The world and the beings within it are related contrapuntally, so that individual beings manifest themselves only when they cease to be innerworldly, and the world functions as a world only so long as individual beings do not manifest themselves.[103] This is Heidegger's justification for rejecting the assumption that knowledge is essentially continuous with the precognitive experience out of which it arises.

2. The world belongs to the being of Dasein as the field of its care and management of things. As such it is necessarily implicit or familiar. The world is thus never encountered as something new and unknown but as something already open, to which Dasein has already related, in which it has already lived, worked, and acted. All knowledge presupposes this prior familiarity, with which it must begin and to which it can only return. It follows that knowledge always comes upon the scene *too late:* "the revelatory possibilities of knowledge simply do not reach." [104] There is no *original* knowledge of the world.

3. The world is organized around some fundamental human project which it is meant to further, and it depends upon this project for its being and organization. We can see this in any workshop: without some project there would be no workshop, and if the project were different, the shop would likewise be different. But the world is the workshop of workshops, and if they are

103. *SZ* 75.
104. ". . . die Erschliessungsmöglichkeiten des Erkennens [tragen] viel zu kurz . . ." (*SZ* 134). See also SZ 76; *Ho* 41 (677–78).

determined by projects which Dasein *happens to have*, it is determined by the project which Dasein essentially *is*. On its structure the being and nature of all innerworldly beings depend. The world, along with everything in it, is thus relative to Dasein and its essential project of what it is to become. In this sense Dasein "projects" the world and everything in it.

Because every project stems from a decision, Heidegger traces the organization of human experience to an origin (*Ursprung*) in a primordial decision which we must conceive as a "leap" (*Sprung*).[105] And he sees an essential bond between Dasein's decisiveness (*Entschlossenheit*) and the openness (*Erschlossenheit*) of beings for it.[106]

But if Dasein projects its world, so that the world is relative to its being, there is a deeper sense in which Dasein is projected into its world and is itself relative.

1. If the world organizes itself around a decision, it is around a decision which *has already been made*. At any given moment Dasein confronts a world which is already determined in its essential structure and must decide within the concrete range of possibility which such a world affords. The decision to which Dasein's world is relative is never an *original* decision and never simply *its own*. This is what Heidegger wishes to convey when he asks, "Has Dasein itself ever freely decided, or will it ever be able freely to decide, whether or not it wants to attain to its 'being there'?" [107]

2. If Dasein brings forth the instrument, it is only by drawing it into the structure of a world and allowing it to be instrumental. In doing so it can only submit to the functional reference implicit in the thing itself. The hammer must be allowed to serve as a tool of construction, not as a scepter, a swizzle stick or a fly-swatter. Similarly with the materials which Dasein discovers in the world as natural products: each entails a specific range of reference with which the user must comply. Leather must be used for shoes and not for hammers, steel for hammers and not for shoes. In projecting the beings of its world, Dasein can ultimately only "let be" (*sein lassen*), can only submit.[108]

---

105. *EM* 4–5 (5–6); *Ho* 64–65 (697–98). On the necessity of a "leap" in thinking see *WD* 48; *VA* 133–34; *SG* 95–96, 106–7, 157–61; *ID* 24–25 (23–24).

106. *SZ* 297, 307; *EM* 16 (21).

107. "Hat je Dasein als es selbst frei darüber entschieden, und wird es je darüber entscheiden können, ob es ins 'Dasein' kommen will oder nicht?" (*SZ* 228, where the sentence is in italics). Compare *BH* 75 (281); *Ho* 41 (677–78); *WG* 19–20, 43, 54; *PL* 50 (269).

108. *Ho* 17–18 (658–59); *SZ* 84–85.

3. Finally, despite its most strenuous efforts, Dasein cannot determine the point or moment at which the breakdown of its world occurs.[109] But it is the sequence of breakdowns which determines the way in which Dasein's world evolves and its own being unfolds. In these last two considerations Heidegger's second principle begins to emerge.

Though dependant on Dasein for its unity and coherence, the world rests on a foundation of natural products and has its roots in the fecundity of "mother earth." The earth does not appear in *Being and Time,* though its necessity is already apparent there, but it appears in "The Origin of the Work of Art" (1935) in *Holzwege* coequal with the world as one of the two poles between which Dasein exists. It is the *terminus a quo,* the womb of being, the prolific source from which all things proceed. The world and the earth are reciprocal notions and must be described together. Out of their conflict Heidegger sees what he calls the "event of truth" occur.

The world is the open, illuminated area in which Dasein lives and works and strives, the cumulative effect of its decisive activity which in turn renders such activity possible. It is the openness and structure which result from what Dasein *has been* and which determine, within a certain range of possibility, what it *can be.* But Dasein does not exist simply in the midst of openness and structure, or its existence would not be characterized by the necessity of *decision.* "Every decision," Heidegger says, "is grounded in something beyond our control, something hidden, something confusing—otherwise it would not really be a *decision.*" [110] Openness and structure imply a reference to the dense and plastic. And so the world, in Heidegger's sense, implies a reference to the earth (*Erde*).

The earth represents the density, enclosure, and darkness in the midst of which Dasein clears an opening and lays out the field in which decisions are possible. In its boundless fertility the earth serves as the inexhaustible material of Dasein's projects; in its darkness and impenetrability it incessantly resists all Dasein's efforts to draw it into light and make it a factor in its designs. It is the sustainer par excellence which refuses to be understood or controlled. Heidegger calls it "the emergent-sustaining . . . the

109. *Ho* 36 (673–74).
110. "Jede Entscheidung aber gründet sich auf ein Nichtbewältigtes, Verborgenes, Beirrendes, sonst wäre sie nie Entscheidung" (*Ho* 43–44 [679–80]). (Italics added in translation.)

effortless and inexhaustible which is nevertheless adamant and cannot be forced." [111]

The earth corresponds roughly to what we call "nature," but not, in the first instance, as the principle of regularity which underlies scientific research. Heidegger asks us to understand it in the original sense of the Greek *physis,* as the moment of emergence in the process of coming forth and commencing to be. "This coming forth and commencing to be in its totality the ancient Greeks called *physis.* The word is meant to summon up that on which and in which man grounds his life. We call it the earth." [112] We could think of the earth as the *mater* of *materia* if the notion of material had not been debased to signify the raw material of the tool or instrument. As the counterpole of the world, the earth is the ground of structure and meaning which is not itself structured or meaningful. It is the nature of which Heraclitus speaks when he says that it "loves to hide." [113] For it presents itself immediately in the instrument, which, as we have seen, embodies the tendency which Heraclitus ascribes to it.

We can understand the earth as "nature" but not as a principle of regularity: it is not the *physis* of physics. The earth has a rhythm, but one which Heidegger would distinguish sharply from the regularity of behavior which renders things "intelligible," predictable, and controllable. He emphasizes rather the *facticity* of the earth, which is "brute facticity" only from an anthropocentric point of view. So if we conceive the earth as nature, we must distinguish it in the first instance from the nature of natural science. But only in the first instance, because the earth is the sustainer of all man's activities and so must sustain his scientific research as well.[114]

The earth announces itself in every breakdown of the world. Such breakdowns bring Dasein to a recognition of the contingency of its designs, to an awareness that the rhythm of the earth is not its rhythm and that the manipulability of things is not unlimited, is often not even sufficient. Surrounding Dasein's world of meaning—or rather penetrating it to the core—is the meaningless

111. ". . . das Hervorkommend-Bergende . . . das zu nichts gedrängte Mühelose-Unermüdliche" (*Ho* 35 [673]).

112. "Dieses Herauskommen und Aufgehen selbst und im Ganzen nannten die Griechen frühzeitig die *Physis.* Sie lichtet zugleich jenes, worauf und worin der Mensch sein Wohnen gründet. Wir nennen es die Erde" (*Ho* 31 [670]).

113. Frag. 123 (Diels). Quoted by Heidegger, *SG* 113.

114. *VA* 61–63; *HH* 27–31; *Ho* 257–58.

source of meaning and the marvelous or terrible ground of every-thing that is familiar. The familiar is not *fundamentally* famil-iar—it is not familiar in its ground or origin. Rather it is essen-tially *un*familiar: terrible or marvelous.[115]

The negative character of the earth as the unfamiliar, like that of the instrument as the inconspicuous, does not merely indicate what the earth *is not*. "The earth is the *essentially* self-concealing."[116] The earth is the sustaining-*and*-self-concealing, each in virtue of the other. Heidegger appeals to the twofold sense of the German verb *bergen*, which means both "to shelter or protect" and "to hide or conceal." The earth sustains Dasein's life and conceals itself from Dasein's scrutiny—and mastery—and is thus *bergend* in both senses of the term. "The earth is the ada-mant and imperturbable coming forth of that which continually conceals itself and so provides shelter and protection."[117] The essence of the earth is best expressed in the inner coherence of these two notions.

But what is their coherence, apart from the fact that they are the same word in German? First we must recall the dialectic of Dasein's original encounter with the instrument. So long as the instrument is functioning properly and thereby sustaining Da-sein's life, it tends to disappear, and being withdraws and conceals itself. But beyond this we must remember that Dasein's being is that of concern, manifesting itself in activities requiring decision, and that decision is rooted in the unknown, uncontrolled, and confusing. In concealing itself the earth not only sustains Da-sein's factual existence but protects its being as concern as well.

The earth is the ground of the constancy of Dasein's world: the resistance which it offers is essential to the abiding or endur-ing aspect of openness. "In the earth as that which essentially conceals itself the openness of the open [area of human experi-ence] finds its greatest resistance and so a place to stand fast and endure, the only place in which it can take permanent shape."[118] This is metaphorical language. Dasein's activity throughout his-tory takes permanent shape against the resistance of the earth in

115. "Das Geheure ist im Grunde nicht geheuer; es ist un-geheuer" (*Ho* 43 [679]). Compare *BH* 107–9 (296–97); *SZ* 188–89.

116. "Die Erde ist das wesenhaft sich Verschliessende" (*Ho* 36 [674]). (Italics added in translation.)

117. "Die Erde ist das zu nichts gedrängte Hervorkommen des ständig Sichverschliessenden und dergestalt Bergenden" (*Ho* 37 [674–75]).

118. "An der Erde als der wesenhaft sich verschliessenden findet aber die Offenheit des Offenen seinen höchsten Widerstand und so gerade die Stätte seines ständigen Standes, darein die Gestalt festgestellt werden muss" (*Ho* 57 [691]).

the way in which the activity of the sea leaves its mark in the contours of the coast against which it washes. If the world belongs to the being of Dasein, which is defined as a source of activity, it requires a counterelement as the source of its permanence and continuity. This counterelement is the earth, which, in Heidegger's thinking, plays the role traditionally ascribed by philosophers to *materia*. Only unlike the *materia* of most philosophers, the earth is not a purely passive medium, as our metaphor with the seacoast might suggest. Heidegger speaks of it as an "opponent." The earth has a rhythm and dynamism of its own, on which Dasein is wholly dependent, which it must exploit, and to which, in the final analysis, it can only submit.

The world and the earth imply each other as openness and density, illumination and opacity, meaning and the source of meaning which is not itself meaningful. For Heidegger the two are active forces—not abstract concepts—and their being can only be seen when they are in conflict with each other. "The juxtaposition of world and earth is a conflict." [119] This conflict is the "event" out of which truth emerges.

World and earth are in themselves essentially contentious and competitive. Only as such do they enter into the conflict between concealment and the clearing. Earth only permeates the world and the world can only sink its roots into the earth insofar as truth occurs as the primeval struggle between concealment and the clearing.[120]

This conflict unfolds in human life; in Heidegger's understanding it *is* human life. It is man who must wage the conflict—or at least provide the arena. He must continually try to draw the mysterious into the illuminated area of his life in order to experience it *as* a mystery, as the resolutely self-concealing. He must make the supreme effort to subject the earth to his designs in order to reveal it as the "inexhaustible" on the one hand and the "adamant" on the other. Man must allow the sustaining, mysterious, and adamant to be what it is. We have already seen how man allows the instrument and the determinate being to be; we now see that he must allow the dimension of beings which transcends the instrumental and determinate to be as well. He does this by giving

119. "Das Gegeneinander von Welt und Erde ist ein Streit" (*Ho* 37 [675]).
120. "Welt und Erde sind je in sich ihrem Wesen nach streitig und streitbar. Nur als diese treten sie in den Streit der Lichtung und Verbergung. Erde durchragt nur die Welt, Welt gründet sich nur auf die Erde, sofern die Wahrheit als der Urstreit von Lichtung und Verbergung geschieht" (*Ho* 44 [680]).

himself up to the conflict which lies at the heart of human existence, the conflict between the intelligibility and control which he demands and the mystery and intransigence with which he is continually confronted—and the more forcefully confronted, the more he demands. Descartes need not have encountered the mystery of the earth when, in the tranquillity of his study, he decided to submit the traditional view of things to universal doubt. The conflict in which the mystery becomes manifest also goes beyond the relentless conflict *of ideas* which Hegel portrays in the *Phenomenology of Spirit.* The hammer must break in man's hand if he is really to encounter the mystery—or, as Heidegger suggests, if there is *to be* a mystery at all. In this conflict man is doomed to "lose." Heidegger's view of life is a tragic vision which he can sustain because of his faith—which is not simply a "necessary presupposition of thought"—that the conflict of human life is a *competitio* in the etymological sense of a "seeking together."

In [any essential] struggle each of the combatants calls out the other beyond himself. In this way the struggle itself continually becomes more intense and so more properly what it is. The more exaggerated the struggle becomes, the more resolutely the combatants give themselves up to the inwardness of simply belonging together.[121]

Man is not one of the combatants; the combatants are the world and the earth—or the familiar and the terrible or marvelous—as these are the poles between which human existence is cast. But Dasein is the arena in which the combat takes place, and without it there would be neither combat nor combatants. The issue at stake is what is to manifest itself: the determinate and instrumental or the dimension of beings which transcends their instrumentality and determination, the mystery which is their terrible or marvelous ground. Man is in the position of one who has staked everything on what he mistakenly conceives to be the issue of the struggle. He does not want to confront the terrible or marvelous in the breakdown of his designs; he struggles to escape the moment of truth in the broken hammer. This is only human nature, and Heidegger does not attribute such a "mistake" to any human failing. On the contrary, the mistake plays a decisive role in the evolution of the struggle.

121. "Im Streit trägt Jedes das Andere über sich hinaus. Der Streit wird so immer strittiger und eigentlicher, was er ist. Je härter der Streit sich selbständig übertreibt, umso unnachgiebiger lassen sich die Streitenden in die Innigkeit des einfachen Sichgehörens los" (*Ho* 38 [675]). Compare *EM* 47–48 (62).

We are now in a position to compare the characteristics of the world and the earth as they are the protagonists in the conflict of human life. (1) The world is a generic and flexible notion, while the earth is unique and abiding. Every man exists in many worlds, and the world which all men have in common is continually evolving. But there is only one earth, and it remains forever the same. Heidegger emphasizes this difference by speaking of *a* world and *the* earth. "To the open area belong a world and the earth." [122] (2) In contrast to the world, which belongs to Dasein's being, the earth appears as the radically other: mysterious and sustaining. Nowhere does Heidegger say of the earth, as he repeatedly does of the world, that it belongs to the being of Dasein. On the contrary, he speaks of man's "belonging to the earth" as something to be achieved.[123] (3) Neither the world nor the earth is properly intelligible, but the world is the principle of intelligibility while the earth is the obstacle on which such intelligibility is continually shattered, revealing a "beyond" which was present all along, and in this sense it is unintelligible *as such*. (4) Finally, both the world and the earth are portrayed as active forces and human being as the arena of their conflict.

The failure to see the world in its necessary conjunction with the earth is the cause of a great deal of misunderstanding in discussions of Heidegger. Karl Löwith says, "Actually nature does not matter at all in Heidegger's ontology, it vanishes in the vague and negative notion of what is merely 'extant' (*vorhanden*) . . . Heidegger does not recognize any kind of autonomous life on the part of nature." [124] Such a reading is based solely on *Being and Time*: the earth of *Holzwege* is not a negative notion but an active force. It is autonomous enough to be adamant, and it is the sustainer of all life. If we do not frequently encounter nature by name in Heidegger, it is probably because the word has become so inseparably tied to the principle of regularity which underlies science and technology, and nature in this sense *has* no autonomous life.[125]

Thomas Langan recognizes the earth but sees it only as the adamant, not as the sustaining, and thereby overlooks the second of the two senses in which it is *bergend* and the necessary

122. "Zum Offenen gehört eine Welt und die Erde" (*Ho* 43 [680]). Compare *Ho* 36 (673–74), 38 (675), 57 (691).

123. *EH* 34.

124. Karl Löwith, *Philosophy and Phenomenological Research*, III (1942–43), 63.

125. For Heidegger's view of nature see *SZ* 65, 70, 112, 388–89; *WG* 36, n. 55; *BH* 68 (278); *Ho* 236, 265–66; *VA* 61–63; *EH* 51–65; *HH* 27–31.

conjunction of the two. He calls it "the brute reality of the *Seiende* which forms the base of all experience." [126] Such a characterization is a far cry from the lyrical language of *Holzwege,* and from the statement:

> It is one thing to use the earth and another to receive the blessing of the earth, making the law of such reception our own, in order to protect the mystery of being and to keep watch over the sanctity of the possible.[127]

A more difficult question is raised by Martin Buber, the question of whether Heidegger's description of human experience leaves room for the encounter of the radically other, whether the self which he portrays can ever get outside or beyond itself.

> The mystery of being which appears to us shining forth in all particular beings Heidegger . . . has doubtless experienced deeply, but not as a mystery which confronts us directly, demanding that we give up our ultimate and most dearly won possession, our own selves in which we abide, that we break through the barriers of the self and venture out toward an encounter with the essentially other.[128]

"Heidegger's self," Buber claims, "is a *closed system.*" [129] Such a criticism raises problems concerning Heidegger's view of the nature of the self which go beyond the scope of the present discussion. But the earth appears to be as radically other as the "God of the philosophers," and not so much an other to which we must break out as one which is continually breaking in.[130]

We can see the earth breaking into human experience in the main outline of the argument thus far. What we call truth, I have argued, depends upon the openness and order which are consequent upon the projection of a world. Dasein projects its world and with it the possibility of truth. It decides what it means for anything *to be:* gold, pleasure, a hammer, a prime minister. But every project depends upon an order of things resulting from some previous project, on the natural resources available as its materials, and on the continual occurrence of breakdowns over

---

126. Thomas Langan, *The Meaning of Heidegger,* p. 134.
127. "Eines ist es, die Erde nur zu nutzen, ein anderes, den Segen der Erde zu empfangen und im Gesetz dieser Empfängnis heimisch zu werden, um das Geheimnis des Seins zu hüten und über die Unverletzlichkeit des Möglichen zu wachen" (*VA* 98).
128. Buber, *op. cit.,* p. 378.
129. *Ibid.,* p. 369. It appears that what Buber means by "a mystery which confronts us directly" is one which we confront in others rather than in things, and this point seems well taken.
130. For Heidegger's attitude toward solipsism see *SZ* 188.

which it has no control. Here Dasein is not creative but passive, does not *make be* but *lets be*. In this sense it is Dasein which is projected into its world and so into the openness and order which make possible what we think of as truth. Here something else, something *other*, determines what Dasein is to be and what things are to be for it. Here the earth manifests its secret presence, and it appears to span the gulf between the Hebrew Jehovah, Whose ways are inscrutable and Whose Being cannot even be pronounced, and the *materia* of the philosophers as it has been the subject of their continual derogation and abuse.[131] Such a notion hearkens back to William Blake's *Marriage of Heaven and Hell.*

The design which renders things accessible and intelligible requires *resources* on the one hand and *resistance* on the other. The more completely any design fulfills its own being, in fact, the more it becomes nothing but a pure catalyst between the resources and the resistance which it confronts. This is roughly Heidegger's conception of man.[132] By providing both the resources and resistance of human design, the earth is the hidden source of the openness and order of the world. Since Heidegger calls openness and order "truth"—the ground of the intelligibility of any judgment—he calls its dense and plastic counterelement "untruth" (*Unwahrheit*). And since it is this counterelement in the form of resources and resistance which gives rise to openness and order, he calls such untruth the ground or essence of truth. "Truth is in its essence untruth." [133] But we are here anticipating the argument of the following chapter. For the moment we can say that if the world is the immediate ground of truth, the earth is its ultimate ground, and the two meet in the being of Dasein in a conflict which allows each to be what it is.

Dasein is cast between openness and concealment, between meaning and the source of meaning which is not itself meaningful, or, as we can now put it, between the world and the earth. If Heidegger begins by emphasizing the openness of the world and

131. Aristotle begins the tradition, defining matter as "what desires form . . . as the female desires the male and the ugly the beautiful—not the ugly or female *per se* but *per accidens*" (*Meta.* 192a21–24). John Locke probably represents the apex of the tradition in his *Second Treatise of Government.* Comparing the relative contribution of human labor and nature (or matter) to the value of things "as they come to our use," Locke ascribes first nine-tenths (v, 25), then ninety-nine hundredths (v, 40), and finally 999/1000ths (v, 43) of the value of any useful object to human processing.

132. Heidegger uses the term *Zwischen*, a "between." See SZ 132, 374; Ho 104, 327; VA 195–96; ID 61–63 (56–58); EH 43, 140; ZS 31 (69–71).

133. "Die Wahrheit ist in ihrem Wesen Un-wahrheit" (Ho 43 [679]). Compare Ho 49 (684); WW 19 (340–41).

the sense in which Dasein's activity is constitutive of truth, he ends by insisting on the impenetrability of the earth and the sense in which Dasein, in and through all its activity, is ultimately passive in the face of truth—and the more active in the immediate sense, the more passive in the ultimate sense. It is at this point that many of Heidegger's critics see a "turning," or reversal of position, and maintain that Heidegger has given us not one system but two, which are either unrelated, or stand in direct contradiction to each other.[134] In opposition to this view I maintain that the later works really grow out of the original intuition of *Being and Time* as its necessary complement, implicitly foreseen all along, and that it is at this point that Heidegger's thinking reveals itself at its most consequent.

Our view of Dasein has now become more comprehensive; we have seen a new aspect of its being in relation to a deeper dimension of being itself. This new dimension appears on the scene as an active force in conflict with a moment of Dasein's own being. In the face of this conflict Dasein takes on a new, and in one sense

134. The leading exponent of this view is Karl Löwith in *Heidegger, Denker in dürftiger Zeit.* Löwith oscillates between the view that, in his later writings, Heidegger says something different from what he said in *Being and Time* (pp. 20–21, 38–41) and the suspicion that the later writings do not say anything at all (pp. 9–10, 37–38).

It is not difficult to find passages in *Being and Time* and in the later works which contradict one another when they are placed side by side. So, for example, Löwith can say, "In *Being and Time* human being relates positively through its understanding of being to being itself. After *Being and Time* it is rather that being involves an intrinsic reference to the being of man. . . . Dasein is no longer responsible for disclosing the sense of being—being itself opens *itself* in the 'there' of 'being there' " (p. 38).

By the same token one can say that Aristotle defines primary substance in the *Categories* as the concrete individual, composite of matter and form (*Cat.* 2a11–13)—*afterwards,* however, as the pure form of a thing taken without its matter (*Meta.* 1031b1–14). This sort of criticism is based upon the assumption that all philosophical statements are made on a single level, that introductory statements are interchangeable with final statements, or that the scholarly monograph properly *contradicts* the primer.

Aristotle himself is certainly aware of the difference. He asks us to "start from the things which are clearer and more knowable to us and proceed toward those which are clearer and more knowable by nature; for the same things are not 'knowable relative to us' and 'knowable' without qualification" (*Phys.* 184a16–18). "Yet the acquisition of [knowledge] must in a sense end in something which is the opposite of our original inquiries. For all men begin . . . by wondering that things are as they are, as they do about self-moving marionettes . . . for it seems wonderful to all who have not seen the reason. . . . But we must end in the contrary and . . . better state" (*Meta.* 983a11–19). Heidegger also appears to be aware of the difference. He repeatedly refers to the investigation of *Being and Time* as "provisional" (*vorläufig* [SZ 17]) and "preparatory" (*vorbereitend* [SZ 41]), and he promises to complete *Being and Time* with a section on "Time and Being" (SZ 39), a project which he has not yet carried out.

reduced, significance: it is now simply the field for the conflict of forces between which it is cast. Its relation to these forces is ambivalent. On the one hand the character of the field is decisive for any conflict. On the other hand it is a natural field, and its contours have been traced by the form which the conflict has previously taken. Since there can be no conflict without a field, however, Dasein still remains essential to truth. It is to this field that we must now return in a final attempt to sketch its character.

6. The Three Moments of Dasein

HEIDEGGER DOES NOT BEGIN with an analysis of Dasein. We are almost a third of the way through *Being and Time* before we come to such an analysis. He first attempts to describe human experience as it is lived and then reflects on his description, first uncovers the data and then proceeds to its analysis. We must proceed in this way, he argues, because common sense and the philosophical tradition falsify man's immediate experience and so fail to provide the data in which his essential characteristics can be seen. Together with the phenomenological description of human experience there goes a continually recurring critique of the way in which experience has traditionally been represented, and especially a lengthy analysis of Descartes, whose thinking represents common sense writ large.[135] Phenomenological description and the "destruction of the history of ontology" go hand in hand.[136]

We have seen that man instinctively misrepresents the way in which he originally encounters things. He thinks that he sees things through a kind of pure and detached vision and subsequently discovers how they can be put to some use, when it is only insofar as things can be put to some use that he can "see" them at all. He does not realize that he reads time, sees symptoms of disease, hears someone at the door, and smells dinner all *directly*, and without the need to interpret or infer.[137] Man also misrepresents his relation to things, conceiving himself as relating to things in the same way in which they relate to one another. Most important, man misrepresents his own being, understanding himself in terms which are appropriate to the things which he encounters in the world. He conceives of himself as a thing—a very special thing, perhaps, even one which is unique, but a thing

135. *SZ* 89–101.
136. *SZ* 19–27.
137. *EM* 26 (34).

nonetheless. When we remove the special characteristic which makes him unique, we are left with a substratum which is indistinguishable from that of any other being. This holds true of anything which is defined in the classic formula of genus and species, as man is when he is called *animal rationale*.[138] So Descartes thinks of man as *res cogitans*, in contrast to all other things, which are simply *res extensae*. And Aristotle says, "Examples of substance are 'man' or 'the horse.' "[139] Even if we deny of man all characteristics attributable to other beings, as Aristotle does in the *De anima* and Kant does in the notion of a transcendental subject, we still understand him in terms of the beings which he *is not*, as a limiting case. So Heidegger says, "Dasein first understands itself ontologically . . . on the basis of the sort of being which it itself *is not* but which it encounters within the world."[140]

It is understandable that we should misrepresent our immediate experience, for as soon as we reflect on it, it loses its immediacy. In reflection we have assumed a different position and point of view: the poet becomes a critic, the dancer a choreographer, the gambler a statistician. And so it is with Dasein when it reflects upon its immediate experience: it is no longer "there" in the same sense. This is expressed in the paradox of trying to imagine a definition of laughter which is itself hilarious. Besides, it is the being of man as care to be outside himself and with things, so that it is not surprising that he should understand himself in terms appropriate to the things with which he is constantly preoccupied. The philosopher particularly embodies both considerations. On the one hand he is the critic, the choreographer, the statistician. On the other hand he has realized a particularly intense—while deliberate and cultivated—form of humanity.

But if it is natural for man—and especially for the philosopher—to misunderstand his own being, we may ask how Heidegger is able to avoid such a misunderstanding. His answer is that by the second quarter of the twentieth century the traditional conception of man has broken down, like the hammer, and that we are consequently driven to recognize a dimension of man which escaped philosophers' attention so long as their initial defi-

138. *BH* 64–66 (276–77); *WD* 66, 95–96; *SZ* 22, 38, 114.
139. *Cat.* 1b27–28.
140. ". . . [Dasein] versteht sich selbst . . . ontologisch zunächst von *dem* Seienden und dessen Sein her, das es selbst *nicht* ist, das ihm aber 'innerhalb' seiner Welt begegnet" (*SZ* 58). (Word order inverted in translation.) See also *SZ* 15–16, 146.

nition was functioning adequately. This is part of what I have called the existential justification of the new problematic.

Dasein's most fundamental characteristics Heidegger calls "existential," and he contrasts such existential characteristics (*Existentialien*) with Aristotle's categories, which were devised on the basis of beings other than Dasein.[141] There are three existential characteristics of Dasein: (1) *existentiality,* which includes the project and understanding, (2) *facticity,* which includes situation, thrownness, and mood, and (3) *decadence,* the condition of being lost in the impersonal "one." [142] The three are not separate and distinct determinations which together go to make up Dasein's being; each reflects Dasein whole and entire, and all three belong to the unity of being-in-the-world.[143] Of the three, the first has been present from the start, the second has made its appearance in the last two sections of this chapter, the third we have not yet encountered.

1. Alone among beings, Dasein exists, standing out from all the specific beings by which it is surrounded and even from itself insofar as it too is a specific being. Only Dasein ex-ists in this way: the table, the mountain, and the star *are,* but they do not ex-ist. Unlike any other being, Dasein is not imprisoned in the self-identity of its own being but exists beyond itself, projecting itself—and other beings along with it—into possibilities of being as it understands them. For this reason all Dasein's characteristic activities and attitudes involve a reference to the inward presence of an *other.* As Alphonse de Waelhens puts it, "Thinking, willing, imagining, perceiving, sensing, loving, we are always thinking *something,* willing *an object,* imagining *the unreal,* perceiving *this* or *that,* feeling *sorrow* or *pleasure* . . . loving *someone.*" [144] In contrast to activities like growing and moving, such intentional acts are specifically human and depend upon Dasein's existence.

141. SZ 12–13, 44–45. Existential characteristics are meant to complement, not to replace, categories. Categories continue to apply to beings other than Dasein and to Dasein itself insofar as it is *a* being. But they are not adequate to comprehend the *being* of Dasein.

142. SZ 142–48, 134–40, 126–30, 175–80. Pöggeler calls our attention to the fact that Heidegger employs the word "existence" in a broader and narrower sense. In the broad sense it is synonymous with Dasein's being as a whole; in the narrow sense it signifies one of Dasein's three existential characteristics. (See Pöggeler, *op. cit.,* p. 56.) Kant employs the word "reason" in the same way: as the supreme power of the mind, in contrast to understanding and sensibility, and as synonymous with mind as a whole. In both cases the ambivalence is intentional and significant.

143. SZ 191, 284.

144. Alphonse de Waelhens, *Phénoménologie et vérité,* p. 98.

Other things are related to one another, but only Dasein *relates to* things in a positive and dynamic sense.

Dasein exists in three ways: outside itself with other beings, beyond itself in the future, and vis-à-vis itself in reflection—that is to say: in the *world*, in *time* and as a *self*.[145] These three modes of human existence must be seen as a unity. Only Dasein has a world and is a self. World-possession and selfhood are correlative as outer and inner, and both are rooted and linked together in temporality.[146] All this belongs to Heidegger's meaning when he calls Dasein essentially "open."

Dasein relates not only to beings (*Seiendes*) but to being itself (*Sein*). Beings are determinate, intelligible, and potentially available; being is not. In relation to human intellection—but not to human life in its totality—being is absolutely opaque and impenetrable. It is a "beyond" which is always present, even in the mode of absence, and human intellection comes closest to it in recognizing its own limitations, in the Socratic knowledge that we do not know. Heidegger sees its clearest traces in history, where it manifests its progressive absence as man comes increasingly to ignore the necessary limitations of his knowledge. Most of all it is absolutely unavailable to human design, and this is what, in Heidegger's view, marks it off from the God of Christian theology, Whom he regards—rightly or wrongly—as *a* being.[147] Properly speaking, we should not say that Dasein relates to beings but that, as the pure catalyst which we portrayed in the previous section, it is the relation of all beings to their ground or origin. Dasein is the focal point of the relation—and difference—between being and beings.

Heidegger sometimes speaks of transcendence in place of existence,[148] but we must not take this to mean that Dasein exists beyond this world in a transcendent realm which is timeless and eternal, for this would break the essential unity of Dasein's three modes of existence: in the world, in *time,* and as a self. Dasein "goes beyond" all beings, but in going beyond them it really comes into their presence and makes them inward to its own being. We have said that Dasein is not a being but a possibility of being which realizes itself in the project.[149] In thus realizing its possibili-

145. Compare these modes of human existence with the references implicit in the work: above, pp. 38–41.

146. *WG* 19–21, 37–39; *SZ* 316–23; *KM* 171–77 (193–201).

147. *BH* 99–103 (292–93); *SG* 169–70.

148. *SZ* 38; *WM* 38 (374); *WG* 16–23; *KM* 212 (244).

149. The formula "a being which realizes itself through its project" unites the three modes of existence to which I refer above: "realizes (in *time*) itself (*self*) through its project (*world*)."

ties, Dasein allows other beings to realize their possibilities as well, sketching out a design from which they draw their meaning and significance. Heidegger insists that it is not necessary for Dasein to transcend beings in the traditional sense—to transcend the sensible world and time to a supersensible and timeless realm or to stand in a special relation to a supreme being—in order to understand them.

But Dasein's relation to and understanding of beings presupposes a relation to and understanding of being. "The disclosure of being first makes possible the openness of beings." [150] Projecting itself and all other beings into possibilities, Dasein understands itself and them *out of* such possibilities—the way a painter understands colors or a gambler the law of averages. This understanding of being is implicit and vague—as vague as the understanding of soldiers and officers in Tolstoi's battles. We have seen, for example, how Dasein misinterprets its own being and its relation to things. But just as we can only handle a hammer because of our implicit comprehension of carpentry, so, Heidegger suggests, we can only relate to any being because of our implicit comprehension of what it means to be. This is the familiarity which knowledge and action presuppose. Heidegger calls this understanding of being "preontological" (*vorontologisches Seinsverständnis*), for it is neither "ontic" (a knowledge of specific beings) nor properly ontological (explicit knowledge of what it means to be) but the source of both.[151]

Dasein misunderstands its own being; this is natural, even inevitable. (And its understanding of itself, as we shall see directly, is fundamental to its understanding of all things.) But *mis*understanding is a form of understanding in a more fundamental sense. I can misunderstand a situation only if I am basically aware of what is going on, or a theory only if I know something of what it is about. In this sense the ontological misunderstanding which Heidegger finds in the views of common sense and in the history of philosophy must be rooted in the primeval comprehension which he calls preontological. Of Dasein's understanding of itself he says, "Dasein is ontically closest to itself, ontologically farthest from itself, and yet preontologically not [wholly] strange." [152]

Existentiality, the project, and understanding constitute the

150. "Enthülltheit des Seins ermöglicht erst Offenbarkeit von Seiendem" (*WG* 13, where the sentence is italicized). See *WG* 13–16; *SZ* 142–48.

151. *SZ* 12–13, 86; *WG* 14–15.

152. "Dasein ist ihm selbst ontisch 'am nächsten,' ontologisch am fernsten, aber vorontologisch doch nicht fremd" (*SZ* 16). Compare *SZ* 43.

active manifestation of Dasein's being as care. They reveal Dasein's positive role in the occurrence of truth, the sense in which Dasein projects what it means for anything to be true.

2. Facticity refers to Dasein's existence as it is confronted with the demand for decisions which are not of its own choosing but with which it is saddled, whether it will or not. Heidegger speaks of Dasein's being "thrown" (*geworfen*) into a specific world of decision, where it is faced with the fact "that it is and has to be" ("dass es ist und zu sein hat").[153] "Thrown into its 'there,' Dasein is always 'factually' referred to a particular world, its own."[154] By virtue of its facticity Dasein finds itself "delivered over" to a concrete situation, and this is something quite different from the factual character of any fact which Dasein encounters within its world, although this is the way it tends to be misunderstood. Psychological mechanisms and complexes represent translations of the facticity proper to Dasein—the "facticity of being delivered over" (*Faktizität der Überantwortung*)—into the factual character proper to things. Thrownness (*Geworfenheit*) is the reverse side of the project.

Unknowingly and involuntarily Dasein finds itself (*sich befinden*) in a certain situation which represents the concrete range of its possibilities. This situation (*Befindlichkeit*), the chrysalis of Dasein's being, Heidegger finds reflected in the mood. Dasein's whole being is always immersed in mood. Its moods may be fleeting and shadowy—they may change suddenly and without any apparent reason—but mood itself is a constant reflection of "being there."[155]

The mood is really not a reflection but a prerequisite of "being there": it is not a concomitant of some of Dasein's activities but a condition of all its activities. For the mood opens Dasein to itself and to the world. It is the basis of man's affective life, rendering him susceptible to the encounter of things, allowing him to be *touched, moved*. Fear makes it possible for us to encounter the dangerous, frustration allows us to experience the adamant or intractable, disappointment disposes us in such a way that we can confront the useless. The mood, which arises neither "from within" nor "from without," binds Dasein to its world and, through the world, to itself. The mood "refers us to innerworldly

153. *SZ* 55–56, 134–35, 144–45; *WG* 45–47; *KM* 212–13 (244).
154. "In sein 'Da' geworfen, ist das Dasein faktisch je auf eine bestimmte—seine—'Welt' angewiesen" (*SZ* 297).
155. *SZ* 134–40. See also *WM* 30–33 (364–67); *SG* 91; *EH* 112–13.

beings in their ability to move us." How are we otherwise to explain how the stimulation of a physical organ of sense can elicit the psychic response of sensation? "Even under the most intense pressure and resistance we could never be sensibly affected by things . . . if our situated being-in-the-world were not referred by mood to innerworldly beings in their ability to move us."[156] Descartes' animal spirits do not in the least explain how *res cogitans* can be stimulated, moved, or affected by *res extensa*.[157] They rather suggest that the philosopher of the Enlightenment had ultimately to have recourse to magic. Every purely speculative inquiry into the relation of Dasein and its world issues in an unbridgeable dichotomy of mind and thing, self and other, subject and object, for the relationship is grounded, and its poles originally united, not in knowledge (or in understanding as a purely cognitive function) but in the mood.

To be "there" is necessarily to be in some mood or other. Dasein can never rise above the mood. Even in purely theoretical contemplation its attitude remains fundamentally moody. Contemplation requires a mood of tranquillity, and tranquillity is a limiting case of mood, representing it in its most privative manifestation. "Even the purest *theōria* does not leave behind all mood: that which is now merely present can manifest its pure visage to [the theoretical] gaze only when [*theōria*], in *quietly abiding by it . . .* , allows itself to be approached."[158] The mood, which binds the self and the world together, allowing the self to be affected by the world, is the source of the two meanings of the word "sense": sensation and primal intelligibility. "Only because the 'senses' belong ontologically to a being whose mode of being is that of situated being-in-the-world can they be 'stimulated' and 'make sense,' so that the stimulus reveals itself in perception."[159]

As that which opens Dasein to itself and the world and

156. "Dergleichen wie Affektion käme beim stärksten Druck und Widerstand nicht zustande . . . wenn nicht befindliches In-der-Welt-sein sich schon angewiesen hätte auf eine durch Stimmungen vorgezeichnete Angänglichkeit durch das innerweltlich Seiende" (SZ 137).

157. *Disc.* V, ed. Haldane and Ross, I, 115–18.

158. "Aber auch die reinste *theōria* hat nicht alle Stimmung hinter sich gelassen; auch ihrem Hinsehen zeigt sich das nur noch Vorhandene in seinem puren Aussehen lediglich dann, wenn sie es im *ruhigen* Verweilen bei . . . auf sich zukommen lassen kann" (SZ 138). Compare Ho 37 (674–75); WP 43.

159. "Und nur weil die 'Sinne' ontologisch einem Seienden zugehören, das die Seinsart des befindlichen In-der-Welt-seins hat, können sie 'gerührt' werden und 'Sinn haben für,' so dass das Rührende sich in der Affektion zeigt" (SZ 137).

provides the basis on which anything can make sense, mood is fundamental to understanding. "Understanding is always moody." [160] Mood is a necessary prerequisite of human awareness, bringing Dasein into the presence of itself and things. "Mood manifests how one is and how things are going. In this 'how one is' the mood brings being into its 'there.' " [161] We have already encountered mood in the context of our discussion of science, and we can now see more clearly why Heidegger calls it the primordial event of Dasein, the genesis of our being there. There it revealed nothing; here it reveals Dasein, whose being we have come to describe as that of a pure catalyst. Mood makes it possible for Dasein to take its direction from things (*sich richten nach . . .*) and so is presupposed by the correctness of judgment (*Richtigkeit*). "At any given moment mood has already disclosed being-in-the-world in its totality and so first makes possible a 'taking direction from. . . .' " [162] Mood (*Stimmung*) is prior to and presupposed by correspondence (*Übereinstimmung*).[163]

It is surprising that Heidegger does not introduce mood into his discussion of the work of art, which we recounted briefly in section 3. For the work of art is certainly permeated by mood, which it succeeds in capturing and holding in what T. S. Eliot calls its "objective correlative." It expresses for a whole age "how things are going." And in doing this it opens us to things in such a way that we are affected, touched, and moved by them. The earth finds expression in the work of art as the human situation finds expression in the mood, and these two stand in the closest relation in Heidegger's thinking.

Facticity, situation, and mood constitute the passive (passionate) manifestation of the being of Dasein as care. They reveal Dasein's passivity in the face of the occurrence of truth. Through them Dasein confronts the hidden ground of openness, or what Heidegger has called the untruth—the mystery—in which truth is rooted.

3. Existence and facticity are presupposed by all awareness and so are necessary to explain the possibility of truth. But there is another aspect of Dasein's being which is essential to any

160. "Verstehen ist immer gestimmtes" (*SZ* 142).
161. "Die Stimmung macht offenbar, 'wie einem ist und wird.' In diesem 'wie einem ist' bringt das Gestimmtsein das Sein in sein 'Da'" (*SZ* 134). Compare *SZ* 339–40.
162. "Die Stimmung hat je schon das In-der-Welt-sein als Ganzes erschlossen und macht ein Sichrichten auf . . . allererst möglich" (*SZ* 137, in italics).
163. See *WG* 12–13; *WW* 18–19 (338–40).

explanation of truth, not to explain its possibility but to describe how it manifests itself concretely. This is the aspect of human being which Heidegger calls decadence (*Verfallensein*). In order to see it in its proper context we must return to the description of human being as it immediately presents itself, immersed in its daily preoccupations, and more especially to the moment at which Dasein comes explicitly to be "there," the moment of breakdown in its immediate activity.

We have said that Dasein is a unique possibility of being capable of realizing itself through its concerned activity in the world. But Dasein's immediate existence is not a realization of the self or of any possibility which is uniquely its own. In the first instance Dasein is lost in its world: preoccupied, distracted, confronting neither its own being nor that of the things which it encounters. This is what Heidegger calls the impersonality of the "one" (*das Man*), the "one" to which we refer when we talk of "what one does" or "how one goes about doing something."

Dasein is first and foremost absorbed in the world of its care. This absorption has chiefly the character of being lost in the impersonal realm of the "one." In the first instance Dasein has always deserted itself as a genuine possibility of selfhood and has "fallen prey to" the world.[164]

In the course of our daily lives we can hardly be said to project a world in the way in which Heidegger talks in characterizing existence as the fundamental principle of Dasein's being. We rather allow a world to be projected for us, and we ourselves simply fit in and go along. The influence which society exerts over us in the form of habit, custom, convention, ritual, and taboo greatly exceeds our power to conceive. What we think of as *conformity* is really only its most superficial manifestation, one that is blatant enough to strike the eye. When it becomes this blatant, an influence has already been outstripped and left behind. It is an exaggeration which no longer fits in, like an instrument which is out of date. When we see it in an old photograph album, we regard it as quaint, and often with considerable nostalgia. We find it hard to conceive that we could appear as quaint to a later generation. But the impersonal one is inescapable, and the bohemian who

---

164. "[D]as Dasein ist zunächst und zumeist *bei* der besorgten 'Welt.' Dieses Aufgehen bei . . . hat meist den Charakter des Verlorenseins in die Öffentlichkeit des Man. Das Dasein ist von ihm selbst als eigentlichem Selbsteinkönnen zunächst immer schon abgefallen und an die 'Welt' verfallen" (*SZ* 175).

turns away from society—the society within society—does not escape its formative influence.

We enjoy ourselves as *one* enjoys oneself; we read, see, and judge literature and art in the way in which *one* sees and judges; but we also "withdraw from the milling throng" in the way *one* withdraws; we are enraged by what *one* finds outrageous.[165]

Existence in the mode of the impersonal one is not a characteristic which Dasein merely happens to exhibit or occasionally assumes. It is the way in which, in the indifference of its daily life, Dasein *necessarily* exists, the immediate and inescapable way of being there.

In the first instance "I" am not I in the sense of my own proper self; I am . . . the impersonal one. This is . . . the way in which I am immediately "given" to myself. In the first instance Dasein is the impersonal one, and for the most part it remains so.[166]

Our normal way of thinking, behaving, and getting things done is the way in which one thinks, behaves, and gets things done. This is a commonplace observation, but for Heidegger it is significant. Who, he asks, *is* this impersonal one? Strictly speaking it is *no one*. To ask how one does something is to ask how it is done, as though no one were there and the contemplated action were to take place of itself. This is the existential no one.

The impersonal *one* which is the answer to the question of the *who* of Dasein's daily existence is the *no one* to which Dasein, in being with others, has invariably delivered itself over in advance.[167]

The *who* is not this person or that, not oneself and not "some people" nor even the sum of everyone. The "who" is the neuter, the *impersonal one*.[168]

165. "Wir geniessen und vergnügen uns, wie *man* geniesst; wir lesen, sehen und urteilen über Literatur und Kunst, wie *man* sieht und urteilt; wir ziehen uns aber auch vom 'grossen Haufen' zurück, wie *man* sich zurückzieht; wir finden 'empörend,' was *man* empörend findet" (SZ 126–27).
166. "*Zunächst* 'bin' nicht 'ich' im Sinne des eigenen Selbst, sondern die Anderen in der Weise des Man. Aus diesem her und als dieses werde ich mir 'selbst' zunächst 'gegeben.' Zunächst ist das Dasein Man und zumeist bleibt es so" (SZ 129).
167. "Das *Man*, mit dem sich die Frage nach dem *Wer* des alltäglichen Daseins beantwortet, ist das *Niemand*, dem alles Dasein im Untereinandersein sich je schon ausgeliefert hat" (SZ 128).
168. "Das Wer ist nicht dieser und nicht jener, nicht man selbst und nicht einige und nicht die Summe Aller. Das 'Wer' ist das Neutrum, *das Man*" (SZ 126).

The impersonal one recalls the description of Dasein's immediate encounter with things prior to the breakdown of the instrument. Only at that time we had not yet attained to awareness—being had not yet come to be "there" in the full sense—so that, strictly speaking, Dasein had not yet come upon the scene. What we find in the early sections of *Being and Time* is really only a prehuman dimension of human being out of which *man* has yet to emerge. In contrast to this abstraction, the impersonal one is real and concrete, a specific way of being there. Heidegger speaks of it as a loss of selfhood, and prior to the breaking of the instrument there is as yet no self to lose.

We have argued that the self is not immediately given in human experience. Together with the world and the innerworldly being, it emerges only when the instrument breaks down. When this happens, Dasein is brought up short to confront its own being with the question, "What do I do now?" This is the first manifestation of the self. But the question really asks, "What does *one* do now?" or "What is to be done now?" The first manifestation of Dasein, the immediate way of "being there" in the full sense, thus necessarily assumes the form of the impersonal one. We may call this the *phenomenological* derivation of decadence.

In the moment of truth in which the instrument breaks down, Dasein confronts the order of the world in which it lives, an order grounded in the project which it *is*. At the same time it confronts its own being projected into nothing, its decisions the source of meaning in the world—decisions into which it is thrown, which it cannot understand, but for which it must assume responsibility. The moment of truth is a moment of anxiety reflecting the necessity of decision in the face of the unknown. But the impersonal one relieves Dasein of all this.

The impersonal one is omnipresent, but in such a way that it has always just slipped away at the moment when Dasein presses toward a genuine decision. By providing a pretense of judgment and decision, however, it relieves Dasein of its responsibility at any given moment. . . . The impersonal one thus *eases the burden* of Dasein's daily existence.[169]

Impersonal existence is soporific: it removes Dasein—or seeks to remove it—from the immediacy of mood and situation. Heideg-

169. "Das Man ist überall dabei, doch so, dass es sich auch schon immer davongeschlichen hat, wo das Dasein auf Entscheidung drängt. Weil das Man jedoch alles Urteilen und Entscheiden vorgibt, nimmt es dem jeweiligen Dasein die Verantwortlichkeit ab. . . . Das Man *entlastet* so das jeweilige Dasein in seiner Alltäglichkeit" (SZ 127). Compare SZ 177, 254, 268.

ger speaks of a "flight from the ominous"—or from "homeless-ness" (*Flucht vor der Unheimlichkeit*).[170] We may call this the *existential* derivation of decadence. The two derivations are not meant to prove that Dasein exists impersonally—this Heidegger advances as a fact—but by appeal to the fact to reinforce the analysis which accounts for it.

We have said that Dasein originally understands its own being in terms of the things which it is not. We can now call this a manifestation of decadence. "For the most part what Dasein *is* depends on what it cares for." [171] Encountering all things as in-struments, *caring* for them insofar as they are instrumental, Da-sein comes to regard itself as an instrument as well. This is more than a simple misunderstanding with unfortunate ramifications for Dasein's *knowledge;* it is fundamental to the way in which Dasein *exists*.

Dasein understands itself first and foremost on the basis of the beings which it encounters and prudently cares for within the world. This understanding is not a simple case of recognition of the self accompanying all Dasein's activities; it involves projecting the self into the possibility of being-in-the-world which presents itself at any given moment, *existing as* this possibility.[172]

In regarding itself as an instrument, Dasein comes *to be* an instrument.[173] Its existence then assumes the form of the imper-sonal one. When we exist as the impersonal one, we fit in with other people in the way in which an instrument fits in with other instruments; we fulfill a function which another could fulfill as well and so become the replaceable parts of a collectivity; and in the course of such activity we lose track of ourselves in a way

170. *SZ* 276. *Unheimlichkeit* is difficult to render into English. It is synonymous with the *ungeheuer* in the conflict of the world and the earth, which I have called "terrible and marvelous." I have used the word "omi-nous" here because it contains the root "omen" as a manifestation of the mysterious. Etymologically the word derives from *Heim,* "home," and so has connotations of "homelessness."

171. "Zunächst und zumeist *ist* das Dasein aus dem her, *was* es besorgt" (*SZ* 141).

172. "Zunächst und zumeist versteht sich das Dasein aus dem umwelt-lich Begegnenden und umsichtig Besorgten. Dieses Verstehen ist keine blosse Kenntnisnahme seiner selbst, die alle Verhaltungen des Daseins lediglich begleitet. Das Verstehen bedeutet das Sichentwerfen auf die jewei-lige Möglichkeit des In-der-Welt-seins, das heisst, als diese Möglichkeit existieren" (*SZ* 387). (Italics added in translation.)

173. For phenomenological description of this condition see *SZ* 332–33, 387–88, 412–13. Compare *EM* 34–39 (45–51); *PL* 49–50 (268–69); *BH* 58–60 (273–74).

which recalls the disappearance of the instrument in the performance of its function.

If Dasein's own being is affected by its understanding of itself, so are the beings of its world. Everything is rendered common, comparable, interchangeable. "All precedence is held in abeyance. Everything loses its original vitality, as though it had been worn smooth overnight and were now thoroughly familiar. Everything hard-won becomes readily accessible. Every mystery loses its motive force." [174] Beings appear as the homogeneous world-stuff of science or as the amorphous raw material of technology. In fact this is what they *become*. This phenomenon, the objective counterpart of the impersonal one, Heidegger calls "flattening" (*Einebnung*) or "leveling" (*Nivellierung*).[175] In decadence we can see why Heidegger makes thinking and acting correlative and why he regards Dasein's understanding of itself as decisive for the way in which things manifest themselves.

We can see Dasein's understanding of itself as an instrument reflected in the history of philosophy. The moral treatises of David Hume and J. S. Mill can be read as studies in the evolution of human instrumentality in history. Even as sublime a moral principle as Kant's categorical imperative calls upon us, in effect, to act as though no one were there. His aim, as he repeats again and again, is to remove moral philosophy from the immediacy of mood and situation. The mainstream of Western moral philosophy has taken its direction from the doctrine of teleology, which understands all things, man included, in relation to a specific end or function, the final cause, and it seems reasonable to suggest that such thinking is rooted in the being of the instrument. But Dasein's being is the ground of the meaning of the instrument, and once it itself assumes the status of an instrument, the ground of meaning in the world is lost. The result is a kind of groundless vortex (*Wirbel*) which sucks up all things—Dasein included—and Dasein, a unique possibility of being, emerges as the impersonal one.[176]

Man is conceived as an instrument wherever his being is interpreted as a combination of body and soul, as in the definition *animal rationale*. Body and soul are applications of the more

174. "Jeder Vorrang wird geräuschlos niedergehalten. Alles Ursprüngliche ist über Nacht als längst bekannt geglättet. Alles Erkämpfte wird handlich. Jedes Geheimnis verliert seine Kraft" (SZ 127).

175. SZ 127, 194–95. This is the one point in Heidegger's thinking at which Husserl's influence (beyond terminology) is apparent: the reciprocity of *noēsis* and *noēma* (*Ideen*, I, iii, 3).

176. SZ 178, 268.

comprehensive notions of matter (*animal*) and form (*rationale*), a distinction which, we have already argued, arises from a consideration of the instrument. Where the duality of matter and form is introduced, matter is invariably subordinated to form, while the form is identified with a thing's function. Like the instrument, man must have an end and function; the goal of life is the attainment of the end through the performance of the function. In this way, taking the instrument as the paradigm of meaning, philosophers have found meaning in human life. The vortex sets in when the philosophers of the Enlightenment—notably Bacon and Hobbes—throw out the final cause. They see that things cannot be conceived to have ends of their own if they are to provide material for the most far-reaching human design, and that man himself, the instrument of instruments, cannot be understood according to the model of the instruments he manipulates. There is a leap here, but not the decisive break which the philosophers of the Enlightenment imagine. Human thinking remains instrumentally oriented, and in its development it gathers speed like a man running downhill. The danger is that, in liberating man and his materials to the full range of their instrumental possibility, philosophers have divested life of meaning according to the old criterion without succeeding in evolving—or conveying—any new criterion. Here Heidegger sees human thinking following inner laws of its own development, paralleling—or even prefiguring—developments in the organization of human life and the technological conquest of the earth. It is the evolution of the impersonal one.

We have argued that the notions of matter and form are not appropriate to the work of art, and it may seem that we are now arguing that they are not appropriate to the being of man. They apply specifically to the instrument, and man, like his artistic creations, is not an instrument. This is true in a sense, but it does not touch the full purport of Heidegger's argument. Man is not an instrument, but instrumentality is an outstanding possibility which he is capable of realizing. Man *can be* an instrument, and to the extent that he becomes one the notions of matter and form *are* appropriate. So Heidegger maintains that the doctrine of man as *animal rationale* arises out of decadence—which we must remember belongs to the being of Dasein as the immediate way of "being there"—*and reflects it accurately.*[177]

To suggest that Dasein originally understands its own being as that of an instrument is an interpretation of Heidegger's thinking

177. VA 72–73, 91–95; SG 147; WD 24–28; PL 49–50 (268–69).

which has to be justified. For Heidegger himself gives us conflict-ing statements on this point. Sometimes he suggests that Dasein originally relates to (and understands) itself as an instrument (*zuhanden*),[178] at other times as a being which is merely present (*vorhanden*).[179] Surprisingly, the latter is the more common ex-pression, for it is inconsistent with the assumption that *every* being is originally approached in its instrumentality. Knowledge, we are told, must "press forward over what is available to human design to lay bare what is *then* merely present."[180] Despite Heideg-ger's own statements to the contrary, there seems to be clear justification for the assertion that Dasein originally understands itself as an instrument. If my analysis is correct, Heidegger him-self exhibits the confusion which he attributes to daily experience.

Existence as the impersonal one is unavoidable: it is the immediate way of "being there." But insofar as Dasein *projects* this form of existence—*chooses* to exist in this way—Heidegger describes it as "inauthentic." He distinguishes two concrete ways of existing: authentic (*eigentlich*) and inauthentic (*uneigent-lich*), depending upon whether Dasein's project is of a genuine self through the realization of unique possibilities or of an imper-sonal "self" through the realization of possibilities which another could fulfill as well.[181] Each is open to being in its own way, and to each there corresponds a distinctive form of truth.[182] The two must be sharply contrasted, but they cannot be allowed to fall apart—a temptation into which many commentators fall—without sacrificing the unity and coherence of Heidegger's think-ing as a whole. Authenticity begins by recognizing inauthenticity for what it is. "Authentic existence is not something which hovers over the decadent tendency of everyday existence but an existen-tial modification of the way in which everyday existence is grasped [taken in hand]."[183] On the other hand, inauthenticity belongs to the human situation as such, to the sense in which Dasein does not so much project a world as it is itself projected

178. SZ 239, 289, 333, 387–88.
179. SZ 59, 114, 130, 201, 225.
180. "[Das Erkennen] dringt erst *über* das im Besorgen Zuhandene zur Freilegung des nur noch Vorhandenen vor" (SZ 71). (Italics altered in translation.)
181. SZ 42–43. See also SZ 239–40, 252–67, 297–99.
182. Heidegger speaks of "truth in the mode of authenticity" (*Wahrheit im Modus der Eigentlichkeit*) and of correspondence as a "derivative modi-fication" (*abkünftige Modifikation*) of truth, which suggests that we must recognize two forms which truth takes. See SZ 221–23.
183. "Umgekehrt ist die *eigentliche* Existenz nichts, was über der verfal-lenden Alltäglichkeit schwebt, sondern existential nur ein modifiziertes Ergreifen dieser" (SZ 179). Compare SZ 130, 267.

into the world. "As thrown being-in-the-world, is Dasein not thrown in the first instance into the public realm of the impersonal one?"[184] In falling prey to the world, Dasein falls "out of itself into itself."[185]

Alphonse de Waelhens suggests that Heidegger confuses an "undifferentiated structure" of Dasein with a particular manifestation of that structure in identifying daily existence with the impersonality of the one.[186] But if I am correct in my interpretation of the phenomenological derivation of decadence, it is understandable that daily existence should be a class with a single member, or that all our immediate experience should be colored by impersonality. We should not call daily existence *inauthentic*, however; we should only say that it manifests an inescapable tendency *toward* inauthenticity, that, of the two fundamental ways of "being there" which Heidegger recognizes, the one comes about as though of itself, while the other requires effort and struggle. As Otto Bollnow puts it, "Inauthenticity can endure as a permanent condition; authenticity, on the other hand, is never a *condition* but an *event*."[187]

The question remains whether the phenomenological derivation of decadence is altogether compatible with its existential derivation. If the impersonality of immediate existence comes about of itself, as I have suggested, why does it require any further explanation, such as the fact that it is reassuring? And if Dasein first emerges dominated by the impersonal aspect of its being, why should this be described as a "fall" (*Absturz*)?[188] There seem to be two points of view simultaneously at work here, as Heidegger variously represents Dasein as *coming to* relate explicitly to being (and especially to itself as a unique possibility of being) and as *falling away* from such an explicit relationship.

It is unfortunate that Heidegger tends to portray all communal or social existence, all being *in the presence of others*—in the family, the club, the profession, the municipality, the market place, and the state—as characterized by the impersonal one. He writes as though the communal dimension of man's being were not capable of being raised to the level of genuine awareness and self-realization, as though there were no such thing as an authen-

184. "Ist das Dasein als geworfenes In-der-Welt-sein nicht gerade zunächst in die Öffentlichkeit des Man geworfen?" (SZ 167).
185. "Das Dasein stürzt aus ihm selbst in es selbst . . ." (SZ 178).
186. Alphonse de Waelhens, *La philosophie de Martin Heidegger*, pp. 33–34.
187. Otto Bollnow, *Existenzphilosophie*, p. 52.
188. SZ 178.

tic "we," one not dominated by the impersonal one. We have seen that the impersonal one is that "to which Dasein *in being with others* has invariably delivered itself over in advance." Unless the *individual* decides, Heidegger seems to suggest, *no one* decides. (The chief exception is the "historical people" in the face of its destiny.[189]) To this Martin Buber objects most forcefully and convincingly. "Just as there is a [genuine] 'you' (*Du*)," he writes, "so there is a [genuine] 'we,'" giving as examples the dedicated group of revolutionaries and the fervent religious community.[190] It is difficult to find justification for this tendency in Heidegger's thinking. It is one thing to claim that genuine human community is never given (as superficial community is) but must be hard-won, and another to suggest that man's existence with others does not offer the possibility of becoming genuine. The deficiency probably stems from the inadequate analysis of Dasein's initial encounter with others. "Only men who are capable of genuinely saying 'you' to one another," Buber says, "can truly say 'we' together." [191] It probably also represents the intrusion of Heidegger's existential commitment into his phenomenological analysis. *Being and Time* points up the sense in which human beings are interior to one another—indeed, the radical distinction between human being and all other beings, on which it insists, may be decisive for an adequate philosophical understanding of human community—but it seems to recognize only the negative aspect of men's "being together."

For Heidegger, being and thinking must be held together: to be in a certain way is to think in a certain way, and conversely. This is generally recognized in Heideggerian criticism. What is often overlooked is that the two fundamental *ways* in which we can think and be must likewise be held together: our being and thinking are poised between authenticity and inauthenticity as though in a tension between magnetic poles.[192] (This is the theme

189. See for example *Ho* 61 (695); *EM* 29 (38); *SZ* 384.
190. Martin Buber, *op. cit.*, p. 373.
191. *Ibid.*, p. 374.
192. Peter Fürstenau does not attach sufficient importance to the positive role which inauthenticity plays in Heidegger's thinking. He argues that being (*Sein*) is not present to inauthentic human being at all, since such a being attaches itself exclusively to beings (*Seiendes*). "Inauthentic 'being there' is precisely *not* the 'there' (allowing-to-appear) of being, understanding of being, but solely and exclusively the understanding of beings" (*Heidegger, das Gefüge seines Denkens*, p. 56). Such an interpretation ignores the fact that a certain comprehension of *being* (*Seinsverständnis*), not simply of beings, is characteristic of Dasein as such, whether authentic or inauthentic (*SZ* 12). It overlooks Heidegger's assertion that authenticity itself is, in the first instance, a "grasp" of inauthenticity (*SZ* 130, 179). On

of Heidegger's studies in the history of philosophy, which we will take up in Chapter 4.) It is in this tension that Heidegger finds what we call truth.

If truth is openness, there is a sense in which inauthentic existence is untrue. It levels or flattens things, deprives existence of its mystery, blurs the contours of its conflict, allows the ground of meaning to be absorbed in a vortex in which meaning becomes illusive and phantasmal, distorts the immediacy of situation and disguises its revelation in mood. This is a form of untruth or concealment which is distinct from the mystery we encountered in the conflict of the world and the earth. It is the situation from which, in our struggle for genuine awareness, we must always begin.

But inauthentic existence is not simply untrue, providing, as it does, the starting point for any ascent to deeper awareness and the realization of more genuine possibilities of being. "In no case does discovery occur on the basis of complete hiddenness; it always takes its departure from what has already been discovered in the mode of mere appearance or illusion." [193] Only out of misunderstanding, in Heidegger's view, can understanding arise. Misunderstanding provides the initial content, the impetus, and even the direction for the process of coming to understand, as Aristotle also suggests when he urges us to follow the difficulties in our thinking. In Heidegger's later works we find that the impersonal one accentuates the conflict which it attempts to conceal, the conflict between the world and the earth out of which openness arises. In the course of rendering things banal it creates the background against which the terrible and marvelous can burst forth with the greatest impact. And so, in the end, inauthenticity comes to play a decisive positive role in the evolution of truth. Inauthenticity is revelatory and in this sense *true*.

Heidegger's twofold sense of truth recalls Aristotle's use of the word "nature" (*physis*). After insisting strenuously that the nature of a thing be identified with its form rather than its matter, Aristotle allows that the word may be understood derivatively as applying to the matter of a thing as well. "For the privation too is, in a way, form." [194] This is what critics who divorce the two

---

this view it is impossible to do justice to Heidegger's interpretation of tradition and to the intimate conjunction of truth and untruth on which he insists.

193. "Erst recht vollzieht sich alle Neuentdeckung nicht auf der Basis völliger Verborgenheit, sondern im Ausgang von der Entdecktheit im Modus des Scheins" (SZ 222).

194. *Phys.* 193b20.

existential modifications of Dasein's being and their two corresponding forms of truth fail to appreciate.

Heidegger regards common sense and the Western philosophical tradition as primarily expressions of inauthentic existence. The human mind tends to be regarded as an instrument, its function to correspond with its object. Everything, including Dasein, is drawn up into the instrumental complex of a world of knowledge. The origin of knowledge in vital activity and the project underlying the order of the world is forgotten. The crucial significance of mood in human existence is overlooked. All these tendencies of the philosophical tradition, which we shall take up in Chapter 4, Heidegger sees reflected in the traditional notion of truth.

With the analysis of inauthentic existence Heidegger's portrayal of the background of the traditional notion of truth has come full circle. He begins by examining the notion, which he concedes to be truth as it has appeared, for its necessary presuppositions. He finds that such a notion presupposes an area of openness and the being of Dasein which provides such an area. But when he analyzes the structure of Dasein's being, one of its moments—decadence—proves to be such as necessarily to manifest itself in the way in which truth has appeared, in a doctrine of correspondence.

3 / The Essence of Truth: Unhiddenness

THE QUESTION OF TRUTH is, in a literal sense, the central question of Heidegger's philosophy. The discussion of truth in *Being and Time* divides the book into two halves of equal length, and the essay *On the Essence of Truth* appears in the middle of his career in 1943. Coming as it does in the middle, the question presupposes all that has gone before, and this is why it was necessary, in the preceding chapter, to sketch Heidegger's initial approach to experience in *Being and Time* and other early works. Against this background we can now make sense out of the terminology in which he expresses his own notion of truth, which is at first disconcerting, appearing arbitrary and willfully obscure. We will follow the argument in the essay *On the Essence of Truth*, the initial steps of which are already familiar, and then correlate this treatment with the one which appears in *Being and Time*, hoping thereby to show that Heidegger's position and approach always remain fundamentally the same.

We should here recall the *status quaestionis* from Chapter 1. If we wish to avoid the initial paradox involved in formulating a notion of truth, we must begin by examining the traditional notion. Whatever truth may be, this is what it has appeared to be: this is the way it has been represented throughout the Western philosophical tradition. Philosophers have traditionally (*a*) predicated truth primarily of the judgment, or in general of knowledge, (*b*) located it primarily in the mind or intellect, and (*c*) defined it as a relation of correspondence between the mind and things, or the intellect and its object. We can begin by asking what such a doctrine presupposes without assuming that we already know what truth is. So Heidegger, as we have said, advances his own notion of truth in the first instance as a presupposition of the traditional view, though he ultimately claims that it is the presupposition of all human experience as well.

In accounting for the traditional view, Heidegger unfolds a series of notions which are meant to be successive "layers" of the human situation out of which it arises: (1) the openness of conduct, (2) freedom and the binding criterion, (3) letting-be, (4) mood, (5) deception and illusion, and (6) history. The analysis is circular, as history leads back into the openness of conduct and accounts for its concrete character. We can now follow this analysis in some detail.

1. Truth and Openness

IF A JUDGMENT is to correspond with its object, it must first discover it. If our thinking is to *re*present things, they must first be present to it. If the mind is to know anything, it and the thing must partake jointly of an area of openness in which the thing can manifest itself as it is. Such an area of openness, Heidegger insists, is not simply given and cannot be taken for granted.[1] In asking what truth is, we must explain how such an area of openness is possible.

Knowledge, as it is expressed in the judgment, presupposes a presence which it does not itself create but on which it can only depend. Knowledge is only possible when an object of knowledge is already present, but it itself does not originally render any object present in this way, much less constitute the presence on which such a thing as an object of knowledge depends. Furthermore, the object of knowledge must be autonomous in order to serve as one of the two poles of a relationship of correspondence. (The same is true of Dasein as the other pole.) But it is not clear where things derive their autonomy—certainly not from their status as objects of knowledge, which *presupposes* such autonomy.[2]

Relating to an autonomous being is what I have called an "encounter." Two inanimate objects do not encounter each other: whatever relationship there may be between them is not *their*

1. WW 10–11 (327–28); WM 15–16 (214–15); PL 33–45 (261–67); BH 100–101 (293–94); Ho 33–34 (671–72), 49–51 (684–86), 55 (689–90); ID 22–23 (21–22).
2. WW 11–12 (328–29); N II 73–74.

relationship but a relationship in and for consciousness or some *tertium quid* which embraces them both. Nor does the beast encounter things, although it is endowed with consciousness and is the center of an organized area which we call its environment. The beast does not encounter the things which go to make up its environment because it is completely immersed *in* its environment; it does not participate in an area of openness which makes an encounter with things, a relationship to things, and ultimately knowledge possible.[3] Even man's original encounter with things, as we have seen, is a tenuous one: his being is immediately characterized not by openness to things but by distraction in his preoccupation with them. In its immediate manifestation the human condition, from this point of view, does not differ essentially from that of the beast. Only when human design breaks down do we attain to the area of openness in which things first manifest themselves explicitly. It is only from this moment on that we can regard the human situation as unique.

In describing the movement by which an area of openness comes about we are forced to employ *negative* terminology: it is a movement toward the dis-tance and de-tachment required for the dis-covery of things in their autonomy or identity. "We gain access to the unhiddenness of beings . . . by withdrawing before them in such a way that they can manifest themselves, revealing what they are and how they are. . . ."[4] This negative movement Heidegger calls *Verhalten*, which includes both "attitude" and "behavior" and perhaps approaches most closely our notion of "conduct." The word is meant to describe the fundamental character of human experience, of which all our concrete attitudes and forms of behavior are specific manifestations. A movement of withdrawal from the immediacy of the environment is the essence of conduct. The beast, which is not open to things, does not "conduct" itself. In Heidegger's sense conduct and openness are reciprocal notions. "Conduct is open to beings. Every open relationship is conduct."[5]

This withdrawal from the immediacy of the environment does not interpose anything *between* Dasein and things. On the contrary, it is meant to explain the immediate *presence* of Dasein *to*

3. On animal nature see *BH* 69–70 (278–79); *FD* 171–72; *SZ* 45–50.
4. "Das Sicheinlassen auf die Entborgenheit des Seienden . . . enfaltet sich zu einem Zurücktreten vor dem Seienden, damit dieses in dem, was es ist und wie es ist, sich offenbare . . ." (*WW* 15 [334]).
5. "Das Verhalten ist offenständig zum Seienden. Jeder offenständige Bezug ist Verhalten" (*WW* 11 [328]).

things. Paradoxically a certain distance is required for the presence of any particular being in its openness and autonomy.[6] Otherwise we would have the immersion characteristic of the beast or the preoccupation and distraction characteristic of the prehuman dimension of human being which we described in the previous chapter. In the moment of withdrawal man stands in the presence of things—confronts things—for the first time, and only in virtue of this movement is he properly human.

Three observations are important in connection with this analysis of conduct. (1) In the notion of *Verhalten*, which includes both attitude and behavior, Heidegger wants to convey the original unity of thought and action, one of his most fundamental presuppositions. (2) The negative movement of conduct was implicit in the previous chapter in the discussion of science, with its specific form of immediate presence to things which we call "objectivity." (3) The reciprocal character of conduct and openness explains why Heidegger speaks of truth as an event, the event out of which human being properly arises.

Conduct always relates immediately to a particular being around which other beings organize themselves in openness. "All conduct entails this essential characteristic: that standing in openness it attaches itself to some particular manifest being as such."[7] The particular being provides, so to speak, the focal point of openness, and it brings with it the distinction between figure and ground, what we encounter and the background against which it is encountered. This is true both of behavior—driving, typing, or looking for a friend in a restaurant—and of attitudes like attentiveness, expectation, or the feeling that our friend is inconsiderate in being late. It is *most* true of knowledge, which, through its abstractions, is able to concentrate on one particular aspect of a situation to the exclusion of all its other aspects. More than any other form of conduct, knowledge severs its object from the web of connections in which it has its tangible existence and which bind it to its background and to the whole of human experience. No form of nontheoretical conduct is capable of this in the same degree. Since all conduct focuses on some particular thing within the area of openness, however, suppressing other things and ignoring the area which it itself constitutes, it necessarily

6. *SZ* 104–10; *WG* 54; *ID* 61–62 (56–57).
7. "Alles Verhalten aber hat seine Auszeichnung darin, dass es, im Offenen stehend, je an ein Offenbares *als ein solches* sich hält" (*WW* 11 [328]). Compare *Ho* 49–50 (684–85).

conceals at the same time that it reveals.[8] This point later plays an important role in Heidegger's argument.

It is the area of openness resulting from conduct that knowledge presupposes. The judgment is one form of conduct which discovers beings and thereby contributes to openness, but only *one* form—not the only one or even the original one. Our most common daily activities discover beings, even though they are not primarily cognitive. Discovering activity need not even be conscious. In typing, for example, we discover the keyboard without being consciously aware of it or of the demands which it makes upon our conduct. All consciousness is a form of open, revelatory conduct, but not every form of conduct need be conscious.

Man's openness assumes different forms, depending on the sort of being which is encountered and the type of conduct in which it is encountered. In whatever man does or makes, in all his dealings and calculations, he occupies and holds fast to a position in the openness of an area in which beings can present themselves, revealing what they are and how they are, taking up their own express place [in human experience] and [thus] becoming susceptible of being named.[9]

Beings are open to every form of human conduct—not only to knowledge or even to consciousness—and to each in a different way. We have already referred to the different aspects which a field presents to a farmer, a military tactician, and a town-planner and to the different way in which a situation takes shape for a moralist, a judge, and a psychiatrist. No one of these points of view can claim to be more "objective" than the others. Heidegger is convinced that there is no point of view from which any being can be definitively ("objectively") represented. He seeks to safeguard the prolific character of things by presenting them in a variety of contexts—not simply conceptual contexts—each of which manifests a distinctive facet of their being.[10] Knowledge is only one form of revelatory conduct, consciousness only a certain range of such conduct, and we cannot assume that things manifest themselves to all forms of conduct in the same way that they do to knowledge or consciousness.

8. WW 18–19 (338–40); Ho 41–43 (677–79), 49 (684), 310–11; PL 32–33 (260–61).

9. "Je nach der Art des Seienden und der Weise des Verhaltens ist die Offenständigkeit des Menschen verschieden. Jedes Werken und Verrichten, alles Handeln und Berechnen hält sich und steht im Offenen eines Bezirks, innerhalb dessen das Seiende als das, was es ist und wie es ist, sich eigens stellen und sagbar werden kann" (WW 11 [328–29]).

10. EM 25–27 (33–35); Ho 10–11 (652–53); FD 9–10, 20.

In his search for the presupposition of the truth of knowledge, it is not enough for Heidegger to explain how Dasein can encounter an object; he must also show how it is possible—even necessary—for Dasein to make of the object the criterion (*Mass*) of its thought and action, how things can—or even *must*—direct and control all our conduct, theoretical and practical. This is a necessary aspect of any explanation of knowledge, but it is also presupposed by all human experience whatever. As de Waelhens puts it, "Why . . . has man given his radical 'consent' to conform to reality in his knowledge, his action, in short, in all his conduct? Why does he submit to reality by drawing from it the substance and value of what he knows and even of what he does?"[11] The fact that we regard it as self-evident that all our thinking and behavior should take its direction from things—that we should be "realistic" or "objective"—only points up how fundamental the question is.

Heidegger argues that no criterion can impose itself *of itself* on human conduct. If there is to be a criterion of conduct, Dasein must impose on itself the obligation of accepting it and *permit* beings to serve in this capacity. Sartre elucidates this point when he says that we mistakenly think that it is the alarm clock which gets us up in the morning, forgetting that it is we who set the clock and must then hear it as a command. Obligation simply cannot come from without. This is the cornerstone of Kant's moral philosophy. Only Kant understands obligation solely in relation to a consciously and deliberately articulated system of rational principles of action. As Sartre's example indicates, Heidegger wants to extend the Kantian principle of self-imposed obligation throughout the whole range of human experience. It is not only in confronting deliberate decisions or in making what we would call a moral choice, he argues, that human being "gives a law unto itself." These are the peaks of human experience, but Heidegger, as we have said, directs his attention to the valleys.

Heidegger is not concerned with elaborating any particular criterion of conduct in an attempt to establish a theory of value. He wants rather to explain the possibility of a criterion as such, whatever it may be. The question is what human being must be like in order to be capable of experiencing a criterion—*any* criterion—and ultimately what being must be like if such a thing as a criterion is to be possible at all.[12]

11. Alphonse de Waelhens, *Phénoménologie et vérité*, p. 92.
12. *BH* 104–19 (295–302).

We have seen that Dasein, through the negative movement of conduct, must open itself to an encounter with things. We now see that it must similarly open itself to their directive power. These are really two aspects of a single event: the former is meant to explain the existence of facts, the latter to account for the weight which facts have in our experience—or what came in the nineteenth century to be called values. Heidegger is deeply concerned not to let fact and value split apart. This second aspect of conduct he calls "setting oneself free to a binding direction" ("Sich-freigeben für eine bindende Riche").[13]

If things are to serve as the criterion of all our conduct— especially of our knowledge—we must be "free" to accept such a criterion and to recognize its binding character. Truth as the correspondence of knowledge with its object must be grounded in freedom in this sense. So Heidegger concludes, *The essence of truth is freedom.*[14] The statement appears to make truth arbitrary and subjective. But before reaching this conclusion we should first see what Heidegger means by freedom.

The freedom which Heidegger calls the essence of truth is not a faculty or property of man: it is not the faculty of free choice or a property of the will which allows us to select between two possible goods or to realize one of two possible modes of conduct. The freedom with which we are here concerned does not refer to exemption from physical or mechanical necessity or to the acceptance of such necessity in the light of reason. It is not the sort of freedom which we exercise now and then, as occasion demands. In short, Heidegger does not employ the word "freedom" in any of the senses, common or technical, in which it is usually understood. Yet the sense in which he does use the word is meant to reveal the event, fundamental to human experience, from which all the usual senses derive.

Heidegger does not predicate freedom exclusively or primarily of the human will, just as he does not predicate truth exclusively or primarily of human understanding.[15] The term is rather a development of the notion of openness and can best be understood by analogy with the spatial sense of "free" as "clear of . . ." or "open." Heidegger frequently speaks of a "clearing" (*Lichtung*) in the density of beings—a clearing without which there could be no light (*Licht*)—and it is in this sense that the term "free" is

13. WW 12 (330). Compare SZ 84–86.
14. "*Das Wesen der Wahrheit ist die Freiheit*" (WW 12 [330]).
15. VA 32–33; WG 43–44. Compare SZ 193–96.

employed in the present context.[16] Such freedom is constitutive of Dasein as a being essentially open to things.

If Dasein can encounter things because its essence consists in being open to them, it can—and must—discover in things the criterion of its conduct for the same reason. Dasein must permit things to provide the binding direction of its conduct because its very being is such as to depend upon other beings, because it is essentially oriented toward the realization of itself outside or beyond itself in the midst of the things it encounters within an area of openness which it itself constitutes. All human actions and attitudes involve an intrinsic reference to an "other." "Our destiny as free beings," as de Waelhens says, "is to 'make' ourselves in a dialogue with the world and with beings. Our selfhood is achieved through that which is other than itself." [17]

The freedom which Heidegger calls the essence of truth is the openness which constitutes Dasein's being. Such freedom does not belong to man as a property; on the contrary, man belongs to freedom as its creature. "Man does not 'possess' freedom. At the best the contrary is true: freedom possesses man." [18] Man belongs to freedom as to the area of openness which he is, but which, for that very reason, does not stand at his disposal. So it is not surprising that Heidegger introduces freedom in conjunction with the notion of binding direction. "Here freedom reveals itself as creating at the same time the possibility of a bond or obligation in general." [19] Freedom here is freedom to obligation, man's freedom to be bound, directed, and obliged by the beings which he encounters.[20]

Such freedom is not arbitrary or subjective in the usual sense. It is nothing less than the obligation *to be* of a being which has no being of its own but must realize itself in a continual commerce with other beings. It characterizes the pure catalyst to which we referred in describing the conflict of the world and the earth. The

16. *SZ* 133, 170, 350–51; *Ho* 41–44 (677–80); *BH* 115 (300); *EH* 18, 55; *ZS* 11 (43); *VA* 247, 252, 258, 276–79. The texts in *Vorträge und Aufsätze* identify freedom and the clearing.

17. De Waelhens, *op. cit.*, p. 98.

18. "Der Mensch 'besitzt' die Freiheit nicht als Eigenschaft, sondern höchstens gilt das Umgekehrte: die Freiheit . . . besitzt den Menschen . . ." (*WW* 16–17 [336]). See also *WD* 153; *SG* 157–58; *EM* 120–21 (156–58).

19. "Hierin enthüllt sich aber die Freiheit zugleich als die Ermöglichung von Bindung und Verbindlichkeit überhaupt" (*WG* 43–44).

20. This conjunction of freedom and obligation recalls the dual sense of "being-to" portrayed in the preliminary sketch of Dasein in the preceding chapter. See above, p. 32.

obligation which it imposes differs from obligation in the usual sense in that, stemming from the area of openness which Dasein *is* but does not control, and bringing in its wake a responsiveness to beings which precedes and transcends knowledge, it is an obligation which man can never adequately understand.

This notion of freedom bears comparison with Kant's. Kant sees freedom as a postulate of thought necessary, in the first instance, to explain a certain range of actions which we call "moral," [21] meaning that they are obligatory.[22] We cannot explain how a specific sort of action like truth-telling can be obligatory unless we assume that we are free. Obligation makes no sense applied to natural phenomena, which we assume to be causally determined.[23] Paradoxically, freedom is thought to be not only a presupposition of moral action but also a condition of being to which man, *through* such action, must attain. In acting morally man—instead of dangling on the puppet strings of nature by pursuing his natural needs, desires, and drives—gives a law unto himself, *determines* himself, and such self-determination is what is properly to be understood as freedom.[24] But to say that man gives a law unto himself in this sense is really to say that the highest element in his being, which Kant regards as reason,[25] exercises a decisive influence over all the lower elements, which can be grouped together under the collective designation of nature. This is why freedom must always appear in the guise of obligation: because, while it originates in man's highest element—reason—it *appears* to the whole man, of which the lower elements are an integral part.[26] Freedom can never be explained or justified—we can never explain why we are free or why we ought to realize our freedom through moral action—because it is the source of our being as men, a *daimon* sitting on our shoulder; and so it is like the eye as the power of vision, which we can never see directly but only in the inverted image of a mirror.[27] As the source of sense in human experience, Kant's freedom cannot itself "make sense."

There are striking resemblances between this conception of freedom and Heidegger's. Heidegger too approaches freedom as a necessary presupposition, sees it indissolubly bound up with obli-

21. *GMS* 447–48.
22. *GMS* 389, 408, 416–17.
23. *GMS* 426–27, 446.
24. *GMS* 446–47.
25. *GMS* 452.
26. *GMS* 453–54.
27. *GMS* 459–63.

gation, makes it the background of a process of self-realization, and denies that it can ever be adequately explained. But the differences go deeper. Kant's freedom is first and foremost the presupposition of a certain range of actions, while Heidegger's is a presupposition of *all* our actions—and it is not a condition to which man must attain but one into which he is thrown. Against the background of freedom Kant portrays human being determining itself independently of the world and nature, while Heidegger regards such self-determination as possible only *through* the world and nature.[28] Kant's freedom binds man to actions, imposing obligations which he can understand. Heidegger's freedom binds man to beings, and the obligation which it imposes transcends human understanding. The difference comes most sharply into focus if we ask each of the two philosophers regarding his source of obligation: "who" obligates "whom"? For Kant it is the highest element in man—reason—which obligates the whole man, and this is why freedom is seen primarily in conjunction with some actions but not all. For Heidegger it is the being of man as an area of openness which obligates man as *a* being within such an area. This is why his freedom is a presupposition of all our actions, not simply of those which we call moral, and why it imposes obligations beyond our understanding, which always occurs *within* openness.[29]

To understand Heidegger's claim that freedom is the essence of truth, we must recognize freedom and binding direction as correlative notions, both rooted in human existence. And we must remember that by existence Heidegger does not understand the reality, facticity, or givenness of a thing but uses the term to signify that essential characteristic of man by which he is not simply present, along with other things, within the world but is present *to* things by virtue of "standing out" from them and relating—relating *himself*—essentially to them. Existence in this sense is the being of man as "being *there*," "being *with it*," present to things, vitally responsive to them, concerned with them as with his own being. To exist in this way is at once to be free in Heidegger's sense *and* to be bound.

The essential characteristic of existence Heidegger describes as "letting beings be" (*Seinlassen von Seiendem*).[30] This is a surprising thesis, for we are all aware of the human tendency to

28. Heidegger criticizes Kant on this point, SZ 316–23. See also WG 19–20.
29. WG 43–48.
30. WW 14–15 (333–34); KM 206 (236).

distort experience, to color everything which it encounters with the bias of subjectivity. Heidegger himself first portrays man encountering things in a practical context, handling them, organizing them, fashioning and improving them, smashing and rebuilding them. Such activities seem to be anything but ways of "letting beings be." Yet Heidegger maintains that Dasein essentially lets beings be "what and as they are." [31] This it does by constituting the area of openness in which beings can attain to identity and autonomy. Such an area of openness creates the possibility of the *what* and the *as,* so that it is only here that any being can be what it is and as it is. We have talked of Dasein's letting a lamp, desk, and chair be what they are, and the same principle holds true of leather and steel, quarries and orchards, frost, drought, and storm clouds. We have also talked of the artist letting bronze and wood, colors, sounds, and words be what they are. Dasein provides the context in which these things can be what they are and the perspective to which they can manifest themselves as they are. This is what Heidegger means by the freedom of Dasein, essential to truth, of letting beings *be,* and of letting them be *what* and *as* they are.

Letting beings be in this sense does not entail a passive or disinterested attitude toward them; it is not synonymous with letting *alone* but with the letting-be of the fiat. It is by explicitly turning toward things, opening ourselves to them so as to permit them to have a decisive influence on our being, that we let beings be. "Letting-be is gaining access to beings." [32] In letting beings be we gain access to them and in turn permit them to have access to our being. In Heidegger's terms, we "ex-pose" ourselves (*sich aus-setzen*) to beings.

This is the beginning of history, the process of human development in the midst of the totality of being and in the immediate presence of beings. "That man ex-ists now means that the history of the essential possibilities of historical mankind is guaranteed him in the disclosure of the totality of being." [33] History does not begin at the moment when Dasein first comes to leave its mark on beings but when it first allows beings to leave their mark on it. The continuity of history requires the presence of the earth in

31. WW 15 (334).
32. "Seinlassen ist das Sicheinlassen auf das Seiende" (WW 14 [333]).
33. "Der Mensch ek-sistiert, heisst jetzt: die Geschichte der Wesensmöglichkeiten eines geschichtlichen Menschentums ist ihm verwahrt in der Entbergung des Seienden im Ganzen" (WW 17 [337]). On the historicity of Dasein see SZ 378–92.

conflict with the world, and this is another aspect of Dasein's letting-be.

It is true that letting-be in the full sense is not characteristic of man's immediate experience as it appears in the early chapters of *Being and Time,* but we should regard this as a description of a dimension of human being which is prehuman. The moment of truth occurs when the instrumental complex breaks down, and it is only from this moment onward that Heidegger's analysis of truth is applicable to human experience. From this point on, however, Heidegger maintains that Dasein is essentially "in the truth." Truth here embraces the notions of openness, freedom, and letting-be which we have just discussed.

2. Truth and Untruth

BECAUSE DASEIN LETS beings be it does not follow that human behavior is always objective or human thinking always true in the usual sense. A definitive revelation of any being, Heidegger argues, is in principle impossible. In letting beings manifest themselves "as what . . . ," Dasein also creates the possibility that they manifest themselves as what they are *not.*[34] So Dasein's letting-be is the ground of subjectivity as well as objectivity,[35] of error and illusion as well as truth.

Dasein is "in the truth." The meaning of this statement is ontological. It does not mean that Dasein, in an ontic sense, is always—or indeed ever—immersed in "the whole truth and nothing but the truth" but that the disclosure [and disclosing power] of its own most proper being belongs to its existential structure.[36]

Truth in the ontological sense is meant to explain the possibility of truth in the concrete ("ontic") sense: the manifestation of any being in its identity. Beings attain an identity—they become a *this*—through human revelation, and yet at the same time they are distorted, for no being is ever simply what it reveals itself to be. In revealing beings, man invariably misinterprets, confuses, and conceals them; he mistakes an aspect of things for things themselves. We have seen how he takes the instrumental being

34. See *SZ* 29–30, 84–85.
35. On subjectivity and objectivity as correlative and derivative see *VA* 258–59; *Ho* 81; *KM* 151 (171–72); *WG* 38; *SG* 99, 139–40.
36. "*Dasein ist 'in der Wahrheit.'* Diese Aussage hat ontolologischen Sinn. Sie meint nicht, dass das Dasein ontisch immer oder auch nur je 'in alle Wahrheit' eingeführt sei, sondern dass zu seiner existentialen Verfassung Erschlossenheit seines eigensten Seins gehört" (*SZ* 221).

to which he first relates as something merely present and how his attitude toward beings as they *are* merely present is almost invariably tinged with the manipulative spirit appropriate in relation to instruments. In this sense Heidegger says that man stands continually "in untruth." It is this untruth which, as we have said, art seeks to remedy: it is the sculptor who must teach Aristotle that a statue of Hermes is not "out of bronze" in the same way as an Athenian spearpoint. But man is only able to mistake beings insofar as he has already revealed them, so that they can manifest themselves in such a way as to be mistaken, and in this ontological sense man stands "in the truth" even when he errs or is deluded or becomes the victim of illusion.

The full existential and ontological sense of the statement "Dasein is in the truth" conveys at the same time "Dasein is in untruth." But only insofar as Dasein is disclosed [and disclosing] is it also closed off, and insofar as Dasein implies that innerworldly beings have already been discovered, it implies at the same time that such beings, in order to be capable of being encountered, are covered over (concealed) and distorted.[37]

Even when man errs, in Heidegger's sense, he lets beings be what and as they are. When we err, we say that we have been deluded or confused. To use such an expression is to ascribe the cause of our error to beings as they have manifested themselves to us. Heidegger refuses to ascribe error simply to the frailty of human understanding: if beings did not deceive, he argues, we could not *be* deceived. But beings *can be* illusive, deceptive, and confusing, and in constituting an area of openness Dasein lets them be *this* as well.

If beings did not distort one another, we could not be upset by them or fumble them, we could not go astray or become lost in our dealings with them, and above all we could never venture beyond our limits in approaching them. That beings can be deceptive in the form of illusion is the condition of our being deceived, not conversely.[38]

In permitting beings to manifest themselves as illusion, Da-

37. "Der volle existential-ontologische Sinn des Satzes: 'Dasein ist in der Wahrheit' sagt gleichursprünglich mit: 'Dasein ist in der Unwahrheit.' Aber nur sofern Dasein erschlossen ist, ist es auch verschlossen; und sofern mit dem Dasein je schon innerweltliches Seiendes entdeckt ist, ist dergleichen Seiendes als mögliches innerweltlich Begegnendes verdeckt (verborgen) oder verstellt" (*SZ* 222). Compare *SZ* 144.

38. "Würde Seiendes nicht Seiendes verstellen, dann könnten wir uns am Seienden nicht versehen und vertun, wir könnten uns nicht verlaufen und vergehen und vollends uns nie vermessen. Dass das Seiende als Schein trügen kann, ist die Bedingung dafür, dass wir uns täuschen können, nicht umgekehrt" (*Ho* 42 [679]). Compare *EM* 83 (108–9); *N I* 277.

sein still stands in the openness of beings, apart from which there could be no "as . . . ," and still lets beings be. The beast cannot become the victim of illusion in this way. In encountering any being as what it is not, as illusion, Dasein still stands in the presence of what it is, in the presence of truth.[39] It is man's destiny, Heidegger believes, to be eternally bound in this way—through error and illusion—to beings as they are and to truth.

At this point Jean Wahl accuses Heidegger of "objectivizing" deception and rendering it intransitive.

> Consequently there is an intransitive deception of some kind, a deception in appearance which is supposed to explain how man can be deceived, although we would have thought it more natural not to abstract from man in this matter. If there is to be deception, there must be someone to deceive himself and be deceived. But Heidegger objectivizes deception, so to speak. . . .[40]

In short, Heidegger holds for "an intransitive deception which does not deceive anyone at all." [41] Such an interpretation is hardly tenable. In regarding Dasein as constituting the area of openness in which it is possible for anything to appear, Heidegger never "abstracts from man." And to say that a magician and a counterfeit coin deceive—that deception is built into the activity of the one and the appearance of the other—is not to overlook the need for someone to be taken in by the deception. Heidegger does not make deception intransitive. On the contrary, he traces the passive—or reflexive—voice back to a source in the active voice, and this is to make it properly transitive.

It follows that error is not to be reckoned solely to human ineptitude or carelessness. Insofar as man stands in the openness of being but does not dispose of such openness, insofar as his essence consists in a freedom which does not belong to him but to which he belongs, untruth cannot be ascribed to human shortcomings—a very widely held view which finds its consummate expression in Descartes [42]—but must be seen to arise from the essence of truth itself.

---

39. On the unity of being, appearance, and illusion see *EM* 75–88 (98–115), esp. 80 (105); *SZ* 28–37.

40. Jean Wahl, *Vers la fin de l'ontologie*, p. 116.

41. Wahl, *Revue de métaphysique et de morale*, LXI (1956), 119.

42. "What then is the source of my errors? This alone, that the will is of wider range than the understanding, and that I do not restrain it within the same limits as the understanding, but extend it to things which I do not understand . . ." (*Med.* IV, ed. Kemp Smith, p. 237). Descartes argues that both will and understanding, though finite, are without defect in themselves; it is man who coordinates them badly.

Because ex-istent freedom as the essence of truth is not a property of man, but man rather ex-ists only as a possession of this freedom, becoming thereby capable of history, the anti-essence of truth cannot arise as a by-product of inability or carelessness. Untruth must rather derive from the essence of truth.[43]

Error and illusion, Heidegger maintains, have their origin in truth; they spring from truth and, in their own way, they *manifest* truth. (We have touched upon this point in discussing the instrumental thinking which characterizes inauthentic existence.) The so-called "problem of error" is not simply a corollary of the question of truth, as it has generally been regarded. Rather an understanding of error—what it signifies and how it comes about—is the "decisive step" toward a comprehension of truth in the ontological sense. "The elucidation of the anti-essence of truth is not an afterthought intended to fill up a gap in the argument; it is the decisive step toward an adequate posing of the question of the essence of truth." [44]

Untruth is not synonymous with error in Heidegger's usage. There are two forms of untruth: the mystery and error. But what we have quoted Heidegger saying of untruth in general can also be said specifically of error. For the two forms of untruth are inseparable, both from each other and from truth as an area of openness in which beings manifest themselves. It is this necessary conjunction of truth, mystery, and error which we must now portray. We find them rooted together in human ex-istence, in the radical finitude of a being characterized essentially by care, whose being it is to be outside and beyond itself in the world, in time, and as a self.

Untruth, whether as mystery or as error, is usually seen as an index of the finitude of human knowledge. Heidegger traces the finitude of human knowledge back to the finitude of human being, of which it is a reflection. We must here recall the salient features of the analysis of the origin of knowledge in *Being and Time*. Knowledge presupposes the familiarity of things which issues from their being organized in a structure which knowledge itself

43. "Weil aber die ek-sistente Freiheit als Wesen der Wahrheit nicht eine Eigenschaft des Menschen ist, sondern der Mensch nur als Eigentum dieser Freiheit ek-sistiert und so geschichtsfähig wird, deshalb kann auch das Unwesen der Wahrheit nicht erst nachträglich dem blossen Unvermögen und der Nachlässigkeit des Menschen entspringen. Die Unwahrheit muss vielmehr aus dem Wesen der Wahrheit kommen" (WW 17 [337]).

44. "Die Erörterung des Unwesens der Wahrheit ist nicht nachträgliche Ausfüllung einer Lücke, sondern der entscheidende Schritt in die zureichende Ansetzung der Frage nach dem Wesen der Wahrheit" (WW 17 [338]).

does not create. Things originally organize themselves around human activity as it proceeds from a project, and not simply a project which Dasein *has* but one which it *is*. The intelligibility and accessibility of things—human knowledge and all other non-cognitive forms of experience—are grounded in this project.

Only a being which is finite can have a project, and only a being which is radically finite can *be* a project: the being which ex-ists must have nothing at its core. The clearing of truth, the source of the intelligibility and accessibility of things, depends upon the finitude of such a being. Philosophers have traditionally ascribed the limitations of human knowledge and the imperfections of human being to man's finitude; Heidegger ascribes to it the possibility of human being and knowledge as well. "More original than man," he says, "is the finitude of Dasein in him." [45] To say that human knowledge and human being are grounded in human finitude is to say that everything man knows is enveloped in what he does not know and that everything he can control depends ultimately upon what he cannot control. This points to the "un-" which Heidegger finds at the source of human experience, the untruth which belongs to the essence of truth, which he emphasizes by insisting that the proper word for truth is negative: unhiddenness (*Unverborgenheit*).[46] So Heidegger does not place untruth, as Descartes does, at the periphery of truth, but at its center: untruth is not simply where truth "leaves off" but the source out of which it arises.[47]

If our experience depends upon the project which we are, we cannot discover the source of the project *within* experience. At any given moment man is already involved in the project which provides the structure within which he encounters things in the world. The human project is in this way preconstituted, or what Heidegger calls a "thrown project" (*geworfener Entwurf*).[48] Thus, while the project around which things organize themselves in an intelligible order is a human project, it does not belong to man or submit to his disposing. For this reason human understanding is excluded on principle from the source of the intelligibility of experience, which is to say from the source of truth. So Heidegger says, "The unhiddenness of beings determines us in our essence in

45. "Ursprünglicher als der Mensch ist die Endlichkeit des Daseins in ihm" (*KM* 207 [237], in italics).
46. *WW* 19–20 (340–42); *SZ* 222; *VA* 220–21, 257–82, esp. 259; *ZS* 34–35 (91).
47. *WD* 72.
48. *SZ* 145, 148, 284–85, 328; *WM* 18 (217); *BH* 84 (285–86); *WG* 54; *KM* 212 (244). Compare *SZ* 192, 221; *WG* 49.

such a way that, in our representative thinking, we always *follow in the wake of* unhiddenness." [49]

This is the hiddenness of beings which is prior to all discovery. If truth is the openness of beings, this is the untruth which is its source and which is presupposed by the discovery of any particular being. This hidden source of openness is what Heidegger calls the mystery (*das Geheimnis*). "The hiddenness of being in its totality—in the strict sense un-truth—is older than the specific openness of this or that being. It is older than letting-be itself . . . the mystery." [50]

Heidegger also calls this form of untruth "truth" in an exceptional sense: the truth of being (*Sein*) in contrast to the truth of beings (*Seiendes*), which we have been discussing all along. If it can be called truth, the mystery must be revealed and revealing. In fact Heidegger holds that the mystery *is* revealed—but revealed *as hidden*—in the mood of anxiety. It is also revealing, as the "inescapable" which manifests its restless presence in the inner conflict of Western thinking and eventually drives man to confront the "unattainable"—the theme of the following chapter. In calling what is untruth in relation to *beings* the truth *of being*, Heidegger could not be more emphatic in expressing the contrast—amounting to a conflict—which he sees between being and beings. This is what he understands by the "ontological difference." [51] We should understand it against the background of the dialectical tension between the individual instrument and its referential complex and the conflict between the world and the earth.

Besides the untruth which precedes openness, there is another form of untruth—error—which necessarily accompanies it. In all his conduct man stands in the midst of the totality of beings, but he conducts himself in the first instance toward this or that being in particular. "All open conduct vibrates in the letting-be of beings and relates at any given moment to this or that being." [52] Letting-be thus involves two moments which stand in necessary di-

49. "[D]ie Unverborgenheit des Seienden bestimmt uns in ein solches Wesen, dass wir bei unserem Vorstellen immer der Unverborgenheit nachgesetzt sind" (*Ho* 41 [677]; italics added in translation).
50. "Die Verborgenheit des Seienden im Ganzen, die eigentliche Unwahrheit, ist älter als jede Offenbarkeit von diesem und jenem Seienden. Sie ist älter auch als das Seinlassen selbst . . . das Geheimnis" (*WW* 19 [340–41]).
51. *SG* 15; *ID* 46 (43), 59–69 (54–64). See above, p. 19, note.
52. "Jedes offenständige Verhalten schwingt im Seinlassen von Seienden und verhält sich jeweils zu diesem oder jenem Seienden" (*WW* 18 [338]).

alectical opposition: letting beings in general be and letting this or that particular being be this or that. The unity of experience is broken up into the tenuous relation of figure and ground, with the figure tending to break free of the ground and realizing this tendency most fully in knowledge. In letting beings be *this* or *that*, man conceals their being *as such*. He comes to identify being with thisness or thatness—"The last differentia," Aristotle says, "is the substance of a thing"[53]—and to look on openness as grounded in something which is open: Descartes' God-Who-cannot-be-a-Deceiver, *lumen naturale*, the regularity of nature, and the like. Every *revealing* of beings is thus at the same time a *concealing*.

Precisely in letting the particular being to which it relates in any specific form of conduct be, and thereby revealing it, letting-be conceals the totality of being. Letting-be is essentially at the same time a concealing.[54]

The dialectical necessity by which Dasein, in revealing beings, conceals being (and other beings) Heidegger calls insisting (*insistieren*), the counterpart or shadow-side of ex-isting (*eksistieren*).[55] Existence, as we have seen, finds its consummate expression in the mood; insistence, as we will see in the following chapter, finds its consummate expression in science and technology. In keeping with the dual character of conduct as attitude and behavior, insistence is both a way of knowing and a way of acting. In both cases insistent conduct fastens upon a specific being or area of beings, which it makes fundamental to the whole of experience. Such a relation submits to control in a way in which Dasein's relation to the totality of being does not. As the word implies, insisting is pragmatic, bringing with it the distinction of ground and figure, which, as Nietzsche saw, is pragmatically based. Out of it emerge the distinction of subject and predicate and the dichotomy of subject and object, both of which are modifications of man's original encounter with things.[56] It is fundamental to the manifestation of human being which we characterized in the preceding chapter as inauthentic. With insistence the integral character of human experience is lost and a second form

53. *Meta.* 1038a19.
54. "Gerade indem das Seinlassen im einzelnen Verhalten je das Seiende sein lässt, zu dem es sich verhält, und es damit entbirgt, verbirgt es das Seiende im Ganzen. Das Seinlassen ist in sich zugleich ein Verbergen" (WW 19 [340]).
55. WW 21 (344).
56. SG 99; SZ 148–60.

of hiddenness emerges, one which is a distortion of the original hiddenness of the mystery. The mystery which lies at the heart of truth is forgotten.[57]

The forgetting of the mystery is an integral part of the event by which openness comes about. For an area of openness can only occur around something—by the same necessity with which consciousness is always consciousness *of something*—and so is concentrated or centered in that thing.

The openness of the open area, i.e., truth, can only be what it is—this openness—insofar as it organizes itself into such an area. To this end there must be a being in the area in which openness can take its stand and endure. . . . It belongs to the essence of truth to organize itself in [and around] beings. . . .[58]

Since the concealment involved in all revelation is necessary, it is not to be attributed to any human deficiency.[59] Dasein, after all, belongs to openness, freedom, and the mystery, so that it is to them and not to Dasein that the second form of concealment is to be attributed. So Heidegger insists that it is the area of openness which conceals itself, or truth which hides itself. "This relation to concealment conceals itself by allowing the forgetfulness of the mystery to assume priority and itself disappearing in it. . . . The mystery refuses itself in and for forgetfulness. . . ."[60] When Heidegger speaks of the "forgetfulness of being" (*Seinsvergessenheit*) we should hear both a subjective and objective genitive: it is being which is responsible for the forgetting as well as that which is forgotten.

With the withdrawal of the mystery into forgetfulness, man's sole concern is for what he encounters *within* the area of openness—with the *thing* in its intelligible character or whatness—

57. *WW* 20–21 (342–44); *SZ* 44, 219, 339, 345, 354; *KM* 210–11 (241–42); *VA* 240–41, 264–65, 281; *Ho* 243–44, 310–11, 336; *BH* 77–78 (282–83); *EM* 14–15 (18–19); *ID* 46–47 (44–45); *EH* 88–89; *WD* 97–98; *WM* 11–13 (211–12); *ZS* 34–35 (91), 40–41 (103).

58. "Die Offenheit dieses Offenen, d.h. die Wahrheit, kann nur sein, was sie ist, nämlich diese Offenheit, wenn sie sich und solange sie sich selbst in ihr Offenes einrichtet. Darum muss in diesem Offenen je ein Seiendes sein, worin die Offenheit ihren Stand und ihre Ständigkeit nimmt. . . . [E]s gehört zum Wesen der Wahrheit, sich in das Seiende einzurichten . . ." (*Ho* 49–50 [684–85]). (Word order inverted in translation.)

59. *WW* 17 (337), 23 (344–45); *WM* 11–12 (211); *Ho* 76–77; *ID* 46–47 (44–45); *ZS* 34 (89–91); *WD* 98.

60. "Doch dieses Verhältnis zur Verbergung verbirgt sich dabei selbst, indem es einer Vergessenheit des Geheimnisses den Vorrang lässt und in dieser verschwindet. . . . [D]as Geheimnis versagt sich in der Vergessenheit und für sie . . ." (*WW* 20–21 [342–43]). (Word order inverted in translation.) Compare *EH* 89.

rather than with the hidden source from which the possibility of encountering a thing arises. Being has retreated behind particular beings, so to speak, and *realitas* comes to be identified with *reitas*. This Heidegger sees as the genesis of the attitude of objectivity.

The movement is one toward human domination, security, and control.[61] Relating solely to the things which he can control—and conversely to the things which force him to take measures of control—man comes to regard himself as the "measure of all things." Subjectivity and objectivity thus arise together in a movement which leads ultimately to science and technology, which Heidegger regards as inseparably conjoined.[62] In this movement the hiddenness out of which openness arises, and which binds subject and object together in a primeval unity, is concealed. The mystery is forgotten.

To turn away from the mystery and to turn toward control are really two sides of the same movement. We have already seen Dasein turn away from the nothingness encountered in the breakdown of the instrument, despite the fact that it alone could reveal the world in which Dasein exists, and it is against this background, as symbol or metaphor, that we should understand Heidegger's present argument. From one point of view this is a movement toward control, but from another point of view it is not so much that man devises ways of controlling things but rather that he is abandoned by the mystery and thereby left to his own devices. For only in the face of abandonment is there *need* of control. "In refusing itself in and for forgetfulness the mystery allows historical man to relate exclusively to what is accessible to him and to support himself by his own powers." [63] Thus left to his own devices, man is driven to incessant activity in organizing and controlling the world and in disciplining himself in order to assure his position in the midst of the totality of beings. This Heidegger sees as true of every period in history—and as the clue to the meaning of history—but pre-eminently true of our age. Man's forgetfulness of being (*Seinsvergessenheit*) is a symptom of his abandonment by being (*Seinsverlassenheit*).[64]

The result is that human being is characterized by systematic preoccupation and distraction, restlessness and incessant activity.

61. *WW* 21 (343–44); *WM* 43 (381); *Ho* 79–87; *VA* 21–24, 28–29, 34–35, 55–61; *SG* 194–203; *EM* 35–36 (47–48).

62. *Ho* 80–81, 85–86; *VA* 258–59; *SG* 99.

63. "Indem das Geheimnis sich in der Vergessenheit und für sie versagt, lässt es den geschichtlichen Menschen in seinem Gangbaren bei seinen Gemächten stehen" (*WW* 21 [343]).

64. *WM* 12 (211); *VA* 90–91; *N II* 27–28.

Such restless activity in distracted preoccupation with the immediate and particular Heidegger calls *Irren;* I have rendered it, for want of a better word, illusion.[65] Its aim is not only to establish control but to elude the mystery: it conceals the concealment which lies at the heart of human existence. Not only do we forget the mystery, we even forget *that we have forgotten.* "The concealment of the fact that being in its totality has been concealed dominates the revelation of every particular being, and this in turn, as the forgetting of concealment, becomes illusion." [66] The final form of untruth is illusion: the concealment of concealing or the forgetting that the mystery has been forgotten.

Only to forget the mystery is not to escape it. Though the mystery disappears, it does not thereby cease to be present and at work in human experience. Heidegger's thinking here takes a Freudian bent: forgetting lends to what is forgotten a unique presence, its effective force heightened by the fact that it *is* forgotten. "Only forgetfulness does not settle accounts with the mystery of Dasein. On the contrary, it lends to the seeming disappearance of what is forgotten its own proper presence." [67] Man feels driven and harried, pressed between the secret presence of the mystery and the repression of illusion. This is the basis of the necessity (*Notwendigkeit*) which Heidegger finds in history, the record of man's continual "turning into need" (*Wendung in die Not*).[68] Out of this historical necessity arise the natural necessity of physical science in the seventeenth century and the possibility of human determinism as it is revealed in the experiments of Pavlov in this century—both possibilities (of knowing and being) which Dasein, the being of possibilities, is capable of realizing.

Heidegger finds reason to hope that history may have eschatological direction. Man may ultimately be driven—Heidegger's reading of history leads him to believe he *is* being driven—by the necessity of history to an inescapable encounter with the mystery. "Man's being there—and this alone—gives rise to the revelation

65. WW 22 (344–46). Compare EM 83 (108–9); Ho 310–11. The German word *Irren* contains three related elements: *Irrtum* is "error" (*sich irren* is "to err"); *ein Irrer* is a "madman"; *irre gehen* is "to go astray or become lost." It is a strong expression, and this at least the word "illusion" retains. The term should be understood as an activity.

66. "Die Verbergung des verborgenen Seienden im Ganzen waltet in der Entbergung des jeweiligen Seienden, die als Vergessenheit der Verbergung zur Irre wird" (WW 22 [345]). Compare EM 14–15 (18–19); VA 264–65.

67. "Allein das vergessene Geheimnis des Daseins wird durch die Vergessenheit nicht beseitigt, sondern die Vergessenheit verleiht dem scheinbaren Schwund des Vergessenen eine eigene Gegenwart" (WW 21 [343]).

68. WW 23 (346); WM 49 (389).

of necessity and consequently to the possible confrontation of the inescapable." [69] A "*possible* confrontation of the *inescapable*"? The confrontation is of the inescapable because Heidegger believes that human development can take no other course, but it is only possible because, prior to attaining it, man may cease to be human or simply cease to be. At the moment when Heidegger speaks of the point of view of the mystery—man's abandonment by being—his thinking merges into faith, and when he sees human history (*Geschichte*) as a "calling" (*Geschick*) he has entered the sphere of hope. [70]

It is at this point that critics have seen a "turning" in Heidegger's thought: a new interest, a new context, a new way of putting the question, in effect a new philosophy. It seems reasonable to talk of a leap, but hardly of a turning or reversal of thought—the continuity of direction is too striking. We began (in *Being and Time*) with a dialectical tension between the work at hand and the world as its necessarily implicit context. Out of this situation awareness arose through an event which occurred in and through Dasein but over which Dasein had no control, and the form which this awareness assumed proved to be decisive for the way in which the situation subsequently evolved. Thus far the young Heidegger. This event we then translated into the issue of a conflict between two primeval forces, the world and the earth (in *Holzwege*), and this conflict has remained continually present as the guiding thread of the argument: first a conflict between authentic and inauthentic aspects of Dasein's being (in *Being and Time* again) and now (in the essay *On the Essence of Truth*) a conflict in which truth and untruth—and more originally the mystery and illusion (the two forms of untruth)—contend for Dasein's being. Thus the old Heidegger. Where is the turning in all this? When a distinction becomes a conflict, when factors become forces or poles become protagonists, we recognize a leap but not a reversal of thought. In rejecting logic as an objective foundation of human knowledge, Heidegger has emphasized the necessity of a "leap" (*Sprung*) in thinking from the start, [71] and it seems likely that such a leap occurred in his own thinking at the very beginning. Certainly once it is under way the argument

69. "Aus dem Da-sein des Menschen und aus ihm allein entspringt die Entbergung der Notwendigkeit und ihr zufolge die mögliche Versetzung in das Unumgängliche" (*WW* 23 [346]). Compare *VA* 62–64.

70. *SZ* 384–85; *VA* 32, 252–53; *Ho* 310–11; *SG* 108.

71. In *Being and Time* Heidegger already talks of the necessity of a leap to break into the "circle of understanding," which reflects the circular character of Dasein's being. See *SZ* 315–16.

seems singularly undeviating in its direction. It always manifests the same tendency, beginning by insisting on the active role of Dasein in the event of truth and ending by emphasizing its passivity in the face of that event, beginning by emphasizing the understanding latent in the human project and ending by emphasizing the mystery latent in the human mood. This does not entail a change of position: the concern is always to show how these two moments of the human situation belong necessarily together.[72]

When factors in human being become forces possessed of an active power of their own, or when the poles between which human life unfolds become the protagonists of a conflict of which human life is the issue, one is open to the charge of mythologizing. Jean Wahl brings this charge in discussing the conflict which Heidegger portrays between being and appearance, but it applies equally well to the conflicts which we have described. There is no such thing as being or appearance as such, Wahl argues, and so nothing which could correspond to the force of being on the one hand and of appearance on the other. Such a criticism is based on assumptions on which Heidegger and Wahl disagree. It assumes that philosophical notions are simply generalizations meant to describe qualities which things have in common. Universals in this sense clearly cannot be possessed of any power. It assumes the very point at issue in Heidegger's thinking: that the truth of thinking consists in correspondence with a given object rather than in the illumination of the situation out of which objects arise. If mythologizing consists in projecting an inner state into the outer world, Heidegger cannot be accused of mythologizing, for he is not talking of the outer world but seeking to reveal a dimension of experience in which the distinction of subject and object appears as derivative and distorting. On the other hand, to the extent that, in the myth, subject and object—fact and mood—have not yet broken apart, Heidegger actually *seeks* to get beyond abstractions to their mythological substratum. One thing must be admitted, however. Heidegger, as we have said, prefaces *Being and Time* by quoting Plato's dictum that the philosopher should not "tell stories about being," and in the second part of his philosophy, which we are now approaching, Heidegger's own thinking comes to take on something of the form of a story.

We have characterized history as a movement away from the mystery and toward control, which means a movement away from

72. This is not to deny the historical unfolding of Heidegger's thinking, which Otto Pöggeler portrays with consummate skill in his book, *Der Denkweg Martin Heideggers.*

the totality to the particular and away from concern for beings as such to a concern for beings as this and that. It is essentially a movement toward positivity, toward dispersal in the particular, which is one aspect of science.[73] But it is accompanied by the attempt to re-establish unity and totality. In speculation this attempt takes the form of system, the complementary aspect of science, and in practical life the form of technology.[74] Since the original unity of things is not a systematic organization of particulars, however, but the vital and mysterious wellspring which makes particulars possible, such attempts to achieve unity and totality *with control* are doomed in principle to failure. The decisive aspect of any system is that it eventually breaks down.

Despite his dispersal in the particular, historical man still stands in the midst of the totality of beings. The mystery is always present in its own unique way. It even "announces itself," as Heidegger puts it; it is expressly experienced—in mood. For this reason Heidegger makes mood central to truth, contrasting its revelatory power with the inadequacy of understanding.

3. Truth and Mood

HEIDEGGER DOES NOT regard mood as a psychic condition, an accidental attribute of human subjectivity, an inner reaction to an outer event, or a by-product of Dasein's relations to things. He regards it rather as the explicit announcement to Dasein of its position in the midst of being in its totality. Mood is the "ex-istent exposure to the totality of beings." [75]

Mood reveals a fundamental aspect of Dasein's being-in-the-world, that of being situated (*Befindlichkeit*). It reveals Dasein's facticity: that it finds itself in the midst of beings, thrown into a situation which it did not create, confronting issues which are not of its own determining, the vital center of a world organized around the project which it is but does not control, and hence radically finite, dependent. Mood is the reverse side of the aspect of human being which Heidegger has called the project, out of which he insists understanding arises. Both refer to Dasein's relation to the totality of beings, a relation which constitutes its own being, but the project points up the active, the mood the passive aspect of the relation.

73. WW 20–21 (342–43); Ho 76–77; VA 58–59.
74. WM 48–49 (388–89); Ho 77–79, 93, 95–96.
75. ". . . ek-sistente Ausgesetztheit in das Seiende im Ganzen" (WW 18 [339]).

Heidegger understands mood in an ontological rather than an empirical sense. It is only because mood in the ontological sense belongs to the structure of human being that we are able to "feel" or "experience" mood in the empirical sense. But no empirical investigation of mood can uncover its ontological significance, if only because it reveals the mood as *a* being—either at hand or on hand, either as a given fact or as a manipulable factor—rather than as a manifestation of the openness which gives rise to beings. The ontological significance of mood is accessible only to philosophical reflection, never to scientific observation; and yet if we look at the history of philosophy, we find that it has been continually overlooked.

Kant approaches a recognition of the ontological significance of mood in his treatment of the feeling of reverence (*Achtung*) in the context of his moral philosophy.[76] Reverence is the passive aspect of man's relation to the moral law as the ground of his being which transcends nature. A pure feeling of reverence for the moral law is not merely a consequence but a condition of moral action—or rather, in a paradoxical sense (as we have already said of freedom), it is at once a condition *and* a consequence, the alpha and omega of significant human experience. For Heidegger, too, mood is not the by-product of conduct but the condition of conduct: of deliberate (moral) action and the habitual behavior out of which it arises, of scientific knowledge and the familiarity out of which *it* arises. It is thus a condition of *all* human experience, significant and insignificant. In this sense we have spoken of Heidegger's effort to widen the scope of the Kantian problematic. What is significant in Kant's doctrine of reverence is that this feeling does not relate to any specific object—otherwise it could not be "moral" in Kant's sense, it would be "heteronomous"—and it cannot properly be understood.[77] From a Heideggerian point of view we may surmise that Kant's reverence cannot attach to any specific object because it reflects the source out of which objects arise, and that it cannot be understood because it lies too close to the source of understanding.

76. *GMS* 401, note. For Heidegger's commentary see *KM* 143–46 (162–66).

77. Unlike any other feeling, reverence is not receptive (*empfangenes*) but self-engendered (*selbst-gewirktes*). From an empirical point of view this is unintelligible. Reverence also subverts the principle that feelings always represent either an attraction to or a repulsion from some object and can therefore be reduced to one of two fundamental categories: desire and aversion (Hobbes). Reverence is neither but is analogous to both.

Kant attributes such importance to this mysterious feeling—which we can understand as a kind of mood—because he presses forward toward a recognition of the decisive role which human conduct plays in constituting an area of openness in which things can manifest themselves.[78] Aristotle is more typical of the way in which philosophers have traditionally approached mood or feeling. We find his treatment in Book II of the *Rhetoric*. "The emotions," he says, "are all those feelings which so change men as to affect their judgments. . . ."[79] He assumes a being of man which is properly his own and endowed with the power of judgment unaffected by feeling. He treats moods in the *Rhetoric* because they are important wherever a decision is to be made, and it is the art of the rhetorician to influence men's decisions.

But since rhetoric exists to affect the giving of decisions . . . the orator must not only try to make the argument of his speech demonstrative and worthy of belief; he must also . . . put his hearers, who are to decide, into the right frame of mind.[80]

Aristotle describes feelings primarily in the context of relations *between men*, only secondarily between man and things, and not at all in the context of man's relation to his experience as a whole (the totality of beings). The issue between Heidegger and Aristotle is whether man is to possess a being of his own above and beyond his affectivity to things, of which mood is the supreme index; whether a certain "frame of mind" is not always fundamental to the way in which things manifest themselves; whether this does not always "affect man's judgment"; whether mood is therefore fundamental not only to men's relations among themselves but to their relation to the whole of human experience as well.

For Heidegger mood has an ontological significance which goes far beyond the pragmatic importance which Aristotle attaches to it. It reveals man's place in the midst of the totality of beings: where we are and how things are going. Through mood we relate not to this or that thing in particular but to things in general. Through mood the totality of beings keeps breaking into human experience. The mood is not caused by any particular event or situation. It may be occasioned by an event, but it really

78. Moral philosophy, the theory of human action, affords Kant deeper insight into reality than theoretical philosophy. Practical reason confirms the existence of noumena (that there is something beyond things as they appear), which, for theoretical reason, must always remain a postulate.
79. *Rhet.* 1378a20.
80. *Rhet.* 1377b21–24.

arises out of and reflects the human situation in its entirety and can only be adequately explained on this basis.

We are always in some mood or other, even if it should be one of total indifference. "At any given moment Dasein is already in a mood." [81] Mood is not something which simply happens to Dasein, least of all accidentally. It belongs to the ontological structure of human being as the reverse side of the project, and in this sense Heidegger calls it the decisive event constitutive of human being as such (*das Grundgeschehen unseres Da-seins*).[82] In revealing where we stand, mood brings human being into the immediate presence of beings and so into the presence of its own being as human. "Mood reveals where we stand and how things are going. In this 'where we stand,' mood brings being to be 'there.' " [83]

Lacking any being (*Seiendheit*) of his own, man is attuned to the totality of beings and is permeated by particular beings—a pure catalyst as we have called him—and this is revealed in the mood, which comes over us suddenly and without our control, revealing our dependence on and subjection to beings and thereby the nothingness which lies at the heart of our own being, our radical finitude as beings of care immersed in a project which is essentially a *thrown* project. It is freedom, as we have seen, which attunes human conduct to the totality of beings. Mood manifests this attunement.

Mood, Heidegger argues, arises neither "from within" nor "from without." It is not a by-product of man's encounter with any particular thing nor is it produced by human subjectivity and projected upon the world, which is then experienced as banal or exciting, threatening or promising, familiar and trustworthy, or terrible and marvelous. The mood embraces both subject and object, both the self and its world, and points to the unity out of which such a duality arises and which continues to permeate the relationship when the two have split apart. It is this original and enduring unity which allows things to manifest themselves, specifies their intelligibility and accessibility, and is therefore decisive for any determinate relation between man and the things of his world. Knowledge is one such relation, and mood reveals the unity which it presupposes but which it itself tends to conceal. In revealing the fact that Dasein is attuned (*abgestimmt*) to the totality of being and permeated (*durchstimmt*) by beings in their

---

81. "[D]as Dasein [ist] je schon immer gestimmt" (*SZ* 134).
82. *WM* 31 (364). Compare *SZ* 384.
83. "Die Stimmung macht offenbar, 'wie einem ist und wird.' In diesem 'wie einem ist' bringt das Gestimmtsein das Sein in sein 'Da' " (*SZ* 134).

particularity, mood (*Stimmung*) is the hidden ground of the notion of truth as correspondence (*Übereinstimmung*).[84]

When man turns away from the mystery and forgets his openness to beings, it is *mood,* the revelation of his finitude and dependence, which he forgets and from which he turns away. Only to forget the mystery is not to escape it, and to turn away from mood is not to avoid the revelation which it entails. "For the most part Dasein evades . . . being as it is disclosed in mood . . . [but] even in such evasion the 'there' is disclosed." [85] We are capable of mood—or bound to mood—because we are open to the totality of beings. The more we concentrate on particular beings, the more we are open to their totality (which makes such concentration possible); the more we strive for control, the more we find ourselves abandoned and dependent, exposed to mood. This is a leading theme of Heidegger's philosophy of history, which we will take up in the following chapter.

If the tendency of knowledge is toward dispersal in the particular, in beings as this and that, mood is the countertendency which relates man to being in its totality. Mood and understanding thus stand in a dialectical tension which reflects the conflict of the world and the earth, truth and untruth, the mystery and illusion. We should not think that Heidegger makes mood, in contrast to understanding, the sole repository of truth. He does not deny the genuine revelatory power of knowledge but seeks to redress the balance of a tradition which has come to predicate truth primarily, or even exclusively, of knowledge. In the revelation of beings, mood and understanding imply each other as the ex-posure and in-sistence which *in conjunction* go to make up human existence in Heidegger's sense; there can no more be mood without understanding than there can be understanding which is not fundamentally moody. It is here a question of priority, and Heidegger insists on the priority of the revelatory power of mood. But so deeply is the priority of knowledge rooted in our Western consciousness that his argument is easily misinterpreted as outright rejection. This observation is essential to a proper understanding of his approach to the history of philosophy.

Finally we might contrast Heidegger's discussion of mood (the manifestation of freedom) with Kant's discussion of freedom. Kant conceives freedom as the mysterious source of a process in

84. *WW* 18–19 (338–40); *WM* 30–31 (363–65); *WP* 35–37.
85. "Das Dasein weicht zumeist . . . dem in der Stimmung erschlossenen Sein aus. . . . Im Ausweichen selbst *ist* das Da erschlossenes" (*SZ* 135).

which man determines himself, or is determined by a higher power—reason—representing the highest element in his being. The ideal goal of the process is "pure activity" (*reine Tätigkeit*) or "pure spontaneity." [86] Heidegger conceives mood as the revelation of a process in which man opens himself to the determining power of things and in which he is, through all his incessant and inescapable activity, ultimately passive. Kant sees freedom as an index of pure activity underlying a process in which man determines himself independently of all other things; Heidegger sees mood as an index of human passivity in the face of a mysterious event from which he and all other things derive their being. The primary mark of a being thus characterized by exposure to beings, finitude, and dependence is not that it is capable of *reason* but that it is capable of *mood*.

In Chapter 1 we asked for a context and focus for knowledge. The context of knowledge Heidegger finds in man's relation to the totality of beings as this is incorporated in the project of being which he is and which embraces both him and his world. This context remains necessarily implicit in all forms of knowledge and activity—we can "know" a context only by placing it in a larger context—but it is revealed *as mysterious* in the mood. The focus of knowledge we can find in the specific concern within the project of human being which serves as its organizing principle and determines for every era of history the objects which man seeks to know and the way in which he seeks to know them—in Heidegger's terms, the being (*Seiendes*) "in which openness can take its stand and endure." The context and focus of knowledge are thus to be found in the exposure and insistence which characterize Dasein's being as care. In both cases Heidegger traces back knowledge to a response to being and beings which precedes and transcends knowledge and is most directly reflected in mood. To de Waelhens' question "why man submits to reality by drawing from it the substance and value of what he knows and even of what he does" we may now answer: because of his essential exposure to beings as this is revealed in mood.

Heidegger's analysis of truth leads to mood as the ultimate presupposition of the truth of knowledge. It is because Dasein is essentially moody, exposed to beings, that it is capable of knowledge. So mood occupies the central position in the essay *On the Essence of Truth*. It divides the essay into two parts, the first (secs. 1–4) examining the traditional notion of truth for its pre-

86. *GMS* 451–52.

suppositions, the second (secs. 6–9) treating the necessary conjunction of truth and untruth as the key to an understanding of history. Between these two sides of the question—which correspond to what we have called the two parts of Heidegger's philosophy—mood represents the apex of the argument, the theme of section 5, entitled "The Essence of Truth." Mood is the necessary presupposition of theoretical knowledge on the one hand, but it is also a necessary condition of history on the other: only a being so exposed to beings as to be capable of mood can have a history. The organization of the essay reveals the crux of Heidegger's argument: that truth is rooted in human finitude, not in man's transcendence of the world, the self, and time through knowledge. Mood is accorded the central position because it is the index of human finitude.

Mood is a more fundamental expression of truth than knowledge because it offers the possibility of a revelation which eludes man's theoretical understanding. It reveals the mystery—the unknown as unknown—human passivity and dependence, the human situation as a thrown project. All this Heidegger finds implied in knowledge as well, only there it is necessarily implicit and has the tendency to be disguised and overlooked. Heidegger's mystery does not lie beyond or behind things—the way in which Kant's thing-in-itself is usually understood—but is immediately present in human experience in the mood. Only it is forgotten when we lose sight of the revelatory power of the mood, when we come to regard the mood as an aspect of human subjectivity which is capable of being manipulated, thereby reducing it, as we have a tendency to do with all things, to the level of being at hand.

4. The Three Propositions of *Being and Time*

HEIDEGGER'S ARGUMENT in the essay *On the Essence of Truth* may be summarized in three theses: (1) that truth is related essentially to human being and, conversely, (2) that it is not primarily cognitive, and (3) that it is to be conceived not as a timeless order but as an event issuing from a conflict of forces (the earth and the world, mystery and illusion), one of which is prior to it. These three theses parallel the three propositions which Heidegger employs as leitmotifs for his discussion of truth in *Being and Time:*

1. " 'There is' truth only insofar as and so long as there is human being."

2. "We must presuppose that there is truth."

3. "Human being is simultaneously in truth and untruth." [87]

In order to compare the two works and to further elucidate Heidegger's understanding of truth, we shall take up each of these propositions in turn. We will see that they reflect the three ontological characteristics of Dasein: existence, thrownness, and decadence.

1. There is truth only insofar as and so long as there is human being because truth as openness is relative to the being of man as it is essentially open and thereby draws other beings out of their original hiddenness. Dasein is open to beings by virtue of its existence, having its being outside and beyond itself in the presence of other beings, and Dasein exists in this way because its being as care necessarily projects it beyond itself. Truth as openness is grounded in existence, and existence in the project of being which is Dasein. Otherwise things could not possess their own identity and autonomy and could not serve as the criterion of thought and action.

Heidegger uses the example of Newton's laws of planetary motion: prior to Newton's discovery, he says, they were not true.[88] This does not mean that they were *false,* but that they were hidden or concealed. Newton's laws do not simply describe the motion of planets, they first *reveal* the planet, permitting the heavenly bodies to assume a position as planets in human experience. Prior to Newton's discovery there *were* no planets, only bodies which correspond to what we now know as planets. In allowing the heavenly bodies to attain to an identity as planets, Newton's laws are fundamental to the truth of planetary motion. Any truth, Heidegger argues, is similarly relative to the discovering presence of Dasein.

The possibility of "there being" anything at all depends upon the being which Heidegger calls "being there," Dasein. The English expression "there is" (like the French *il y a*) does not merely indicate brute facticity but a place within some framework or context: *"there* is" (*il* y *a*). But it is Dasein's existence as a project of being which creates the framework or context in which place is possible. Heidegger does not deny the existence of "facts." He

---

87. (1) "Wahrheit 'gibt es' nur, sofern und solange Dasein ist" (*SZ* 226, in italics).

(2) I have taken the statement out of the form of a question: "Warum müssen wir voraussetzen, dass es Wahrheit gibt?" (*SZ* 227, in italics).

(3) "Das Dasein ist gleichursprünglich in der Wahrheit und Unwahrheit" (*SZ* 223).

88. *SZ* 226–27. See also *EM* 64 (84–85).

insists that we encounter facts (being on hand) within the context of human design—at the point of its breakdown—but he does not object to facticity in the usual sense, only to the attempt to find purely given facts in human experience or to make them serve as the basis of its intelligibility. His own analogue of facticity in this sense appears in the notion of the earth as the abiding and inexhaustible which engulfs and forever eludes human design, but the earth belongs to the untruth which precedes openness rather than to truth.

The project which creates the context and openness in which "there can be" things is one which Dasein does not itself determine but into which it is thrown. So Dasein does not determine truth, any more than it determines that there be things. Since Dasein does not determine *that* things be open or *how* they are open but is rather itself determined (as a being) by the way in which things manifest themselves in openness, it is really Dasein which is relative to truth. Dasein, as we have tried to show, is thrown into openness by an event which is not of its own determining, and in this sense it is truth which "gives itself" to Dasein. This "giving" of truth Heidegger finds implied in the German expression *es gibt Wahrheit.*[89] As in the expression "it is raining," where the real subject is rain, Heidegger reads truth as the subject of the expression.[90]

2. All speculation presupposes that there is truth. But Heidegger insists that we have not yet recognized the real sense of the presupposition or the ground of its necessity. Why *must* it be possible for the mind to correspond with the things which it knows? That the task of justifying the presupposition of truth is frequently assigned to God, as in Descartes, is the best indication of how enormous a problem it poses. Kant offers a transcendental justification of the presupposition by showing that it is a necessary condition of the possibility of scientific knowledge and moral action, but Heidegger objects that this approach (*a*) sees truth only in relation to two special moments of human experience, (*b*) leads to the notion of an ideal subject or pure ego—an

89. SZ 227–28. See also *Ho* 80–83; *WD* 115–16; *US* 193–94, 258.
90. The same is true of the expressions "the world worlds" (*die Welt weltet* [WG 44]), "nothing nihilates" (*das Nichts nichtet* [WM 34 (369)]), "the thing things" (*das Ding dingt* [VA 172]), and "temporality renders itself temporal" (*die Zeitlichkeit zeitigt sich* [SZ 328]). In each case we are asked to conceive the notions dynamically, as quasi-events rather than as quasi-things. Like raining, these quasi-events have no subject other than themselves; one could as well say that "it" worlds, nihilates, things, and renders temporal. Despite their justification, the expressions are still unfortunate. In employing them Heidegger puts too great a strain on language.

isolated center of knowing and acting—which is a phantasmal idealization, and (c) appeals to the being of a subject which itself remains unknown except in the context of the aspects of experience which it is meant to explain.[91]

Heidegger greatly extends the sphere of the validity of the presupposition of truth. It is not only a presupposition of thought and deliberate action but a presupposition of human experience in its totality. The assumption that there is such a thing as truth underlies not only man's cognitive and deliberate activities but every form of human conduct, whether cognitive or not—love, work, artistic creativity, habitual behavior, moods—and we only obscure its sense and the ground of its necessity if we ascribe its validity solely—or even primarily—to human thinking and deliberation rather than to human being as it precedes and transcends thought.[92]

What does it mean to make a presupposition? It means to recognize the ground of one being in another, that is to say, outside itself. This is only possible because Dasein exists outside itself in an area of openness in which other beings can exist outside *them*selves, e.g., as instruments, which have their being in the function they are meant to perform. Dasein can only recognize what a presupposition means because it has its own being "in another," in its world. To make a presupposition (*Voraussetzung*) is to "posit (something) in advance" (*voraus-setzen*), and it is only because Dasein exists in advance of itself as care that it can "posit in advance." Heidegger thus traces back the possibility of any presupposition to the worldliness and temporality of human being. "In the ontological structure of Dasein as care, in being in advance of oneself, we find the original 'presupposition.'"[93] The presupposition belongs to human existence, not simply to human thought, so that the ground of its necessity must be seen in the character of human being, not—as in Kant—in the character of human consciousness or knowledge. The original presupposition is not the postulate on which theory is erected but the active projection of self (*Sichvoraussetzen*) which makes such a thing as theory possible.

If the possibility of the presupposition is grounded in the openness of human being, this openness is what Heidegger calls

91. SZ 229, 318–23.
92. SZ 148–53.
93. "In der Seinsverfassung des Daseins als Sorge, im Sichvorwegsein, liegt das ursprünglichste 'Voraussetzen'" (SZ 228).

truth. In this sense it is not we who presuppose truth but truth which renders possible all our presuppositions.

It is not we who posit truth in advance but truth which makes it ontologically possible for us to *be* in such a way as to be capable of positing something in advance. Truth first *makes possible* such a thing as positing in advance, the presupposition.[94]

But man does not *have* an area of openness at his disposing, he *is* it—the human projection of openness is inescapable. In the final analysis it is human being which is projected by the openness which it is and cannot escape and which determines that it be exposed to beings through its project. So truth not only makes the presupposition possible but renders it inescapable. "Because the projection of self belongs to the being of Dasein, we *must* presuppose ourselves as determined by openness."[95] Ultimately it is not man who projects the possibility of truth but truth as openness which projects the possibility of "being there" which we call man.

If the first proposition tends to make truth relative and subjective, this is counterbalanced by the second proposition, which makes man the creature of truth. Yet the second proposition does not conflict with the first but provides its necessary complement. The first is a reflection of existence, the second of thrownness, and the two together go to make up the being of Dasein as a thrown project. In the first instance it is Dasein's decisive conduct which projects an area of openness, and in this sense truth is relative to the being of Dasein. But every decision of Dasein's depends upon the concrete problems and possibilities which present themselves at any given moment, upon previous decisions which cast the framework within which the present decision must be made, and upon the breakdowns in its world over which Dasein has no control. So in the final analysis Heidegger finds that it is not truth which is relative to Dasein but Dasein which is relative to truth. Here we see the germ of Heidegger's philosophy of history, its necessity if truth is not to be relative and subjective, and

94. "Nicht wir setzen die 'Wahrheit' voraus, sondern *sie* ist es, die ontologisch überhaupt möglich macht, dass wir so *sein* können, dass wir etwas 'voraussetzen.' Wahrheit *ermöglicht* erst so etwas wie Voraussetzung" (*SZ* 227–28). Compare *Ho* 41 (677–78).

95. "Weil zum Sein des Daseins dieses Sichvoraussetzen gehört, müssen 'wir' auch 'uns,' als durch Erschlossenheit bestimmt, voraussetzen" (*SZ* 228, in italics).

its connection with the analysis of immediate experience in *Being and Time*. Here is the transition, which I maintain is a necessary transition, from the first to the second part of Heidegger's philosophy, and we find it clearly prefigured in *Being and Time*.

3. Since the possibility of truth is grounded in human finitude, it is not surprising that man is always necessarily in untruth as well as truth. Truth is the openness which results from some essential project. Insofar as man *is* this project he is necessarily in the truth. On the other hand, being already in the project and capable of encountering things only as they are rendered open and accessible by it, man can never have access to the source of openness, and in this sense he is in untruth. This untruth Heidegger calls the mystery. Beyond this, the project reveals any particular being in one or several of its aspects but not in all its aspects. Yet knowledge, which is consequent upon the project, ignores its origin and purports to reveal its object in all its aspects—at least in all its *essential* aspects—laying claim to an absolute character which is in principle impossible. This untruth Heidegger calls illusion. Man is always essentially in the openness of truth and the concealment of mystery and illusion; his being results from a primeval conflict between mystery and illusion which produces openness.

In *Being and Time* Heidegger says that Dasein is "co-originally" (*gleichursprünglich*) in truth and untruth. In the essay *On the Essence of Truth* he speaks of the mystery as untruth which *precedes* revelation and of illusion as the untruth which *accompanies* it. From the word "co-originally" in the third proposition of *Being and Time* we can conclude that Heidegger has not yet clearly distinguished between the two forms of untruth whose conflict he later portrays as the source of openness.

Why does Heidegger make illusion indispensable to truth? We have argued that absolute revelation is in principle impossible—what is totally transparent thereby becomes invisible. Conversely we must say that there is no absolute discovery, no discovery which begins with complete hiddenness. The discovery of beings can occur only on the basis of what has already been revealed, though partially and inadequately. Yet the partial revelation draws us away from what is yet to be revealed—from its own limitations and imperfections—and thereby becomes an obstacle to further revelation, an illusion which has to be overcome. We may think of illusion as the element of inertia involved in the activity of revelation. Every discovery of beings, Heidegger says, conceals at the same time that it reveals; yet this concealment

provides the starting point for any specific revelation and is therefore indispensable to truth. "Every new discovery is made not on
the basis of complete hiddenness but begins with discovery in the
form of illusion." [96]

Heidegger regards this as true of all human conduct, but
especially of knowledge. More than any other form of conduct,
knowledge breaks the unity of experience into figure and ground,
concentrating on a single thing or aspect of things to the exclusion of other things and of the web of connections which binds
things together in an original unity. It produces a familiarity with
things beyond the prudent vision of immediate experience and so
increases the intrinsic tendency of things to disappear in their
autonomy and identity. In short, the abstraction in which knowledge is rooted has an intensified form of distraction as its
shadow-side.

But this is only the negative aspect of knowledge, which plays
a decisive positive role in revelation as well. Knowledge is necessary to preserve revelation—even at the cost of distortion—and so
to confer continuity on human experience in history. By increasing the familiarity of things and extending the scope of Dasein's
world it contributes to the possibility of deepened revelation when
that world breaks down and is stripped of its familiarity. And in
seeking relentlessly to reduce the mystery, it actually reveals,
through its inadequacy, the mystery *as mystery.* The positive role
which the illusion of knowledge plays in the evolution of revelation cannot be overlooked—as it frequently has been—if we are to
understand Heidegger's philosophy of history in the following
chapter.

That illusion—or at least confusion—is indispensable to any
quest for truth has long been recognized. Why does man think at
all? We have already seen both Plato and Aristotle answer: in
order to resolve contradiction. And how do we know what we are
looking for when we are in search of truth—Meno's paradox, with
which we began? We do not know *this solution,* Aristotle suggests, but we know that we require the solution *of this difficulty.* If
we regard the confusion of contradiction as a manifestation of the
breakdown of illusion, we can see the extent to which Heidegger's
notion of the intimate relation of truth and illusion is prefigured
in Greek philosophy. Both Plato and Aristotle suggest that the
illusions of the sensible world provide the impetus to thinking;

96. "Erst recht vollzieht sich alle Neuentdeckung nicht auf der Basis
völliger Verborgenheit, sondern im Ausgang von der Entdecktheit im Modus
des Scheins" (SZ 222).

Aristotle goes further in suggesting that they also provide thinking with its direction.

But we have also seen the difference which separates Heidegger from the Greeks. Both Plato and Aristotle speak of these difficulties which impel us to reflect in theoretical terms as difficulties of thought which can best be expressed in an analogy with vision. Heidegger conceives illusion—as he conceives truth—in the wider context of human existence as it precedes and transcends the vision of knowledge. And while Plato seems to speak, and Aristotle certainly speaks, as though there were a point at which knowledge could finally transcend illusion and divest itself of all difficulties, Heidegger maintains that untruth—illusion as well as the mystery—is the abiding shadow-side of truth, of which truth can never fully divest itself.

One further point is worthy of mention. When we look at the doctrine of substance which Aristotle expounds in the central books of the *Metaphysics*, we cannot help being struck by its affinity to Plato's doctrine of ideas. Here Aristotle identifies the substance of a thing with its immaterial essence,[97] which is the object of knowledge.[98] Being immaterial, such substances are immutable,[99] and they are the cause of both the being and intelligibility of the transient, corporeal things of which they are the forms.[100] How does substance in this sense differ from Plato's immaterial, immutable, purely intelligible ideas? Beginning from different starting points—Plato with human virtues or man's inner experience, Aristotle with corporeal things or man's outer experience—the two philosophers seem to arrive ultimately at the same conclusion. But such a judgment is facile and misleading; it obscures the genuine differences which divide the two thinkers. This is because it regards conclusions of thought as though they had meaning *in themselves* rather than in relation to the whole movement of thought which has gone before. Statements only make sense in context, and the context in which philosophical conclusions make sense is provided by the entire argument which leads up to them. The starting point, then, is as important for speculation as its conclusions, for which it must provide the ultimate source of sense and meaning. Now both Plato and Aristotle find the starting point of philosophical reflection in illusion: Aristotle in the "self-moving marionettes" that men wonder at, Plato

97. *Meta.* 1032b14, 1038a20, 26.
98. *Meta.* 1031b7, 18–22.
99. *Meta.* 1033b16–19, 1039b20–40a2.
100. *Meta.* 1037a25–30.

in the shadows of the cave and the confusion of the lowest segment in the analogy of the line.[101] From the vantage point of the central books of the *Metaphysics* does it not seem like illusion to call species *"secondary* substance" and to give corporeal things ontological precedence over their forms by saying that "if these did not exist, it would be impossible for anything else to exist"? [102] Yet Aristotle not only makes these statements in the *Categories*, a work intended as an introduction to philosophy; he even returns to this form of expression in the central books, immediately following a critique of Plato, when it is necessary to go back to the beginning to make *his* meaning unmistakably clear to listeners who have been imbued with Platonism.[103] This is Aristotle's method: he must begin with what "has little or nothing of reality"—what I am here calling illusion—in order to "end in the contrary and better state." [104] Both in his statements and in his practice Aristotle suggests that the starting point of speculation is the source of the sense and meaning of its conclusions, that illusion must provide the material of knowledge as well as its impetus and direction. If this is so, knowledge can never fully divest itself of its illusory origins if it is to make sense. This is the theme of Hegel's *Phenomenology of Spirit,* to which we shall return when we portray Heidegger's interpretation of Hegel.

Heidegger regards truth as an event; [105] illusion provides the situation in which the event occurs. Truth is the overcoming of illusion, the wresting of being out of its original and abiding hiddenness. "Truth (discovery) must first be wrested from beings. Beings are torn from hiddenness. Every given discovery is at the same time a case of *robbery.*" [106] The Greeks originally recognized the negative character of truth, Heidegger argues, in calling truth *a-lētheia,* "un-hiddenness." [107] We have already seen the event of truth at its most primitive level in the preceding chapter. It is a "negative event," producing the distance required of vision and the negativity required of the determinate judgment. Awareness

101. *Meta.* 983a11–19, *Rep.* 509d–511e.
102. *Cat.* 2a11–b6.
103. *Meta.* 1042a24–32.
104. *Meta.* 1029b4–12, 983a11–20; see also *Phys.* 184a16–21.
105. *Ho* 50 (685); *VA* 40–43; *PL* 21–22 (255). See also *ID* 28–33 (27–32); *EM* 146 (191).
106. "Die Wahrheit (Entdecktheit) muss dem Seienden immer erst abgerungen werden. Das Seiende wird der Verborgenheit entrissen. Die jeweilige faktische Entdecktheit ist gleichsam immer ein *Raub*" (*SZ* 222). See also *EM* 128–29 (168–69); *PL* 32–33 (260–61).
107. *SZ* 33, 219, 222; *Ho* 39–43 (676–79), 310–11; *PL* 32–33 (260–61); *VA* 220–21, 259; *EM* 77–78 (102).

arises out of distraction and beings emerge out of hiddenness when the instrument with which man is immediately concerned breaks down and the things of his world are suddenly divested of their familiarity. Out of this event reflection necessarily arises: both a concern for beings, stripped of all pragmatic considerations, and the drive to control—the effort to insure that the breakdown does not occur again. Philosophy and sophistry, Heidegger says, were born twins.[108] The event is one which occurs in human being, not in human thinking, for it is the source of thinking. It is also the source of history.[109]

History begins when man knowingly turns back toward his broken world. Knowledge introduces a new and increased distraction, and there emerges that concrete form of human being which Heidegger calls inauthentic. When the things of the world are known and organized, they become more familiar than ever and possessed of an increased tendency to disappear in their identity and autonomy. But no matter how well things are known and organized, the breakdowns continue to occur, and they are increasingly severe. The greater the organization of things, the more far-reaching the revelation its breakdown entails; the more familiar things become, the more forcefully they manifest themselves when they are divested of their familiarity. This is basically the pattern which Heidegger sees in human history as the evolution of openness. Knowledge as it is preserved and handed down in tradition confers on Dasein the continuity which makes such an evolution possible. But the direction of the process is determined by the breakdowns of the world which elude Dasein's knowledge and control. Here we see the intimate conjunction of Heidegger's three propositions: the interplay of truth and untruth, the sense in which truth "gives itself," and the source of truth not in thinking but in being.

It is not because of what man does not know that he stands in untruth as mystery, and it is not because of what man mistakenly *thinks* he knows that he stands in untruth as illusion. For Heidegger the case is the other way around: untruth is not primarily an attribute of knowing but of being, and it is not to be found where the being of man "leaves off" but at the center of his being as radically finite, as existence, project, or care. Truth and untruth belong together to the being of man, and not merely to the being of man but to the totality of being as such. For man is only the open area in which beings unfold and manifest their being. The

108. WW 24 (348).
109. WW 16 (336).

attainment of truth is therefore not exclusively a human accomplishment, and neither is illusion solely the result of human deficiency. Insofar as man apprehends truth, beings manifest themselves to him in truth, and, if he is deceived, it is because beings themselves are deceptive. So Heidegger makes error and illusion as transcendent as truth, ascribing them not merely to human knowledge but to the manifestation of being. "To being itself as appearance belongs [the 'mere appearance' of] illusion." [110] Aristotle seems to recognize such an "objective" ground of illusion when he says that "the difficulty of our thinking points to a knot *in the object*." [111] But if illusion is rooted in being, we must recognize that it too is real and, in its own way, true; we must recognize that truth reigns even in illusion.

5. Truth and History

THE NOTION THAT TRUTH reigns even in error and illusion is the original contribution of Hegel in philosophy and—in a very different sense—of Freud in psychology. For both Hegel and Freud the past is of decisive significance in understanding the present. Both insist that truth can only be approached by penetrating human illusions. Both find the vital data of inquiry and the clue to its interpretation in history. Heidegger's notion of truth similarly culminates in history as the scene of the disclosure of the radical finitude of human being in which both truth and untruth are grounded. Man forgets being in favor of beings, turns away from the mystery toward calculation and control, ignores openness and his own being as an area of openness in his preoccupation with the structure which reveals itself *within* openness. But to forget or turn away is not to eradicate or escape: man experiences the mystery as a turning in the direction of need, as necessity (*Not-wendigkeit*). He feels driven or compelled; the direction of history surpasses his control. This is man's calling (*Geschick*): to be thrown into a project of being which is not of his own choosing, to be exposed to the things which stand at his disposal in a way which is not one of his disposing, or to be situated in an area of openness which is not itself open to him. This is the origin of history (*Geschichte*).[112]

110. "Zum Sein selbst als Erscheinen gehört der Schein" (*EM* 83 [108]). Compare *WW* 17 (337–38); *WM* 11–12 (211); *Ho* 42–43 (678–79), 244, 310–11; *VA* 32–33; *N* I 620.
111. *Meta.* 995a30.
112. *SZ* 384–85; *Ho* 243–44, 310–11; *BH* 81–90 (284–88); *VA* 32, 224; *SG* 107–10, 119–20, 137–38, 157, 176.

Heidegger sees history as the evolution of the area of openness in which man confronts beings in such a way as to allow them to have a decisive influence on his being. Man always confronts things within the context of a world which is in varying degrees *his* world, and only within such a context can anything be meaningful or make sense. This is the insight of *Being and Time*. Only Heidegger wants to illumine the "worldliness" of the world and to see it in such a way that it itself makes sense. This is the goal of the later works, which set the insight of *Being and Time* into motion. Having portrayed man's encounter with things against the horizon of the time of an individual life, Heidegger then opens out the horizon to encompass the time of mankind, the time of history. The continuity which underlies his works as a whole must be seen in the fact that the insight of *Being and Time* cannot ultimately remain static; it demands to be set in motion.

The insight that the accessibility and intelligibility of things depend upon human decision carries us necessarily into the realm of history. For every decision is rooted in the past, in previous decisions which set the framework of difficulties and possibilities in which the present decision is to be made and determine the intelligibility of the data on the basis of which it must be made. Man's world, the clearing in which he lives, is constantly changing. "By virtue of the clearing, beings are unhidden in a way and to a degree which is constantly changing." [113] The evolution of openness is what Heidegger understands by history. In view of the necessary interrelation of decisions, it implies continuity—possibly meaningful continuity—as well as change.

Whatever happens to historical man issues from a decision concerning the essence of truth which [at any given moment] has already been made and so does not stand at human disposing. And yet it is this decision which determines what is sought and held fast as true and what is discarded or passed over as untrue within the open area of the essence of truth as it has taken concrete shape.[114]

History is the sphere in which ontological truth issues in ontic truths. Heidegger's philosophy of history is the culmination of his

---

113. "Dank dieser Lichtung ist das Seiende in gewissen und wechselnden Massen unverborgen" (*Ho* 42 [678]).

114. "Was immer sich mit dem geschichtlichen Menschen begibt, ergibt sich jeweils aus einer zuvor gefallenen und nie beim Menschen selbst stehenden Entscheidung über das Wesen der Wahrheit. Durch diese Entscheidung ist je schon ausgegrenzt, was im Lichte des festgelegten Wesens der Wahrheit als ein Wahres gesucht und festgehalten, aber auch als das Unwahre verworfen und übergangen wird" (*PL* 50 [269]).

effort to trace back the truth of knowledge—indeed any concrete truth—to an origin in being as it precedes and transcends knowledge. It is essential if his notion of truth is not ultimately to be relative and subjective. And it is necessary if he is to find meaning in human life beyond the meaning characteristic of the instrument—meaning within structure related to a given end—which he rejects as a possible basis of the meaning of life but which, he argues, man has an inescapable tendency to regard as the only sort of meaning possible.

Being and Time not only leads into the later, historical works by requiring completion in a philosophy of history, it also provides the key to the understanding of history and so prefigures the broad outline and direction of the later works. In individual life, the immediate and inescapable way of "being there" Heidegger calls inauthentic: man implicitly conceives himself after the model of the instruments which he encounters within his world and relates to things, without being aware of it, exclusively in their instrumentality. Dasein first emerges as the impersonal one. This is a contraction of Dasein's being and of the being of the things to which it relates, but being in its totality continues to be present in the form of unrest or disquiet. Approaching history with this key, Heidegger sees it as predominantly the record of human instrumentality, the evolution of the impersonal one. It is characterized by the unrest of technological progress, the increasing organization of human life, and by inner conflict between the two modes of being human—authentic and inauthentic—reflected in the philosophical works which give us the deepest insight into the Western tradition.

History is the product of conflict in man's being out of which unhiddenness emerges: the conflict of the earth and the world, of mystery and illusion, of authentic and inauthentic modes of "being there." The conflict becomes progressively more acute with the evolution of the impersonal one, manifesting itself in crises in human thinking and the organization of human life of more and more serious proportions. Conflict and crises are the dominant themes of Heidegger's philosophy of history, though it is a question to what extent history manifests these themes to one not in possession of the categories of *Being and Time*. The goal is to show that there is a significant issue at stake in the conflict and that the crises reveal signs of the direction characteristic of a meaningful movement.

Aristotle, we have said, finds significance in the conflict in thinking which we call contradiction. It provides man's thinking with direction. Reality first reveals itself to the knowing mind in contradictions; the task of the knowing mind is to resolve each contradiction as it arises and thereby to take its direction from reality itself.[115] The direction of such thinking is not arbitrary, and it is not laid down by thinking. Reality "leads" through the medium of contradiction, and thinking "responds." The same principle applies to Heidegger's conception of the unhiddenness which precedes thinking. Dasein's world is sketched out by its decisions, but its decisions arise in response to breakdowns in its world over which it has no control. Dasein's historical development thus takes on a direction which is not of its own determining. Its immediate response to the breakdown of its world is to take steps to insure that such a breakdown does not occur again and so to evolve a more complex and tightly structured world. The crises in such a world become increasingly severe. But the deeper the crisis, the greater the possibility of the revelation which it entails. Heidegger thus sees history as Aristotle sees thinking: as man's response to the call of being. He values what he calls "essential thinking"—in Plato, Kant, Hegel, and Nietzsche for example—not for the instructions which it gives us on how to organize our lives and our view of reality but for the insight which it offers into the historical conflict of which our traditional way of living and thinking is the product. The notion of truth as correspondence, he seems to suggest, is a contracted and illusory expression of Dasein's original (precognitive) responsiveness to being.

Heidegger's reasons for making inauthenticity, forgetfulness, and illusion necessary to unhiddenness and history may be classified into two groups. The *phenomenological* reasons all reflect the contention that being first manifests itself in an event in which it is contracted or that human conduct necessarily conceals at the same time that it reveals. The *eschatological* reasons find in this necessity the significance of a movement toward deepened revelation. Forgetting lends to what is forgotten a unique presence: in forgetting the mystery, man exposes himself all the more to its directive force. The drive to control spawns crises which eventually drive man to recognize the impotence of willing in the face of the mystery and so to confront the mystery in a deeper

115. *Meta.* 995a23–b4. In recounting the historical evolution of his four causes, Aristotle also speaks of his predecessors' being "forced by the truth itself . . . to inquire into the next kind of cause" (*Meta.* 984b10). Heidegger quotes this text in introducing his notion of truth (SZ 213).

way. The vital principle of history Heidegger thus sees as "the reigning presence of the mystery in illusion" (*das Walten des Geheimnisses in der Irre*). [116]

Because truth manifests itself in history through illusion, we can best approach it—or *only* approach it—by penetrating illusion in order to allow it to reveal its truth. The Western tradition may be dominated by illusion, but this does not mean that we should—or *can*—turn our backs on it. For we are ourselves part and product of tradition. It has given us our power to see, and whatever we are to see we must see from within it. We can only expose ourselves to its illusion, experiencing it *as* illusion.

However and whatever we attempt to think, we can only think within the bounds sketched out by tradition. Its presence reigns when it frees us from a thinking *back* to a thinking *ahead* which is no longer planning.[117]

This is a form of letting things be: letting the illusion of tradition lead us where it will. "Then decisive openness to the mystery begins to penetrate illusion as such." [118] The truth at which Heidegger finally aims is the truth of history, and this he expresses as "insight into the mystery from within illusion" (*Ausblick in das Geheimnis aus der Irre*).[119] In this way we allow ourselves to be led by reality in a more concrete and historical sense than Aristotle in following the path of contradiction.

Every illusion has its own truth. Just as Freud finds in the illusions of his patient the expression of the truth of this particular life, Heidegger finds in the Western philosophical tradition the expression of the truth of Western man in the concrete form in which he has evolved in history, an account of his ascendant inauthenticity. We are part and product of this tradition—its illusions are our illusions—and in coming to understand it we come to understand ourselves. The history of philosophy teaches us what we are, where we stand, and how we have come to be where we are. It provides us with insight into our own being which would not otherwise be open and accessible to us. This is why it is so important for us to come to grips with our tradition.

116. *WW* 23 (347).
117. "Was immer und wie immer wir zu denken versuchen, wir denken im Spielraum der Überlieferung. Sie waltet, wenn sie uns aus dem Nachdenken in ein Vordenken befreit, das kein Planen mehr ist" (*ID* 34 [33]).
118. "Dann ist die Ent-schlossenheit zum Geheimnis unterwegs in die Irre als solche" (*WW* 23 [347]).
119. *WW* 23 (347).

"Our own way emerges out of such [traditional] thinking. For this reason it remains necessarily a dialogue with past thinking." [120] We should remember that Heidegger characterizes authenticity in the first instance as a grasp of inauthenticity possessed of a power to modify our whole way of being.

In this way Heidegger wants to allow illusion to take the lead in the quest for truth. For him as much as for Freud the process of concealment has a revelatory power of its own.

Illusion dominates man by misleading him. In the very process of misleading man, however, illusion contributes to the possibility, which man can bring forth out of his ex-istence, of *not* being misled by experiencing illusion *as such* and not losing his orientation on the mystery of "being there." [121]

Even though it is dominated by inauthenticity and illusion, by concern for determinate objects of knowledge, the history of philosophy must lead of itself to a more original confrontation of truth as the mysterious source of the being and intelligibility of all objects of knowledge. The history of philosophy must reverse itself. This is what Heidegger means by the cryptic statement which takes the form of a simple reversal, "The essence of truth is the truth of essence." [122] The "essence of truth" is openness to the mystery; the "truth of essence" I take to be the revelatory power of the illusion of tradition, with its concern for the determinate object of knowledge, the "essence" or nature of things.

When a tradition rigidifies, it can become a burden and an inhibiting force. This is possible because, as the word *Überliefern* ["to deliver over"] implies, tradition [*Überlieferung*] is a delivering-over in the sense of *liberare,* an emancipation. As a freeing, tradition brings to light hidden treasures of the past, even if the light is only that of a hesitant daybreak.[123]

120. "Unser eigener Weg kommt aus diesem Denken her. Darum bleibt er auch notwendig in die Zwiesprache mit dem bisherigen Denken einbehalten" (*WD* 62).
121. "Die Irre durchherrscht den Menschen, indem sie ihn beirrt. Als Beirrung schafft die Irre aber zugleich mit an der Möglichkeit, die der Mensch aus der Ek-sistenz zu heben vermag, sich nicht beirren zu lassen, indem er die Irre selbst erfährt und sich nicht versieht am Geheimnis des Da-seins" (*WW* 22–23 [346]). (Italics added in translation.)
122. "[D]*as Wesen der Wahrheit ist die Wahrheit des Wesens*" (*WW* 26 [350]).
123. "Eine Überlieferung kann, wenn sie erstarrt, zur Last und zum Hemmnis ausarten. Sie kann es, weil die Überlieferung eigentlich, was ihr Name sagt, ein Liefern im Sinne des liberare, der Befreiung ist. Als ein Befreien hebt die Überlieferung verborgene Schätze des Gewesenen ans Licht, sei dies Licht auch erst nur das einer zögernden Morgendämmerung" (*SG* 171).

It follows that the importance which Heidegger attaches to tradition cannot be overemphasized. Far from breaking with tradition, like Descartes, Heidegger insists that there is no *other* approach to truth *except* through constant and resolute reflection on tradition. For " 'being' always speaks historically and therefore in a way which is permeated by tradition." [124] Such reflection is the subject of the following chapter. Heidegger regards it as the decisive step in "renewing the question of the sense of being," and it is equally essential to an adequate understanding of his notion of truth.

Peter Fürstenau does not recognize the decisive role which the history of philosophy plays in Heidegger's thinking. This is because he draws too sharp a distinction—amounting to separation—between the authentic and inauthentic modes of being human and their corresponding expressions of truth. He interprets the statement, "The essence of truth is the truth of essence" without any reference to inauthenticity, illusion, or tradition. Truth manifests itself to the degree that Dasein comes to exist authentically—that is all.

In the course of the evolution of the "essence of truth," the essence of authentic openness to being manifests itself with continually increasing clarity as the "truth of essence" (being), as the transparency of the way in which the authentic understanding of being . . . is present.[125]

Such an interpretation overlooks the context in which the statement occurs in the essay *On the Essence of Truth,* immediately following two sections which deal with untruth and illusion and one which treats the question of truth in the history of philosophy. If Heidegger is here talking of the way in which truth manifests itself to authentic human being—an expression which nowhere occurs in the essay—his choice of context could not be more misleading. Fürstenau sees tradition as the history of illusion in the pejorative sense alone, failing to recognize the positive role which it plays—and *must* play—in the process by which unhiddenness itself comes to be unhidden. He refers to tradition as "mere tradition" (*blosse Tradition*),[126] an expression which Heidegger never uses and which it is really unthinkable that he should use.

124. " 'Sein' spricht je und je geschichtlich und deshalb durchwaltet von Überlieferung" (*ID* 47 [44]). On the power of tradition see also *SG* 83, 164, 176; *ID* 64 (59); *KM* 14 (5); *US* 95; *EM* 96 (125–26).
125. Peter Fürstenau, *Heidegger, das Gefüge seines Denkens,* p. 94.
126. *Ibid.*, p. 87.

For Heidegger there is no such thing as illusion pure and simple, illusion which does not nourish itself on reality and is not permeated through and through by the mystery. Reality and illusion go hand in hand: *"Wieviel Schein jedoch, soviel 'Sein.'"* [127] His aim in approaching the illusion of tradition is to reveal the inner conflict of thinking and being which it conceals and which gives it its vitality and motive force. The point is important because of the widely held view that Heidegger's aim is to *refute* tradition and its spokesmen—Plato, Kant, Nietzsche, Hegel—or to condemn and reject the spirit of science and technology. "All refutation within the sphere of essential thinking," Heidegger tells us, "is nonsense." [128] His historical studies of the spokesmen of tradition invariably reveal two motifs which are not ultimately reconcilable with each other, but this is not meant to prove the existence of a contradiction which makes the philosophy in question unacceptable or to point up improvements which are necessary if the doctrine is to be made consistent. Such conflict is inescapable, and a thinker's ability to penetrate to the depths of human being where it occurs and to bring it to expression is the real index of his greatness. [129]

Heidegger speaks of his aim as the "destruction of the history of ontology." [130] But he understands such destruction in a positive sense. "The destruction is not intended to bury the past in nothingness: its aim is positive, and its negative aspect always remains unthematic and indirect." [131] The positive aim is to break through what appear to be the fixed and tranquil doctrines of tradition in order to reveal the conflict in Dasein out of which they arise but which they tend in the first instance to conceal. In such an undertaking the concern for theoretical contradiction—especially as the basis of refutation and rejection—can only remain "unthematic and indirect." *De-struction* must here be understood in the literal sense of a reduction of fixed *structure* which is to bring to light its dynamic source. This is necessary, Heidegger argues, if we are to apprehend what has really been going on in history. "Destruction means to lend an ear, to open ourselves to

127. SZ 36.
128. "Alles Widerlegen im Felde des wesentlichen Denkens ist töricht" (*BH* 82 [285]). See also *N I* 503.
129. See, for example, *ID* 44–47 (41–44); *N I* 617–18.
130. SZ 22–23.
131. "Die Destruktion will aber nicht die Vergangenheit in Nichtigkeit begraben, sie hat *positive* Absicht; ihre negative Funktion bleibt unausdrücklich und indirekt" (*SZ* 23). Compare ZS 36 (93).

what speaks to us out of tradition as the being of all beings." [132] Destruction is re-collection or renewal (*Wiederholung.*)[133]

The history of philosophy must lead to its own destruction in this sense. To the questions how he *can* and why he *must* apprehend the truth of the Western tradition Heidegger has a single answer: because it has broken down, revealing its being as inescapably as the hammer which breaks in our hands, revealing the conflict which has been going on—and this means the mystery which was present—all along. The breakdown takes the form of both a theoretical cul de sac and an existential debacle.

Heidegger sees the breakdown of tradition—for our purposes the breakdown of the traditional notion of truth—in the philosophy of Hegel.[134] Hegel draws out the most extreme consequence of a tendency implicit in tradition from the start. For the truth of individual propositions he substitutes the truth of a system in which all individual propositions are absorbed. But since the proposition has traditionally been regarded as an instrument for the acquisition and preservation of truth, and since the being of the instrument, as we have seen, is to be found in the context of the instrumental totality of which it is a part, the traditional notion of truth finds in Hegel its fullest and final expression. In Hegel's system subject and object become one, the mystery vanishes—or is always on the verge of vanishing—and genuine decision in the face of the unknown is no longer possible. Knowledge becomes absolute. But if Hegel is the culmination of tradition on the one hand, he is its nemesis on the other. For starting with the traditional notion of truth as the truth of a proposition expressing the correspondence of a mind and a thing, Hegel proves that, on this basis, *nothing is true.* Knowledge is thus made absolute and is destroyed at the same time, and the conflict in tradition reaches its climax, coming out of the hiding from which it has exercised the decisive directive force in human thinking and being from the time of Plato. Consciousness comes to despair in knowledge— Hegel himself speaks of the argument in the *Phenomenology of Spirit* as a "way of despair"[135]—and the mystery is never more urgently present, as human being is driven toward the

---

132. "Destruktion heisst: unser Ohr öffnen, freimachen für das, was sich uns in der Überlieferung als Sein des Seienden zuspricht" (*WP* 34 [73]). For Heidegger's similar interpretation of the Kantian "critique" see *FD* 92–94.
133. *SZ* 26. Compare *US* 130–31.
134. *EM* 144 (189). Compare *SG* 145–46.
135. *PG* 67 (135).

confrontation of a decision regarding what it means *to be* which eludes its conscious control. It is not long before Nietzsche, following in the same tradition, defines truth as a kind of "error," without which a conscious, deliberate being like man could not live.[136]

Hegel actually plays a dual role in Heidegger's thinking. His conception of truth is important as a symptom of human development and the evolution of beings which Heidegger strives to penetrate—like the dream for Freud, a symptom without which the theory devised to explain it would scarcely be thinkable. On the other hand, Hegel too conceives truth as the truth of illusion, or as the truth of history, the revelation of what has actually been going on in history to which history itself necessarily leads. Hegel speaks of the "cunning of reason" in much the way Heidegger speaks of the secret presence of the mystery.[137] Obviously Hegel is more than a symptom in Heidegger's philosophy of history.

We began with an impossible question—the question "What is truth?"—and we have maintained all along that man must be driven to pose such a question, to confront what Heidegger has called the "unattainable inescapable." This requires a crisis in human thinking and in human being such as to shake our conception of what is possible. Heidegger claims that he is not precipitating such a crisis but only recognizing its existence. The crisis begins in the *Phenomenology of Spirit,* where Hegel questions not only what is true but what truth is, making truth itself "questionable." Since Heidegger regards Hegel as the culmination of tradition and tradition as the record of man's response to being, he calls the question of being a question "of being" in two senses: not only a question *about* being but one which being itself poses.[138] The same may be said of the question of truth. We might even add a third sense: the historical question of truth—how man has conceived truth and why—is the question of the truth of Western man and his tradition. This is the necessary background to the question of truth as such, since it alone can justify such a question and serve as the basis of its meaning and significance. All three themes will recur in the following chapter, in which we will briefly recapitulate Heidegger's philosophy of history as it centers upon the evolution of the traditional notion of truth. Our task will be to find the "reigning presence of the mystery in illusion."

136. *WzM* #493. See *PL* 44–45 (266–67).
137. *PG* 46 (114), 64 (132).
138. *BH* 56–57 (272–73).

4 / The History of Truth: Conflict

1. The Key to the Interpretation of Tradition

HEIDEGGER'S ACCOUNT OF TRUTH IN *Being and Time* opens with a reference to the history of philosophy—Parmenides' identification of being and knowledge. This opening reference to history is significant, for history plays as decisive a role in Heidegger's thinking as it does in Hegel's, though a very different one. It is safe to say that no other original philosopher—not even Hegel—has shown as constant and widespread an interest in the history of philosophy as Heidegger.

Like Hegel, Heidegger regards his thinking as a direct product of the Western heritage and an appropriation of its truth. We have said that his immediate aim is to discover the presupposition of the traditional notion of truth and only indirectly the presupposition of all human experience and that he finds in tradition the justification for posing the impossible question of what truth is. Werner Marx is true to Heidegger's conception of the order of reality in beginning his book *Heidegger und die Tradition* with an account of Aristotle and Hegel as an introduction to the new problematic. Only the order of reality, as Aristotle suggests, need not be identical with the order of investigation or the order of exposition. Heidegger himself speaks of approaching history with the insight obtained in *Being and Time*.[1] This is my justification for putting off until the end what really provides the starting point and initial impetus of Heidegger's thinking.

1. *BH* 72 (280); *Ho* 195.

Heidegger finds the notion of truth as correspondence to be fundamental to the whole Western tradition. He insists that the notion is not original, that it presupposes a further ground of truth which it itself tends to conceal. In this sense he regards it as an illusion. But an illusion reflects the experience out of which it arises, and the traditional notion of truth reflects the experience of Western man in this way. We are all of us part and product of the Western tradition; its illusion is *our* illusion. "In its factual being Dasein is always 'what' and as it has already been. Whether explicitly or not, it *is* its own past. . . . Dasein's past does not *follow along after* it but is always in advance of it." [2] If we wish to attain to the truth of our being and of the world in which we live, we must first come to grips with the Western tradition, in which we have our being and as a result of which we are what we are. [3]

We have seen that an analysis of the traditional notion of truth leads to one which is more original. It must therefore be tied to the original notion by an inner bond, and in this sense it is true. Illusion does not replace truth; it presupposes it and is permeated by it. Though it is the great illusion of Western man, the traditional notion of truth cannot simply be "consigned to the flames." Heidegger's aim in his historical studies is to show how illusion arises out of truth[4] and finally leads necessarily back to it.[5]

Truth according to the traditional notion is primarily the truth of knowledge. Such a notion presupposes (*a*) that there is a distinction between the knower and the object of his knowledge, (*b*) that the object belongs to an intelligible framework, and (*c*) that the knower has accepted the object in advance as the criterion of his knowledge. We have seen Heidegger ask how these conditions are possible and conclude that the last two are *not* possible if there is ultimately a distinction between human being and the world, or if human being relates to the world exclusively or primarily by way of knowledge. Man's being, Heidegger claims, is of such a sort as to realize itself only outside itself in the midst of things, as care. Care involves man in activities from which the intelligible structure of the world derives, and it is in the course of such activities that man originally encounters things. Knowledge is a form of careful activity, but not the original or primary form.

2. "Das Dasein ist je in seinem faktischen Sein, wie und 'was' es schon war. Ob ausdrücklich oder nicht, *ist* es seine Vergangenheit. . . . Seine eigene Vergangenheit . . . *folgt* dem Dasein nicht *nach*, sondern geht ihm je schon vorweg" (*SZ* 20).
3. *EM* 96 (125–26), 156 (204–5); *N II* 202.
4. *SZ* 220, 223; *EM* 83 (109–10), 146–47 (192).
5. *SZ* 26.

It is because knowledge derives from care, while care necessarily subordinates itself to the object of care, that we recognize the demand for "objectivity" in our thinking, accepting the object as the criterion of knowledge. This is the presupposition of the traditional notion of truth which it itself tends to conceal.

When human experience is grounded in knowledge, a gulf opens up between man and his world. Knowledge is conceived after an analogy with vision: it is primarily theoretical or speculative. The distance essential to vision is presupposed, spanned by a light in which things are visible—in which objectivity is possible—and this light is simply natural, *lumen naturale*. Decision is consequent upon speculation, will is subordinate to reason, and moral philosophy is a corollary or appendage of theoretical philosophy. But the object of theoretical knowledge is always some determinate being or determinate aspect of beings generally. Hence being (*Sein*) is equated with determinate beings (*Seiendes*), or at least with some principle of determination; the determinate being qua determinate is taken for being itself. The index of this reduction of being to the status of beings is the definition of man as *a* being, *animal rationale*. These implications of the notion of truth as *adaequatio intellectus et rei* reflect not only the way in which man has come to *think* but the way in which he has come to *exist*. They characterize the mode of being which we have called inauthentic: the turning away from the mystery and the immediacy of mood and situation. This is the sphere of history. The traditional notion of truth expresses the inauthenticity of Western man as he has evolved through history. Because Heidegger regards Western history as decisive for world history, he calls the traditional notion of truth the "fundamental reality of world history" (*Grundwirklichkeit der Weltgeschichte*).[6]

Such thinking falsifies the immediacy of the human situation, suggesting that man first sees things and then, on the basis of his vision, organizes and handles them. Heidegger reverses the order of knowledge and practical activity: man relates immediately not to the thing or object but to the instrument, and his attitude in this relation is prudent but not contemplative or visual. Things only appear to man's vision when the instrument breaks down and he stumbles upon a void in the world in which he lives. Now for the first time we have the presuppositions of theoretical knowledge which the traditional notion of truth simply takes for granted, divorcing knowledge from its roots in life and rendering it original and autonomous. Now there are subject and object (as

6. *PL* 50 (269).

there were not, so long as the work was in progress) and a distance between them rooted in the void. The negative has emerged as the basis of determination and intelligibility. And man is now predisposed—indeed compelled—to "stop and look." This is the knowledge situation as it has been represented in the history of philosophy, but it is not original or autonomous.

There is something deceptive in the notion of pure, disinterested vision. For vision requires distance, or what we have called a "gap" between man and his world, and it is just this gap which makes control possible—even necessary. Of all the senses, vision makes the most direct claim to be detached and disinterested, and yet of all the senses it is the most fundamental to the technological conquest of nature. So it is with much of our detached, objective thinking. It appears to be pure and underived, but in reality it is crisis-rooted and covertly control-oriented.

Such deception is characteristic of the inauthentic mode of being human. To recognize this is the first step toward becoming authentic, for it entails the awareness that intelligibility is rooted in a project which is not itself intelligible, that our destiny is bound up with things in a way which we cannot ultimately control, and that genuine revelation emerges from a breakdown which manifests the presence of the terrible and marvelous. Authenticity and inauthenticity always belong together; we cannot conceive either in isolation from the other.

We have seen authenticity and inauthenticity—the awareness of being and the turning away from its revelation in an effort to insure that it does not occur again—emerge together out of the breakdown of human design which I have called the moment of truth. This is the genesis of human presence, which emerges with its two concrete modes in necessary conflict with each other, reflecting the conflict of the world and the earth, concealment and openness, the mystery and illusion. Its source is the inner bond which we said unites the traditional notion of truth to a more original notion. This theme runs through all of Heidegger's studies in the history of philosophy.

The history of philosophy is the history of increasing inauthenticity for the reasons which Hume and J. S. Mill suggest in arguing that history is on the side of the utilitarian moral principle. Inauthenticity gives rise to the public, impersonal world, and it is this which abides and evolves; it "endures as a permanent condition," as Bollnow puts it, whereas authenticity "is not a condition but an event." It follows that the conflict between authenticity and inauthenticity for man's being becomes increasingly more serious. But the history of philosophy is not simply an inauthentic history. Inauthenticity may be the basis of its continuity and direction, but it is the struggle against inauthenticity which is the source of its vitality. Philosophers struggle relentlessly against the tendency, and the measure of their greatness is the extent to which they are able to sustain the conflict and give it expression in their writings.[7] Only by continual reflection on the great philosophers of history can we obtain insight into the conflict which lies at the heart of our historical being and as a result of which we are what we are.

In each of the philosophers whom he studies Heidegger finds a duality of themes which struggle with one another without reaching any final resolution. Since it is a conflict in which he himself is involved, Heidegger's attitude in his historical studies always has both a positive and negative side. The failure to appreciate this ambivalence is the cause of much misinterpretation. Critics see only the positive side of Heidegger's attitude and accuse him of reading *Being and Time* bodily into the writings of his predecessors. Or they see only the negative side of the criticism and read the studies as simple refutations, overlooking the positive significance which Heidegger finds in every philosopher whom he studies. The conflict of the two motifs—the one authentic, the other inauthentic—is the a priori with which Heidegger approaches his historical studies and provides the key with which we can best ascertain their meaning and assess their role.

The conflict is one of which the philosopher himself is not aware; it is the hidden source of the vitality of his thinking. "The more original thinking is, the richer it is in that which is unthought. The unthought is the supreme gift which thinking is capable of bestowing."[8] In the conflict the authentic dimension of human being invariably succumbs. But Heidegger finds in the process a rationale and direction. Each effort to create a greater and more comprehensive system of thought in which to hold truth fast accentuates the conflict and occasions deeper revelations of the ground from which it springs when—as every system must—it eventually breaks down. There is a phenomenological reason why history had to take the direction which it has: inauthenticity is inescapable. But Heidegger also offers a kind of eschatological explanation of the direction of history: inauthenticity

7. *ID* 41–42 (38–39); *FD* 151; *N I* 617–18; *N II* 239.
8. "Je ursprünglicher ein Denken ist, um so reicher wird sein Ungedachtes. Das Ungedachte ist sein höchstes Geschenk, das ein Denken zu vergeben hat" (*WD* 72). Compare *SG* 123–24; *ID* 44–45 (41–42); *N II* 8; *VA* 122.

produces crises in thinking and being which are possessed of increasing revelatory power.

We have called the moment at which openness emerges in human experience a vanishing moment. For the broken instrument immediately becomes material for repair and is thereby drawn once again into the complex of human design. Once again we are faced, not with a simple object to be known, but with an instrument to be handled, and the dialectic of human preoccupation is again set in motion. The cycle of experience is: distraction—breakdown—awareness—distraction. Within this cycle the historical evolution of the impersonal one adds a new dimension to the distraction by which experience is immediately characterized.

For Heidegger truth consists primarily in surmounting the distraction entailed in the cycle of human experience as a consequence of the fact that man relates to beings first and foremost as instruments. He therefore casts his notion of truth in the negative: un-hiddenness. And his first appeal to history is to claim that this is the original way in which truth is conceived and that the notion of correspondence is a later derivation from it. So the Greeks, who named things *pragmata*, called truth *alētheia*, unhiddenness. Man must surmount the *lēthe* which envelops *pragmata*, overcoming the distraction which immediately attends his being-in-the-world. This is the ascent to truth: *a-lētheia*. Heidegger argues that his notion of truth is the original notion, not only in the sense of being presupposed by correspondence but in the literal sense of preceding it in its appearance in history.[9]

2. Plato: *Alētheia* and *Idea*

THE ORIGINAL GREEK INTUITION of truth as unhiddenness can be found in Plato, only intertwined with a new notion, truth as form (*eidos*) or idea (*idea*). In *Plato's Doctrine of Truth* (1942) Heidegger traces the interplay of the two notions through the analogy of the cave in Book VII of the *Republic*. Plato begins with the original notion of truth, but, as the analogy unfolds, there occurs a metamorphosis of thought out of which the traditional notion emerges. Heidegger sees this as the hidden key to Plato's thought and to the tradition of which he is the father. He calls it a "transformation in the essence of 'truth' " (*Wandel des Wesens der "Wahrheit"*).[10]

9. *EM* 130 (170–71), 144–47 (190–92); *Ho* 39–40 (676–77).
10. *PL* 42 (265); *EM* 145 (190).

Once one is familiar with Heidegger's phenomenological description of man's immediate experience, one cannot help finding affinities to it in the analogy of the cave. Heidegger has man immersed in his project, preoccupied with instruments which disappear beneath his touch. Plato has man chained to a parapet, watching the shadows of objects on the wall of the cave opposite him. Heidegger's man lacks the distance required for vision; Plato's man is not in a position to see reality—or really to see. It is interesting that what Plato's man does see are the shadows *of artifacts*. "In every way, then, such prisoners would recognize as reality nothing but the shadows of . . . artifacts." [11] Plato's metaphor is ideally suited to Heidegger's conception of our daily experience as it is characterized not by knowledge or awareness but by distraction. It is out of this situation that knowledge must arise.

Plato has the ascent to knowledge begin with the breaking of the prisoners' chains, an event which recalls the breakdown of human design. It is not a pleasant experience.

Suppose one of [the prisoners] were set free and forced suddenly to stand up, turn his head, and walk with eyes lifted to the light; all these movements would be painful, and he would be too dazzled to make out the objects whose shadows he had been used to seeing.[12]

The break with the familiar is always painful. But familiarity is primarily a matter of prudence, not of knowledge. It is above all the tool that is familiar: man knows his tools, he can reckon with them, rely on them. This is his world, and he is at home here. If he is now to leave this world, he must be "forced, shoved, dragged forcibly."

And if he were forced to look at the firelight itself, would not his eyes ache, so that he would try to escape and turn back to the things which he could see distinctly, convinced that they really were clearer than these other objects now being shown him? [13]

Such descriptive language is not far removed from Heidegger's portrayal of man's encounter with nothing. (Who, we want to ask, is doing the forcing, shoving, dragging?) Heidegger explains the confusion and perplexity—amounting almost to anxiety—which is present at this stage of the ascent: "The removal of the chains entails a certain liberation. But simply being cut loose is not real

11. *Rep.* 515c.
12. *Ibid.*
13. *Rep.* 515e.

freedom." [14] We do not transcend our preoccupation with instruments simply because they break down.

It is only at the third stage of the ascent—after the initial breaking of the chains and the slow and arduous climbing of the passageway—that one attains genuine freedom, the freedom of the great outdoors, where everything lies open to the clear light of day. Here man confronts things as they are in themselves and not as they originally present themselves in the inverted and deceptive images of shadows. This is the realm of the authentic—of openness and freedom—which is the apex of the philosophical quest.

But the apex of the quest is not the end of the journey. The liberated soul must return once more to the darkness of the cave, to rejoin the other prisoners there and "to take . . . part in their labors and rewards." There is no pure authenticity, pure openness or freedom—no "pure truth." We must continue to live in the world of human preoccupation surrounded by the distraction and illusion which it necessarily entails. Heidegger reads the analogy of the cave as a unity, stressing the importance of its fourth and final stage, which is usually assigned only political or pedagogical significance. He argues that Plato's original intuition of truth is of a process or event, and one which is cyclical. We have described the cycle as: distraction—breakdown—awareness—distraction.

Plato's term for truth is negative because his original intuition of truth is negative: truth which must be rescued from the confusion and inversion of shadows. "The unhidden must be torn from hiddenness—in a sense *stolen* from it. . . . Truth originally means whatever is wrested from a certain hiddenness." [15] Plato originally conceives truth as rooted in untruth, unhiddenness in hiddenness, the awareness of knowledge in the distraction of life. This is expressed in the privative Greek term *alētheia*. Only in relation to such a notion does an analogy with a cave make sense. The cave is an opening in the earth shut off from the light of day and yet having access to it through a passageway which is narrow and arduous. Within the cave everything is obscure and inverted. This is the situation of a being characterized by distracted concern for things and yet capable of attaining awareness of them. Man encounters things insofar as he is involved with them, and yet just

14. "Die Abnahme der Fesseln bringt zwar eine Befreiung. Aber das Losgelassenwerden ist noch nicht die wirkliche Freiheit" (PL 28–29 [258–59]).

15. "Das Unverborgene muss einer Verborgenheit entrissen, dieser im gewissen Sinne geraubt werden. . . . Wahrheit bedeutet anfänglich das einer Verborgenheit Abgerungene" (PL 32 [260]). Compare SZ 222.

to the extent that things figure in human involvement they tend to disappear or be distorted. In this situation beings are open and yet concealed; everything is obscure and inverted, as in a cave. But if obscurity is caused by the fact that man originally relates to things as instruments (issuing, that is to say, from the same source as the initial possibility of the relationship), the impetus to clarity is provided by the fact that instruments invariably break down. In this way obscurity itself leads upward into light: the shadows in the cave point in themselves to something outside the cave. Unless truth is conceived as unhiddenness, Heidegger argues, there is no point to such an analogy.

Unhiddenness is Plato's original intuition of truth, and the only one appropriate to an analogy with a cave. Yet another and quite different notion asserts itself here and comes ultimately to dominate the analogy: truth as intelligibility guaranteeing vision, a positive notion of truth which tends to make knowledge original and underived. The ascent to openness now becomes an ascent to *vision*. It is the visibility of things in the outside world which renders them open and accessible; to be accessible is to be accessible to vision. The principle of a thing's accessibility to vision Plato calls its form or idea. The idea permits a thing to manifest itself by giving it an intelligible identity. The Platonic *idea* unites the notions of intelligibility, identity, and self-manifestation. In it visibility comes to take precedence over unhiddenness as the essence of truth.

Everything comes to devolve on the manifestation of what is to appear and how its visibility is to be rendered possible. Unhiddenness is still referred to . . . but it is considered only insofar as it renders what is to appear accessible in its visage (*eidos*), making visible what manifests itself (*idea*) in this way. . . . Our proper concern is now for the *idea*. . . . The essence of the idea is its manifest character and visibility.[16]

Heidegger sees five consequences of this shift of thinking which influence the subsequent course of Western speculation. (1) It is the determinate character of a thing which makes it visible or intelligible. To make the idea the ground of truth is thus

16. "Alles liegt am Scheinen des Erscheinenden und an der Ermöglichung seiner Sichtbarkeit. Die Unverborgenheit wird zwar . . . genannt, aber sie wird nur daraufhin bedacht, wie sie das Erscheinende in seinem Aussehen (*eidos*) zugänglich und dieses Sichzeigende (*idea*) sichtbar macht. . . . Die eigentliche Besinnung gilt der *idea*. . . . Das Wesen der Idee liegt in der Schein- und Sichtsamkeit" (*PL* 34–35 [261–62]). Compare *EM* 138 (180–81); *VA* 252; *N I* 199–216; *N II* 217–19.

to identify the being of anything with its essence, the principle of its determination. (2) Since the idea is the proper object of knowledge, to make it the ground of truth is to orient oneself toward the encounter of objects of knowledge. (3) The notion of truth as idea determines the character of awareness in terms of a determinate (in principle completely determinable) object. Knowledge and awareness now become a matter of correct vision, truth the correctness of vision (the correspondence of knowledge with its object). (4) This entails a change in the locus of truth. As unhiddenness truth is a characteristic of man's being; as idea it is rather the character of man's attitude toward determinate beings. Truth thus comes to characterize a project which man *has*—his knowledge—rather than one which he *is*. (5) Finally, the notion of truth as idea makes it into a relation between seeing and the thing seen. It is thus bifurcated into poles which have somehow to be held together.

Unhiddenness now refers to what is unhidden in the sense of being accessible through the manifest character of the idea. Insofar as such access is necessarily obtained through "seeing," however, unhiddenness is stretched apart into a "relation" to seeing. . . . What determines the character of seeing and the seen in relation to each other? Wherein does their polarity consist? What yoke (*zygon* [*Rep.*] 508a1) holds the two together? [17]

Plato's answer is the supreme idea, the idea of ideas, which he calls the idea of the good. The idea of the good should not be understood as a compound entity, as though "the idea" were one thing and "the good" quite another. The idea is the principle of a thing's intelligible identity. For the Greeks, Heidegger suggests, the good is the source of a thing's fitness or function (*das Tauglichmachende*). The two notions are correlative, since it is by virtue of its identity that a thing exhibits fitness or function. The idea of the good confers such identity on all other ideas, allowing *them* to be in the way in which they allow things to be. In it idea and goodness—intelligible identity and fitness or function— merge. By allowing all other ideas to function as ideas, the idea of the good is the principle of function *as such*. "Hence the idea of

17. " 'Unverborgenheit' meint jetzt das Unverborgene stets als das durch die Scheinsamkeit der Idee Zugängliche. Sofern aber der Zugang notwendig durch ein 'Sehen' vollzogen wird, ist die Unverborgenheit in die 'Relation' zum Sehen eingespannt. . . . Wodurch sind das Gesehene und das Sehen, was sie in ihrem Verhältnis sind? Worin besteht die Bogenspannung zwischen beiden? Welches Joch (*zygon* 508a1) hält beide zusammen?" (*PL* 35 [262]). On the shift and its consequences see *PL* 35 (262); see also *PL* 41–42; *EM* 140–41 (184–85).

ideas is the source of fitness or function as such, *to agathon.*"[18]
Knowing and being are held together by a supreme being from
which all things derive their function, on the one hand, and their
intelligibility, on the other. Henceforth Western speculation becomes essentially metaphysical, explaining beings through some
other being, and metaphysics becomes essentially theological,
grounded ultimately in a supreme being.[19]

As a consequence of making the idea the ground of truth,
being is equated with essence, knowledge is cut loose from its
roots in man's being-in-the-world, reason is understood as correctness of vision, and the locus of truth is transferred to the mind, so
that there opens up a gulf between man and his world which can
be bridged only by having recourse to a supreme being. This
theme is taken up in greater detail in the *Introduction to Metaphysics* (1953), where we find one further consequence: the
human tendency toward technology. With the gulf between knowing and being there opens up a similar gulf between nature and
value: value descends, so to speak, from above. In comparison
with an ideal realm, this world proves to be deficient. If this is a
gulf which metaphysical man finds it necessary to bridge, it is one
which technological man is driven to exploit.[20] In Plato, Heidegger
suggests, we find only the first, barely perceptible, rift. But the
distinction is fundamental for Kant and attains its consummate
expression variously in Schelling, Nietzsche, and Marx.

The original Greek experience of truth, according to Heidegger,
was the emergence of the hidden into unhiddenness, a process
by which the familar becomes strange, mysterious, and wonderful. Here truth is synonymous with the manifestation of being
and is cast in the context of human experience as a whole. This
original intuition of truth as unhiddenness, *alētheia,* is preserved
in the analogy of the cave. But here it is interwoven with another,
derivative notion: truth as vision, *eidos,* or *idea.* Truth in this
sense is contrasted with falsehood and located in the mind. Because of the interplay of the two notions a marked ambiguity
appears in Plato's exposition, and the word truth (*alētheia*) is
used where correctness (*orthotēs*) is meant. So in one passage
Plato calls the idea of the good the "cause of the correct and the
beautiful" and in another the "mistress of unhiddenness and

18. "Daher ist die Idee der Ideen das Tauglichmachende schlechthin, *to
agathon*" (*PL* 38 [263]). Compare *EM* 150 (196–97); *N* II 222, 225–26.
19. *PL* 48 (268). See also *WM* 19–20 (217–19); *Ho* 179; *ID* 50–70
(46–64).
20. *EM* 147–52 (193–99). See also *PL* 46–50 (267–69).

awareness." [21] In the first case the idea of the good is synonymous with truth; in the second it is the *mistress* of truth, which is now equated with correctness of thinking. Unhiddenness should make vision possible; instead it is equated with vision and subsequently made possible *by* vision—or at least by a principle of visibility. "*Alētheia* comes under the yoke of *idea*." [22] This is the "transformation in the essence of truth" which Heidegger finds in the analogy of the cave.

Heidegger sees this transformation as the event which gives rise to Western history as we know it. In sundering the mind and its object it provides the basis for the emergence—centuries later —of the scientific and technological point of view. The search for truth becomes an effort to transcend immediate experience. [23] Philosophy becomes humanistic. Man is regarded as the being who occupies a special position at the pinnacle of creation, and every effort must be made to develop the powers required by that position. Concern for truth centers on concern for man, and especially for his reason as its proper locus. At the end of a long historical development anthropology becomes the decisive area of philosophical inquiry. [24] As Kant puts it, the question at which all other metaphysical questions aim is the question "What is man?" Man occupies the same central position in technological organization; of all the factors involved in such organization he is the most erratic, and every effort must be made to make him reliable. So Heidegger regards technology and metaphysics as parallel and complementary developments. [25] Plato is the founder of the tradition which gives rise to both.

Three points are of general interest in this interpretation. (1) Approaching the analogy of the cave as a unity, it views Plato's conception of truth as a process rather than as a condition (the third stage of the process considered in isolation). (2) Against the all too common version of a rapturous ascent to blessedness, it emphasizes that it is a *painful* process. (3) It raises the question of the negative—the shadows—in the analogy. It seems clear that the shadows must "point." The issue between Heidegger and classic Platonic interpretation is the question of *how* the shadows

21. *Rep* 517b, c. See PL 43–44 (266). "The correct and the beautiful" recall the two poles of experience which we portrayed in Chap. 2, sec. 5: instrumentality and beauty.
22. "Die *alētheia* kommt unter das Joch der *idea*" (PL 41 [265]).
23. PL 46–47 (267–68); WP 23. Contrast BH 107–9 (296–97).
24. PL 49–50 (268–69); Ho 85–87, 91–92; VA 69, 86–87; BH 63 (275), 89 (288); KM 185–97 (212–26).
25. Ho 69.

point: through their form, which is a reflection of sharper and more precise forms visible in the sunlight outdoors, or through their darkness, as a presence in the form of absence.

3. The Translation of Greek Philosophical Experience into Latin

THE NEXT DECISIVE STEP in the development of the Western tradition Heidegger sees in the translation of Greek philosophical concepts into Latin, a translation which provides the conceptual framework for medieval thought and survives substantially intact into the modern era. The translation of philosophical concepts from one language into another—and especially from Greek into Latin—is not the harmless and relatively conventional matter which it might seem. In Latin translation, according to Heidegger, the vitality of the original Greek notion is lost and the word becomes a *term*. What he calls "the power of the word to *name*" is irretrievably lost.

Words arise out of experience as plants grow out of the soil from which they draw their nourishment.[26] This is the difference between the *word* and the *term,* which is devised with specific reference to its function within a conceptual framework. The Romans take over Greek words without the Greek experience out of which they grew; they are not *their own,* and their roots are either lost or grafted onto an altogether different experience. What Heidegger calls the "groundlessness of Occidental thought" [27] begins with this translation.

With this Latin translation the original content of the Greek word . . . is suppressed, its philosophical power to name destroyed. The occurrence of this translation of Greek into Roman is not arbitrary and harmless but the first step of a process in which the original essence of Greek philosophy becomes fixed and estranged.[28]

The most significant such translation is that of the Greek *alētheia* into the Latin *veritas.* The Greek word loses its negative character and becomes positive and underived, paralleling the

26. See *N I* 169–70; *US* 192.
27. *Ho* 13 (654–55).
28. "Mit dieser lateinischen Übersetzung wird aber schon der ursprüngliche Gehalt des griechischen Wortes . . . abgedrängt, die eigentliche philosophische Nennkraft des griechischen Wortes zerstört. . . . Der Vorgang dieser Übersetzung des Griechischen ins Römische ist nichts Beliebiges und Harmloses, sondern der erste Abschnitt des Verlaufs der Abriegelung und Entfremdung des ursprünglichen Wesens der griechischen Philosophie" (*EM* 10–11 [13]).

new conception of knowledge.[29] What we *call* truth Heidegger regards as not simply a question of etymology or semantics; it reflects the fundamental intuition which the word expresses, either negative and derivative or positive and underived.

Heidegger calls a number of other translations into question. The Greek *logos,* which he reads as a "pressing" or distillation, becomes the Latin *ratio,* a principle of system (Hobbes's "accounts of money").[30] *Physis,* the emergent, becomes *natura,* the born.[31] *Theōrein,* the vision of insight, becomes *contemplatio,* the result of analysis or dissection.[32] *Energeia,* a calling-forth, becomes *actualitas,* the manifestation of being in activity.[33]

The loss of its linguistic roots is the fate of the Western tradition. It reflects the transition from speaking out of one's own experience to speaking from hearsay, which appears in *Being and Time* as a manifestation of Dasein's everyday existence and decadence.[34] Language becomes instrumental.[35] Henceforth, Heidegger thinks, philosophy is really in search of language.[36] It is safe to say that his own influence on philosophical expression in Germany—and on the Continent generally—has been greater than any other philosopher since Kant.

4. Kant: Finitude and Transcendence

HEIDEGGER FINDS THE SAME duality of theme which we have portrayed in the analogy of the cave in Kant's *Critique of Pure Reason.* Once again the tension between two irreconcilable motifs constitutes the inner dynamic of the argument. Only this time there is a tangible manifestation of the conflict in the significant shift of emphasis from the First to the Second Edition. The fact that Kant rewrites crucial passages of the *Critique* provides the initial foothold of interpretation. *Kant and the Problem of Metaphysics* (1929) is Heidegger's first major work after *Being and Time* and retains its intuition in its sharpest focus. But it also

29. The Latin has not strayed too far from its Greek source, however. *Ver,* the root of *veritas,* is "spring," which survives in the Italian *primavera.* And April, T. S. Eliot tells us in *The Waste Land,* "is the cruellest month, breeding / Lilacs out of the dead land, mixing / Memory and desire, stirring / Dull roots with spring rain."
30. WD 127; SG 176–77.
31. EM 10 (13); EH 55.
32. VA 54.
33. VA 50–51; Ho 342.
34. SZ 167–70.
35. BH 58–60 (273–74); US 263–64.
36. See Ho 342; WD 83; US 236.

makes a contribution to an understanding of Kant in his own terms such as we encounter rarely in the writings of original philosophers commenting on the works of their predecessors.

The question is: are there two or three ultimate principles underlying human experience? Kant's answer, as it survives into the Second Edition, is that there are two: sensibility and understanding, the receptive power to which objects are given and the spontaneous power by which they are thought.

Our knowledge arises out of two basic sources in the mind: the first [the power] to receive representations (the receptivity of impressions), the second the power of recognizing an object in such representations (the spontaneity of concepts). . . .[37]

Sensibility and understanding are the two sources of experience and the *only two*. "Besides these two sources of knowledge we have no other. . . ." [38] The First Edition wavers between this answer and another and quite different one, that there are three original sources of experience: sense, imagination, and apperception.

Now there are three original sources (powers or faculties of the soul) which provide the conditions of the possibility of all experience and which cannot themselves be derived from any other power of the mind: sense, imagination, and apperception.[39]

Here Kant recognizes imagination as an original source of human experience coequal with the passivity of sensibility (sense) and the spontaneity of understanding (apperception). It is a power of the mind which cannot be derived from any other. Only this answer is stricken from the Second Edition.

In the Second Edition imagination disappears as an original source of experience and is derived from the activity of understanding operating upon the passive medium of sensibility.[40] The change is more than one of emphasis: it is not as though the weakest member of a triumvirate were reduced to a subordinate position by his stronger colleagues. For in the First Edition imagination appears as the dynamic *center* of experience, sensibility and understanding as mere facets ("opposite ends") of its activity. It is the fundamental power of the soul which, *more than the other two*, provides the a priori basis of knowledge.

37. A 50, B 74.
38. A 294, B 350.
39. A 94.
40. B 151–52.

We thus have a pure power of imagination as a fundamental power of the soul which provides the a priori basis of all knowledge. Through it we bring the manifold of intuition, on the one hand, into conjunction with the condition of the necessary unity of pure apperception, on the other. The two opposite ends, sensibility and understanding, must necessarily cohere by virtue of this transcendental function of the power of imagination.[41]

Even in the Second Edition the decisive significance of imagination has not disappeared altogether. In one passage Kant represents the activity of synthesis, upon which all human experience depends, as the "exclusive effect" of imagination.

Synthesis as such . . . is the exclusive effect of the power of imagination, a blind but indispensable function of the soul, without which we would have no knowledge whatever, but of which we are rarely so much as conscious.[42]

If imagination is dislodged from its central position as the source of all synthesis, the consequences for Kant's speculation must be decisive.

As in his study of Plato, Heidegger finds Kant's thought gravitating between two conflicting themes, the one laying primary emphasis upon imagination, the other subordinating imagination to understanding, the former the dominant theme of the First, the latter of the Second Edition. The change of attitude from one edition to the other Heidegger sees as indicative of a conflict running through the work as a whole and reflecting the vitality of its original insight.

Kant approached the *Critique of Pure Reason* with a twofold speculative aim. On the one hand it was his desire, in the face of Hume's criticism, to provide scientific knowledge with a secure theoretical foundation. But even more than this he regarded it as his obligation, in the face of apparent scientific encroachments on the moral and religious basis of human dignity, to "push back knowledge in order to make room for faith."[43] His speculative achievement was to accomplish both these aims in a single stroke. For it is by pushing back scientific knowledge—recognizing necessary limits to its scope and validity—that he provides it with a secure foundation, and these limits in turn serve as the guarantee of human faith and morals. The Kantian bulwarks which support science on the one hand provide a barrier against any incursion

41. A 124.
42. A 78, B 104.
43. B xxx. Kemp Smith's rendering of *aufheben* as "deny" is inexplicable.

into the domain of faith on the other. Both aspects of Kant's philosophical endeavor thus culminate in the portrayal of the *essential finitude of human knowledge.* Knowledge and its finitude have the *same source:* human knowledge is what it is only *because it is finite.* This, for Heidegger, is Kant's original intuition, and one which portrays human knowledge as an illuminated clearing in the midst of the density of the unknown.[44]

Keeping in mind that his aim is to reveal its essential finitude, we may briefly recapitulate the way in which Kant analyzes knowledge. Our knowledge is always the representation *of* something *as* something—I know this as a book, this book as green, and so on. All human knowledge involves this duality, and so Kant traces its origin to two principles: *intuition,* by which a certain object (which we can only specify as a *this*) is present to the mind, and *thinking,* by which such an object is represented *as such and such.*[45] If we wish to understand the essential finitude of knowledge, we must recognize the finitude of its two component elements.

Human intuition is finite because it is passive rather than creative, because its object must be *given.* Finite intuition can relate only to an object which is *already there,* and in the passive mode of being affected. Such passive intuition Kant calls sensibility. Human intuition is finite because it is sensible, which is to say essentially passive or dependent on its object's already being there.[46]

The function of thinking is to mediate and re-present what is given (present) in finite intuition. Thinking determines the object of intuition *as such and such,* draws it into a system of relations, and thereby renders it open and accessible. Only finite intuition requires this sort of mediation, for, if the object of intuition were not simply given, it would not have to be rendered accessible. Only a being whose knowledge is rooted in finite intuition—only a sensible being in Kant's sense—needs to represent its object *as such and such;* only such a being has to *think* at all. Kant's term for the activity of projecting an intelligible framework in which a given object can become accessible to human experience is *synthesis,* and the synthetic function of thinking directed toward objects in intuition is *understanding.* Understanding is thus the index of the finitude of human knowledge.[47]

44. *KM* 28–29 (27–28), 45 (45–46).
45. *KM* 33–34 (32–34); *FD* 106–7.
46. A 19, B 33. See *KM* 31–33 (31–33); *FD* 111–12; *WG* 29.
47. *KM* 31 (30), 35 (34).

Understanding is not creative, any more than the sensible intuition which it mediates, but it is at least spontaneous or productive, since it draws the data of sensibility into an intelligible framework which it itself projects. Such a framework, however, must always remain subordinate to the passive intuition by which it is required.[48] So while understanding may be the *mark* of the finitude of knowledge, intuition must be its ultimate *ground*.

Finite intuition is not an autonomous notion: it could not exist without the mediation of understanding. The human mind cannot encounter a *this* without at the same time encountering it *as such and such*. So human experience can arise only out of the conjunction of finite intuition and understanding. But this does not mean, Heidegger insists, that the two can be leveled to an indifferent correlation as "matter" and "form" of experience.[49] When such a distinction is introduced, as we have already seen, form—in this case understanding—invariably comes to assume primacy. But thinking must play a role in knowledge subordinate to the intuition which it mediates and re-presents. Knowledge must always have intuition as its focal point.

In order to be a possible object of experience, a thing must accord with the essential structure of human intuition-*cum*-understanding. In its empirical knowledge the mind must correspond with the things which it knows, but such correspondence is made possible by the fact that, in a deeper sense, the things which the mind knows, in order *to be* possible objects of knowledge, must correspond with *it*. This is Kant's way of putting the paradox that all knowledge requires some prior knowledge: all empirical knowledge presupposes a priori "knowledge" grounded in the structure of the human mind. In Heidegger's formulation: all ontic knowledge, or knowledge of things, depends upon ontological knowledge, the mind's determination of what it means to be a "thing," a sort of "knowledge" which is not directly concerned with things, or dependent upon them, at all.[50] Heidegger's contention is that, in Kant's original intuition, a priori "knowledge" has more in common with his own notion of man's being-in-the-world as a thrown project than with traditional conceptions of knowledge or with the knowledge in the strict sense—scientific knowledge—which it is meant to explain.

Our task is to trace this ontological knowledge to its source. Its

48. *KM* 29–31 (28–30); *FD* 112–15.
49. *KM* 39–40 (39–40).
50. *KM* 19–26 (14–22), 115–16 (127–28). Compare *SZ* 10–11.

source is the act of synthesis by which the mind unifies and organizes experience. Heidegger insists that it is not enough to explain such synthesis solely as the result of the interaction of intuition and understanding; one must show the essential unity of the two principles and their necessary and exclusive orientation toward each other, the aim which Kant projects in his transcendental deduction of the categories of understanding. It is the same sort of question as the one in the study of Plato, "What determines the character of seeing and the seen in relation to each other? Wherein does their polarity consist?" [51]

Human intuition is essentially dependent upon thinking, human thinking essentially oriented toward intuition. Each of the elements of knowledge is what it is only in relation to the other; both are moments of the unified activity of knowing as thinking-intuition. Such elements cannot be understood in isolation: the more we attempt to isolate one for inspection, the more it cleaves to its counterpart. "The more radically we attempt to isolate the pure elements of finite knowledge, the more forcefully we confront the impossibility of such isolation and the dependence of pure thinking on intuition." [52] But if we cannot understand the elements in isolation, we cannot understand knowledge itself simply as a product of its elements. "If examination in isolation cannot even succeed in fully grasping the elements as such, their unity can scarcely be achieved by subsequently joining together the isolated pieces." [53]

Neither of the elements of the synthesis underlying all experience can explain their necessary *unity*. This, Heidegger argues, is the function of transcendental imagination, which in this sense provides the ground of synthesis and the real source of experience. In contrast, sensibility and understanding are only *aspects* of the activity of synthesis considered in abstraction. So Kant, as we have seen, describes synthesis as the "exclusive effect" of imagination, of which sensibility and understanding are "opposite ends."

It is the unique character of imagination in its original

51. Compare above, p. 151.
52. "[J]e radikaler man versucht, die reinen Elemente einer endlichen Erkenntnis zu isolieren, um so eindringlicher wird die Unmöglichkeit einer solchen Isolierung, um so aufdringlicher die Angewiesenheit des reinen Denkens auf die Anschauung" (*KM* 58 [61]). *Aufdringlich* recalls one of the three ways in which the broken instrument manifests itself (*SZ* 73).
53. "Wenn jedoch die isolierende Betrachtung nicht einmal die Elemente als solche völlig zu fassen bekommt, dann wird erst recht ihre Einheit nicht durch eine dazukommende Verknüpfung der isolierten Stücke gewonnen werden können" (*KM* 59 [61]).

transcendental sense that it is both receptive and spontaneous, so that sensibility and understanding each reflect one of its aspects. Heidegger sees its essence in the conjunction *both-and*. Should sensibility and understanding assume priority in the analysis of knowledge, becoming the separate and independent sources of receptivity and spontaneity, imagination inevitably falls awkwardly between two stools.

This "formative power" [imagination] is at once a passive (receptive) and a creative (spontaneous) "forming." Its essential structure is properly to be seen in the expression "at once." If receptivity comes to be synonymous with sensibility and spontaneity with understanding, imagination must fall in some peculiar way between the two.[54]

The unity of human experience, along with the primacy of intuition in knowledge, is at stake in the question of what is to become of transcendental imagination. If it loses its central position in experience, receptivity and spontaneity fall apart and have to be united by an "extrinsic bond" (*äusseres Band*)—Heidegger's expression.[55] If, on the other hand, it retains its position, each of its aspects must reveal distinct traces of the other: all receptivity must be *spontaneous* receptivity, all spontaneity *receptive* spontaneity. In order to safeguard the decisive role of imagination, Heidegger therefore attempts to uncover the spontaneous element in sensibility and the receptive element in understanding and thinking.

Space and time, the forms of sensibility, are the spontaneous element in sensibility. Kant calls them "original representations" (*ursprüngliche Vorstellungen*).[56] Heidegger understands space and time to be "original" not as innate or given in the mind prior to all empirical representations but as giving rise to all our empirical representations by *permitting* an object *to appear* in intuition. We can encounter objects only because they are spatial and temporal. But "permitting to appear" is the function of imagination. In this sense space and time are *original* by virtue of belonging to imagination. They are the invisibles which make vision possible: by not being seen they make it possible for *things* to be seen.

54. "Diese 'bildende Kraft' ist zumal ein hinnehmendes (rezeptives) und ein schaffendes (spontanes) 'Bilden.' In diesem 'zumal' liegt das eigentliche Wesen ihrer Struktur. Bedeutet aber Rezeptivität soviel wie Sinnlichkeit und Spontaneität soviel wie Verstand, dann fällt die Einbildungskraft in einer eigentümlichen Weise zwischen beide" (*KM* 119 [136]).
55. *KM* 126 (144).
56. B 40, A 32, B 48. See also A 41, B 58.

Though they are in no sense creative, space and time nevertheless go toward constituting things—contributing to the determination of what it means to be a thing—and thereby reflect a spontaneity which can be understood only if sensibility is recognized as belonging to imagination, which also embraces the spontaneity of understanding as its "opposite end." Kant himself classifies space and time under the heading of *ens imaginarium*.[57]

But if sensibility reveals an element of spontaneity, reason and understanding similarly reveal an element of receptivity. Human understanding is not only finite in relation to human intuition, it is finite *in itself*. But for Kant the essence of finitude is relation to a *given*, i.e., receptivity. Understanding accordingly manifests a spontaneity which is through and through *receptive*. As the "power of rules" [58] reason is the direct opposite of arbitrariness. On the contrary, it is essentially submissive, and in this sense passive or pathetic. (1) It is submissive to its object, in which its activity terminates.[59] (2) It is submissive to the transcendental ideas of God, self, and world as the ultimate sources of its rules.[60] (3) And it is submissive, finally, to the architectonic demand of knowledge, the demand that all knowledge be regarded as belonging to a possible system.[61] The essentially finite, submissive, receptive character of theoretical reason, Heidegger argues, reveals its origin in imagination.[62]

Even in its practical employment reason reveals the receptivity of submissiveness. Here it takes the form of reverence, man's feeling for the moral law. Morality, the highest expression of pure reason, reveals itself to Kant in two aspects: objectively as law and subjectively as the pure feeling for this law.[63] These two aspects of morality are inseparable. Through his reason man gives a law unto himself, but it is a law which is utterly indifferent to his personal interests and to which he can only submit. Only through reverence is such a law accessible to man. So reverence is not the *result* but the *condition* of moral action, the first principle of responsibility and selfhood. The free giving of the moral law to oneself—what is this, Heidegger asks, but spontaneity? Total devotion and submission to the law—what is this but receptivity?

57. A 291, B 347. See *KM* 130–34 (149–52).
58. A 126.
59. A 96, 105.
60. A 643–45, B 671–73.
61. A 474, B 502.
62. *KM* 134–42 (153–62).
63. *GMS* 400 and note.

And what is the original unity of these two aspects of morality but a reflection of the *both-and* structure of transcendental imagination? [64]

The spontaneous element of sensibility and the receptive element of understanding and reason force us to recognize the primacy of transcendental imagination in human experience. This primacy appears clearly in the First Edition of the *Critique,* but in the Second Edition there is a shift of orientation. Imagination becomes simply the effect of the activity of understanding upon the passive medium of sensibility.[65] The formative center of knowledge is replaced by an extrinsic bond uniting autonomous elements, and the decisive role of imagination is taken over by understanding. It is no longer essential to Kant's purpose, as it was in the First Edition, to "investigate the cognitive faculties upon which understanding rests"; [66] there *is* no other faculty upon which understanding rests. The so-called subjective deduction of the categories is never carried through.[67] The explanation of experience now simply culminates in the synthetic a priori power of understanding. Kant refers the ground of synthesis to the Logic, giving it precedence over the Aesthetic, even though intuition (the subject matter of the Aesthetic) should be the primary element of knowledge, with thinking subordinate to it as its instrument. At this point Heidegger asks, "Has not the slave here transformed himself into the master?" [68]

Imagination is now dispossessed. It becomes a "refugee." As a "power of intuition" [69] it ought to be treated in the Aesthetic, but instead it is assigned to the Logic, where, so long as Logic is concerned exclusively with thinking, it has no place.[70] Imagination is now defined in terms appropriate to *empirical* imagination as "the power of representing an object *independent of its presence in intuition."* [71] With this definition, what was previously the source of experience becomes a special function *within* experience, a "power of the soul." It is no longer the transcendental power of

64. *KM* 143–46 (162–66).
65. B 152.
66. A Preface xvi–vii.
67. *KM* 151–52 (171–73).
68. "Wandelt sich da nicht der Knecht zum Herrn?" (*KM* 73 [79]). In his lectures on Kant (1935–36), published under the title *Die Frage nach dem Ding,* Heidegger speaks only of the "apparent precedence of thinking" in Kant's philosophy as a whole. This is the other side of the conflict. See *FD* 113–15.
69. Cassirer, *Kant Werke,* VIII, 54. Quoted by Heidegger, *KM* 118 (135).
70. *KM* 125 (143).
71. B 151.

presenting objects as such, determining what it means to be an object and constituting the presence in which objects can be encountered. It is simply the power of *representing* a particular object which is not immediately present.[72]

Heidegger claims that transcendental imagination is the unifying source of sensibility and understanding. It must be the "common root, unknown to us," which Kant speculates that the two "stems" of knowledge "may have." [73] This common root is "unknown to us," not in the sense of something which we have never encountered, but in the sense of being upsetting or disquieting—which rather presupposes that it *has* been encountered. "For the unknown is not that about which we know absolutely nothing but that which presses forward in what we do know as the disquieting." [74] Kant peers into this disquieting unknown. But in the end, like Plato, he turns away. "Kant shrinks from this unknown root." [75] The turning is marked by the appearance of the Second Edition.

It is not difficult to associate this unknown with the "blind power of the soul," which is the ground of all our knowledge but of which we are "seldom even conscious." Cast in Heideggerian terms, it recalls the hiddenness out of which awareness arises, the mystery which is the source of knowledge, the *lēthe* which lies at the heart of *alētheia*. We come closest to the direct (phenomenal) experience of it, in Kant's view, in the unique feeling of reverence—Heidegger's "mood"—which transcends our powers of understanding by appearing at one and the same time as a kind of attraction and repulsion.[76] So Heidegger claims, "Transcendental imagination is the disquieting unknown." [77]

If transcendental imagination is the unknown "root" of human experience, why should it be disquieting? Heidegger's answer hearkens back to *What Is Metaphysics?* Transcendental imagination is a "standing out into nothing" (*Sichhineinhalten in das Nichts*).[78] Unlike *empirical* imagination it is not essentially oriented toward *beings* but constitutes the presence in which it is

---

72. *KM* 118–23 (135–41).
73. A 15, B 29. Compare A 835, B 863.
74. "Denn das Unbekannte ist ja nicht das, wovon wir schlechthin nichts wissen, sondern was uns im Erkannten als das Beunruhigende entgegendrängt" (*KM* 147 [166]).
75. "Kant ist vor dieser unbekannten Wurzel zurückgewichen" (*KM* 147 [166]). See also *KM* 153 (173), 193–94 (221); *SZ* 23.
76. *GMS* 401 n.
77. "Die transzendentale Einbildungskraft ist das beunruhigende Unbekannte . . ." (*KM* 148 [169]).
78. *KM* 71 (77). Compare *WM* 35 (370–71), 38 (374).

possible for anything *to be*. Such presence cannot itself be a being—it can only be nothing. Standing out into nothing, transcendental imagination creates a presence in which there can arise that which is *not* nothing, viz., a being. It provides the dis-tance which we have argued is required for presence. So Kant himself, as we have seen, speaks of the forms of sensibility—space and time—as categories of "nothing" (*Nichts*).[79]

Transcendental imagination, the unity of receptivity and spontaneity in human experience, must be the source of both time and selfhood. Time and the self (the "I think . . ." which Kant says accompanies all our representations) cannot be regarded as separate and autonomous. Heidegger claims that they are "one and the same." "The pure finite self is essentially temporal in character. . . . Time and the 'I think . . .' no longer stand over and against each other as heterogeneous and irreconcilable—they are one and the same." [80] In order to show that time and the self are rooted together in transcendental imagination Heidegger attempts to reveal time as pure self-affection and to exhibit the radically temporal character of the self.

Kant traces the source of human knowledge and experience to the finitude of intuition, to receptivity. So Heidegger must argue that time is the source of receptivity. Receptivity refers to the possibility—indeed the necessity—of being affected by objects. But empirical receptivity, being affected by objects in experience, depends upon "pure" receptivity, being affected by the self independent of experience. Time is this pure affection. "The form of sensibility [viz., time] . . . can be nothing other than the way in which the mind is affected by its own activity . . . that is to say, *by itself*." [81] As pure self-affection, time is inseparable from the self. This is why Kant can maintain, in a text which is at first very surprising, that we ourselves "produce" (*erzeugen*) time.[82]

Out of the pure self-affection of time arises the presence in which it is possible for objects to be encountered in empirical experience. In Heidegger's terms, time is the basis on which we "let" objects "be." But the self is the subjective correlate of objects. In letting objects be, time therefore lets the self be as well. The being of the self is thus radically temporal.[83]

79. A 291, B 347. See *KM* 132 (150–51).
80. "Das reine endliche Selbst hat in sich Zeitcharakter. . . . Die Zeit und das 'ich denke' stehen sich nicht mehr unvereinbar und ungleichartig gegenüber, sie sind dasselbe" (*KM* 174 [196]).
81. B 68.
82. A 143, B 181.
83. *KM* 171–72 (193–95).

Time and the self are united in the activity of transcendental imagination. By projecting a temporal horizon of beings, determining what it means for anything to be, time makes it possible for the finite self to be affected by objects, at the same time determining the self as radically finite, dependent upon the objects which it encounters within experience. It is because the self is originally temporal that it can be affected by objects as beings with which it is essentially concerned, and only because it can be affected by objects in this way can there be such a thing as a "self" at all. Only insofar as selfhood is grounded in time can human experience be what, for Kant, it must be: thinking *sensibility*, activity grounded in receptivity.

"The abiding and enduring self," Kant says, "is the correlate of all our representations," [84] representations which depend upon the projection of a temporal order by transcendental imagination. But if the self is abiding and enduring, so is time itself, the order of experience projected by imagination. "Time," Kant says, "does not pass away"; time is "immutable and enduring"; it "remains and does not change." [85] Such time is not simply *given* but must be projected by transcendental imagination, and only against this horizon is it possible for anything to be *either* enduring and abiding *or* fleeting and transitory. If the self is not conceived in its original unity with time, it becomes either a kind of soul-substance or a purely logical postulate. [86] The self is not "in" time, as things are, but from this it does not follow that it is timeless but that it is so temporal as to be one with time itself. [87]

On the one hand Kant insists that reason is essentially architectonic, that it must regard all knowledge as belonging to a possible system. "Human reason is by its very nature architectonic, i.e., it regards all knowledge as belonging to a possible system. . . ." [88] On the other hand he reminds us—in the First Edition at least—that all our representations are "subject to time" and insists that this observation is fundamental to any consideration of reason.

All our knowledge is nevertheless ultimately subordinate to the formal conditions of inner sense, i.e., subject to time, in which all objects of knowledge without exception must be ordered, conjoined,

84. A 123.
85. A 144, B 183; A 182, B 225.
86. SZ 229, 318–20; FD 179–81.
87. KM 174–76 (198–200).
88. A 474, B 502.

and brought into relation with one another. This is a general observation which is fundamental to everything which follows.[89]

Does not time, in which all objects of knowledge are "ordered, conjoined, and brought into relation with one another" here appear as a necessary aspect of the "possible system" to which reason must regard all our knowledge as belonging, and as one with the "abiding and enduring self" which is the "correlate of all our representations"? But this passage is stricken from the Second Edition. Here the unity of time and selfhood is forgotten, and we confront Kant's assertions that "pure reason cannot be subordinate to the conditions of the temporal order" and that time cannot be implicated in the principle of noncontradiction, the highest principle of thinking.[90]

If time and selfhood are held together in the activity of transcendental imagination, time is not only the cause of the *finitude* of knowledge but the original *source* of such knowledge as well.[91] And this is decisive for Kant's original insight: that knowledge and its finitude have the same source, that knowledge is only possible *because it is finite*. Kant's original view of human selfhood is of a being which is essentially finite: receptive, temporal, dependent upon beings which it is *not*.[92] "More original than man," Heidegger affirms, "is the finitude of human being in him." [93] Kant uncovers this truth, but in the end he turns away from it.

Among the consequences of this turning we have already mentioned the sundering of experience into opposed and autonomous elements and the sacrifice of receptive intuition to spontaneous understanding as the focal point of knowledge.[94] We may now add that it is a question of whether human experience is to be regarded as projecting in the midst of darkness or as judging in

89. A 99.
90. A 551, B 579; A 152–53, B 191–92. In *Die Frage nach dem Ding* Heidegger directs his argument toward destroying the primacy of the principle of noncontradiction in the *Critique of Pure Reason*. Noncontradiction is the sufficient ground of analytic judgments but not of the synthetic a priori judgments on which all experience depends. The highest principle of thinking need not be—in fact cannot be—the highest principle of experience. The difference is reflected in Kant's distinction between formal and transcendental logic. The principle of noncontradiction is grounded in thinking independent of its object; synthetic judgments are grounded *in the object*, and this is what ultimately makes experience possible. See *FD* 119–45.
91. *KM* 178–80 (201–4).
92. *KM* 195–97 (223–26), 204–7 (233–37).
93. "Ursprünglicher als der Mensch ist die Endlichkeit des Daseins in ihm" (*KM* 207 [237], in italics).
94. *KM* 147–50 (167–70).

the midst of light [95] and whether truth is to be grounded in the temporality of human being or in a timeless order in which man partakes—in the finitude of man or the transcendence of reason.[96] What is significant for Heidegger is not the final answer which Kant gives to these questions but the interweaving throughout his thinking of two different and radically opposed answers. The difference between the First Edition and the Second is the index of this inner conflict, but it by no means represents the successful separation of the two conflicting motifs.

In the beginning Kant peers deep into the finitude of human being to explain knowledge and experience. Knowledge is primarily intuition; finite knowledge is *sensible* (i.e., passive), and therefore *thinking*, intuition. It is sensible because it depends upon its object's already being given. But objects are not *simply* given; otherwise knowledge of them would not be possible. So intuition, which is primarily receptive, must also involve an element of spontaneity. This element of spontaneity is embodied in the notion of the *already* given, an intrinsic reference to time. Time provides the horizon against which objects can be given, and it itself is *not* given but is projected by transcendental imagination in order that objects *may be* given. This spontaneous element must be traced back to thinking, which projects the horizon of time against which it is possible for objects to be given. But thinking is always subordinate to sensibility, in which objects *are* given. So human knowledge is at once sensible and thinking, receptive and spontaneous. The two elements have a common root in the activity of transcendental imagination, the *both-and* character of which is a direct manifestation of human finitude as spontaneous receptivity—or what Heidegger calls a "thrown project." This is a vision of human being as (*a*) radically finite, dependent upon objects, with which it is essentially concerned, (*b*) rooted in time, without which there could be no object, (*c*) its very being the projection of a temporal order in which, by virtue of its concern, it can and must be affected by beings other than itself.

But alongside this vision of human finitude is another vision which transcends the finite. Human reason is a species of reason in general, with understanding and sensibility as its two most fundamental elements. Understanding represents a timeless

95. *KM* 138–39 (158–59), 210 (240–41), 221 (254); *FD* 139–40. In *Die Frage nach dem Ding* Heidegger argues that Kant so transforms the traditional notion of (ontological) judgment that the question of correspondence becomes irrelevant. See *FD* 146–48.

96. *KM* 174–77 (198–201), 215–17 (249–50), 220 (252–53).

architectonic order. The primacy of the Logic is not questioned: the categories of understanding and the ideas of pure reason are conditions of reality *as such* which do not have to be derived from any human activity "on which they rest." Knowledge is not primarily projection but judgment. The sphere of time and sensible intuition is reduced to the status of *"mere* appearance." In this way knowledge comes to dominate experience, and all forms of experience are understood and evaluated according to the model of knowledge.

It is the same inner conflict and the same eventual outcome which Heidegger finds in Plato's analogy of the cave. Beginning with a notion of truth which reflects the wholeness and unity of human experience as an activity which is primarily submissive or passionate, we are left in the end with a notion which distinguishes higher and lower parts of the soul (reason and sensibility) and corresponding orders of reality (noumenon and phenomenon) and culminates in the vision of eternal and immutable truth which is pure activity. Truth as *alētheia* once again comes under the "yoke" of truth as *eidos* or *idea*.

5. Hegel: Skepticism and the System

OF ALL THE PHILOSOPHERS of the Western tradition none has thought through the conflict which lies at its heart as thoroughly as Hegel. "There is only one thinker in the West who has thoughtfully encountered the history of thinking, and that is Hegel." [97] Hegel sees the Western tradition as a history of conflict, and not simply of external conflict between philosophers of different persuasions but of internal conflict at the very source of Western thinking. The crucial task of philosophy in its mature manifestation, for Hegel, is the mediation of the countless dualisms which have arisen in the course of its history: of the intelligible and the sensible, of the eternal and the temporal, of upper and lower regions of being and corresponding parts of the soul, of subject and object, theory and action, freedom and determinism, fact and value. His *Phenomenology of Spirit* is an attempt to show that reality cannot be ascribed to such polar notions—least of all to one at the expense of the other—but only to the conflict in human experience which is the vital source of their polarity. [98]

We have seen Kant attempt to establish the ultimate presuppositions of scientific knowledge. Hegel's aim in the *Phenomenol-*

97. "Der einzige Denker des Abendlandes, der die Geschichte des Denkens denkend erfahren hat, ist Hegel" (*Ho* 298).
98. *PG* 10 (68), 26–27 (89–90), 30–31 (94–95).

ogy is to uncover the presupposition of all conscious experience, whether scientific or not. Kant is concerned in the first instance with knowledge, Hegel with the consciousness out of which knowledge arises. Yet consciousness in Hegel's portrayal is essentially *under way to becoming* scientific. The *Phenomenology* represents the "definitive history of the development of consciousness . . . to science." [99] So Heidegger says, "Hegel employs the words 'consciousness' and 'knowledge' synonymously. The two illuminate one another reciprocally." [100]

Hegel's initial concern is to circumvent the paradox which we sketched in Chapter 1: that the pursuit of truth presupposes that we begin from a starting point which is true and are already in possession of a criterion of truth from which the pursuit can take its guidance. His solution to this paradox is to avoid any initial assumption of what truth *is*, beginning simply with an expression of what it *appears* to be. But how *does* truth appear? If he gave any answer of his own to this question, Hegel would slip back into the dilemma from which he seeks to extricate himself, for he would be making a dogmatic statement about how truth *really* appears. We cannot ask how truth *really* appears but only how it *seems* to appear, and for this we must ask how people have testified to the way in which truth has appeared to them. This is a question of *fact*, Hegel argues, and escapes the dilemma posed by the question of what truth really is.

For testimony on the way in which truth has appeared we must go to the history of philosophy; the writings of philosophers provide the only reliable expression of the way in which things have appeared. Like Heidegger, Hegel sees the history of philosophy as dominated by the view that truth consists in the correspondence of the mind with the object of its knowledge, and this view provides the hypothetical basis of the argument of the *Phenomenology*. The attitude of mind which views truth in this way Hegel calls "natural consciousness" (*natürliches Bewusstsein*) and the way it sees things "appearing knowledge" (*erscheinendes Wissen*).[101] Natural consciousness corresponds to what we usually call common sense. Appearing knowledge must be understood in the first instance as *apparent* knowledge, or the knowledge of "mere appearance," but eventually it proves to be more than this.

99. *PG* 67 (136).
100. "Hegel gebraucht die Namen 'Bewusstsein' und 'Wissen' für das Selbe. Beide erläutern sich wechselweise" (*Ho* 133).
101. *PG* 66–68 (135–37).

Natural consciousness, as Hegel portrays it, strives to reduce the whole of reality to one or several of its aspects. It sees truth as grounded in things and in the judgments which reflect things, guaranteed by the principle of noncontradiction. Truth is ultimately self-evident: to attain it we have only to adopt the correct point of view from which to see things in their self-evidence. The fundamental characteristic of this form of experience is that it is *static,* or at least strives to attain a state of static equilibrium with its object.[102] Hegel's description is modeled on the philosophical attitude which we call naïve realism. We find the same attitude in daily life in the heated argument in which each of the protagonists begs his opponent to open his eyes and *see.* But Hegel regards natural consciousness as underlying all immediate experience and as reflected in all previous philosophical systems, however covertly. When it undertakes to articulate its experience into a system, he calls it "understanding" (*Verstand*).[103]

In contrast to the understanding of common sense, Hegel portrays a more reflective form of consciousness which recognizes every aspect of experience as a moment in human experience as a whole, determined by its position within the whole as the lamp is determined by its position within the study. For this form of consciousness nothing is properly *self*-evident: the thing and the judgment are both limited expressions of truth, which embraces them on every side. Hegel sees the essence of this form of consciousness in its *fluid* character. It is the form of consciousness to which he argues all consciousness must ultimately come. He calls it "science" (*Wissenschaft*) or "real knowing" (*reales Wissen*) or "reason" (*Vernunft*).[104]

Common sense and real knowing, or natural and scientific consciousness, must be kept as closely united as possible, integrated within the unity of consciousness as a whole, of which each by itself is an abstraction, like a figure and its background or a word and its context. "Consciousness itself," Heidegger comments, "is neither natural consciousness alone nor real consciousness alone. It is also not simply the conjunction of the two. Consciousness itself is the original unity of the two." [105] What alone is real is consciousness, which is constantly in motion. But

102. PG 31 (94–95), 37 (103), 49–50 (118–19).
103. PG 17 (76–77), 29 (92–93), 44–45 (111–12).
104. PG 12 (70–71), 24 (85–86), 44–45 (111–12), 67–68 (135–36).
105. "Das Bewusstsein selbst ist weder nur das natürliche Bewusstsein, noch nur das reale Bewusstsein. Es ist auch nicht die blosse Verkoppelung beider. Das Bewusstsein selbst ist die ursprüngliche Einheit beider" (*Ho* 145).

since consciousness is constantly in motion, we can understand it only by resolving it into abstractions as the poles of the field within which it moves. In interpreting the *Phenomenology* we must follow this movement and show its necessity.

Since he does not claim to begin with a starting point which is true, Hegel can argue that he is in no need of a criterion of truth. He begins simply by adopting the standpoint of common sense. There is no question of whether things really are as they appear—fixed, given, and autonomous—or whether self-evidence really is the criterion of knowledge. That this *seems* to be the case is the only question, and Hegel's reading of the history of philosophy gives him ample assurance that it is.

We are no longer concerned with the validity of these determinations, for insofar as our object is appearing knowledge, its determinations must initially be taken at face value, as they immediately present themselves, and there can be no question that the way in which they are formulated here *is* the way in which they present themselves.[106]

Taking natural consciousness as his starting point, Hegel approaches it without any criterion. Natural consciousness must be allowed to judge itself. Its criterion, as we have said, is self-evidence based upon the law of noncontradiction. Since this criterion belongs to the consciousness to which things appear, it can only be an apparent criterion. But this does not mean that it can be dismissed. On the contrary, it is peculiarly adapted to the appearances which it is meant to judge.

Hence it is not necessary for us to bring any criterion to the investigation or to apply our own thoughts and insights to it. It is rather precisely by refraining from doing this that we succeed in viewing the matter as it is, in and for itself.[107]

In allowing the criterion of his inquiry to be determined by common sense, Hegel insists that his approach to experience is radically empirical. He himself—or the real knowing which he personifies—has nothing to do but look on; the inquiry itself is conducted solely by and for natural consciousness. We might describe this approach as "methodological *naïveté*."

But because natural consciousness must undertake the whole inquiry by itself, it does not follow that it alone is present from the start. Hegel presents the traditional notion of truth *as a phenomenon;* he adopts the attitude of common sense as a working

106. PG 70–71 (139–40).
107. PG 71–72 (141).

hypothesis, allowing it to articulate its view of reality while we the readers look on. But this we can do only if, while identifying with common sense on the one hand, we guard a certain distance from it on the other. We could never observe common sense, or probe its notion of truth as a phenomenon, if we were not confronted at the same time by another notion, presenting itself in opposition to the first and so helping to constitute the distance required of vision. Hegel can only observe the traditional notion of truth because it has broken down, like the hammer. The consciousness with which he begins his inquiry is already a split or sundered consciousness. As Heidegger puts it, "With its first step—or even before its first step—the portrayal takes leave of natural consciousness as being by nature utterly incapable of following such a portrayal." [108]

In fact Hegel *is* confronted with a second form of consciousness, which is at odds with common sense. Prior to the *Phenomenology* Fichte and Schelling have insisted that truth consists in the *identity* of the mind and its object rather than in their correspondence. In the Preface and Introduction to the *Phenomenology* they are as much the subject of attack as any English empiricist. In view of this we must admit that Hegel is confronted at the outset of his exposition with *two* notions of truth, and it is not clear why one should be regarded as *the* phenomenon of truth any more than the other.

Be this as it may, Hegel's initial assumption is that, if we wish to let truth unfold of itself—without mixing anything of ourselves into the process and so corrupting it with our own subjectivity—we must begin with the assumption of natural consciousness that subject and object are substantially distinct and that truth is attained when the two are brought together in a stable relation of agreement free of all contradiction. We have then to see what follows from this assumption.

Consciousness is always consciousness of a given object within a context of meaning which is not simply given. (In our discussion of Kant we called this knowing something *as such and such*.) The object and its context constitute two aspects of conscious experience which, as we saw in the dialectical relation of the world and the innerworldly being in Chapter 2, are in constant conflict with each other. In following Hegel's portrayal of experi-

---

108. "Vielmehr verabschiedet die Darstellung mit ihrem, wenn nicht gar vor ihrem ersten Schritt das natürliche Bewusstsein als dasjenige, das seiner Art nach überhaupt unvermögend bleibt, der Darstellung zu folgen" (*Ho* 132).

ence, we may identify natural consciousness with the cognition of an object, and science or real knowing with the recognition of its context. This identification serves to remind us that the two are abstractions and that what is real—consciousness itself—is the tension between the two or the movement from one to the other. There is no such thing as an object *in itself* or a context *in itself:* there are only *objects in context.*

To the extent that I am conscious of any object—of the tree in the quadrangle, for example—the context in which the object appears and the "I" which is conscious of it both tend to disappear. My consciousness is filled with the tree and loses itself in it. The object may depend for its meaning on the context in which it occurs, but as background the context necessarily remains implicit. It *becomes* explicit, in our example, when I turn my attention from the tree to the quadrangle, but it then presupposes a further context—in this case the college—which in its turn necessarily remains implicit. When such a shift of consciousness occurs, the old object is reduced to the status of a part or moment of a more comprehensive object. Recognition of a context in experience thus always occurs through the "destruction"—or reduction to the status of a part or moment—of the object of which it is the context. This is what Hegel means when he says, "The genuine, positive realization of any beginning is at the same time just as much a negative attitude toward it." [109]

It follows that, if there is an ultimate context in which the meaning of every object of consciousness is grounded, recognition of it can come about only through the destruction of every possible object. It follows also that such an ultimate context cannot itself become an object of consciousness properly speaking, and this is the basis of Hegel's objection to Fichte and Schelling, both of whom approach the absolute as though it were capable of becoming the object of a special sort of consciousness. Hegel's conviction is that there is such a total context, though there is no special sort of consciousness through which it can be directly apprehended. It is rather coextensive with consciousness itself, the "I" which, along with the context of the quadrangle, did not manifest itself so long as I was conscious only of the tree, though it was implied in the experience. Hegel portrays the life of consciousness as the gradual unfolding of the total context implied in the consciousness of any object, a movement which occurs only through the destruction of all objects of consciousness in order finally to reveal consciousness to itself.

109. PG 23 (85).

Our example of the tree and the quadrangle is only a meta-phor—Hegel is concerned with conceptual objects like matter, substance, energy, desire, conflict, art, and religion—but it helps to explain why Hegel opposes the immediate awareness of objects, which he calls "familiarity," to the reflective awareness of the context from which they derive their meaning, which he calls "(real) knowing." "Whatever is familiar (*bekannt*)," he says, "is per se not known (*erkannt*)." [110] And conversely, "knowing is irrevocably opposed to the fixed representation and to everything familiar. . . ." [111] The process by which objects are divested of their familiarity—and their autonomy—by being seen in their proper context Hegel calls "destruction" and sometimes even "death." [112] This is the process through which truth emerges in human experience, for Hegel regards the context as the ground of the meaning and being of everything within it and accepts Aris-totle's principle that "that which causes derivative truths to be true is most true." So truth can emerge only out of universal destruction. "[Spirit] attains to its truth only when it finds itself in the midst of being utterly rent apart." [113]

Natural consciousness may seem to lose itself in its ob-ject—my consciousness of the tree may seem to be only of the tree—but, implicity, consciousness of any object is also con-sciousness of its context and ultimately, Hegel argues, of the total context in which it occurs. Human experience, like knowledge, is implicitly systematic: it necessarily organizes itself into a system, and the system is implicitly present from the start, as the sentence is implicitly present from the articulation of its first word. Hegel is really referring to human experience as a whole (and not simply to what we would regard as knowledge properly speaking) when he says, "[K]nowledge is only possible as science or as *system,* and only in this way can it be articulated." [114]

The process by which the ultimate context of meaning unfolds Hegel calls "experience" (*Erfahrung*).[115] It is the same for any individual consciousness and for the history of consciousness as we find it reflected in the history of philosophy. Consciousness evolves through experience, and experience manifests a necessary order beginning with the *cognition of things,* for which the con-text of meaning is presupposed, and ending in the *recognition of*

110. *PG* 28 (92).
111. *PG* 28 (92).
112. *PG* 51 (120), 67 (135–36), 69 (138).
113. *PG* 30 (93).
114. *PG* 23 (85).
115. *PG* 32 (96), 73 (142).

the context, of which everything is merely a moment. Consciousness itself is the tension between the two or the movement from
one to the other—a movement which always proceeds in the same
direction.

Experience is a process which is always going on. There is no
first moment of the emergence of reflective awareness out of the
immediate consciousness of an object, whether in the history of
philosophy or in individual consciousness. On this point Hegel
bears comparison with Aristotle, for whom there is no first moment of the life of nature, which he portrays as a movement from
matter to form.[116] Hegelian experience is likewise a process which
has no simple goal in which it finally comes to rest. The movement of consciousness which Hegel portrays is circular, so that
the truth which emerges out of it is not simply a result but a
"result together with the process of its realization," [117] a result
which is constantly being realized. Here Hegel takes leaves of
Aristotle: in Hegelian experience there is no Unmoved Mover.

The total context implied in the knowledge of any object Hegel
calls the "whole" or the "absolute" and identifies it with truth as
the source of all meaning in human experience. It is like the
sentence which confers meaning on each of the words in it. The
sentence model fits ideally Hegel's formula for truth: "What is
true is the whole . . . a process of becoming itself, the circle
which projects its end as purpose, has its end as its beginning, and
is only real in its end and its realization." [118] Such a total context of
meaning, Hegel argues, makes possible our consciousness of any
object on the one hand and the object of which we are conscious
on the other. It is the middle term in which Hegel seeks to ground
the identity of subject and object, explaining how the two pure
poles of human experience necessarily relate to each other—
Hegel's equivalent of Plato's "yoke" (the idea of the good) and
the "extrinsic bond" which we have seen Heidegger claim Kant
requires to explain the necessary coherence of receptivity and
spontaneity.[119] Understood in this way, Hegel's absolute loses
much of the mystical quality which is often ascribed to it.

The ultimate context of intelligibility can never be made manifest once and for all. We have compared it to a sentence, but a

116. "[T]here is no such thing as a beginning of a process of change
. . ." (*Phys.* 236a14). "[E]verything that is in motion must have been in
motion before . . ." (*Phys.* 236b34). Hegel himself draws the comparison at
PG 22 (83–84).

117. PG 11 (69).

118. PG 20–21 (81).

119. See above, pp. 150, 161.

sentence is no ultimate source of meaning—it points on toward the paragraph. It is like the *opus magnum* which the novelist never finishes writing. So Hegel describes the absolute as both "bacchic tumult" and "simple tranquillity." [120] The movement of consciousness is forever going on, and the task of philosophy is to draw individual consciousness and every possible object of knowledge into its movement. [121]

Every attempt on our part to attain to the absolute would be futile "if it were not and did not want to be with us from the start." [122] The absolute *is* with us from the start as the context implicit in our awareness of any object and (only) *wants to be* with us insofar as it is *only* implicit, manifesting its hidden presence in the form of unrest or disquiet. Natural consciousness experiences unrest in seeking to ground its truth in some particular object—like matter or substance or energy—while it is continually driven on by the contradictions which result from its effort to a recognition of the total context of intelligibility which is coextensive with consciousness itself. [123] Hegel is speaking quite technically of "natural consciousness" when he says, "The inner necessity by which knowledge becomes science is to be found in its *nature*. . . ." [124] It follows that Hegel does not abrogate the principle of noncontradiction, as is often assumed. On the contrary, it is indispensable to the life of consciousness which he portrays.

We may briefly recapitulate one step of the process by which an object of knowledge is divested of its autonomy and familiarity, allowing its context to emerge. Natural consciousness attempts to conceive its object—let us say—in terms of substance and accidental qualities. It then immediately confronts two possibilities which are mutually incompatible: the substance of a thing is either the sum of its qualities or an unknown something ($= x$) underlying them. Natural consciousness cannot find satisfaction in either mode of conception; it cannot conceive substance as either one or the other, and in view of its own principle of noncontradiction it cannot conceive it as both. Consciousness then confronts an impasse which it experiences as unrest in the face of contradiction. When its object proves to be contradictory in this way, natural consciousness negates it and seeks to conceive it

120. *PG* 39 (105).
121. *PG* 26–27 (89–90).
122. *PG* 64 (132).
123. *PG* 25–26 (87–88), 47 (115), 69 (138). Hegel uses the terms force (*Gewalt*) and compulsion (*Zwang*), which recall the "forcing . . . shoving . . . dragging" of the analogy of the cave.
124. *PG* 12 (70).

anew. Substance is now no longer seen in contrast to its qualities but as the principle of their organization, which is in a way the qualities themselves and in a way something distinct from them.[125] Contradiction thus causes consciousness to replace its old object with a new one. But consciousness itself is only a way of conceiving objects, so that the replacement of one object by another is accompanied by the replacement of one form of consciousness by another—in this case, we might say, of an "atomistic" point of view with an "organic" one. Both subject and object are thus taken up into the movement which Hegel calls "experience," out of which their identity is ultimately to emerge.[126]

The development takes the immediate form of *negation*. "The genuine, positive realization of any beginning is at the same time a negative attitude toward it." [127] As experience unfolds, consciousness comes to negate every particular way of conceiving its object which purports to be definitive. Everything proves to be true only *in a sense*. Regarded as final or definitive, every point of view manifests contradiction, creates an impasse, and has to be superseded. As every point of view from which an object can be conceived proves to be inadequate, natural consciousness experiences first doubt (*Zweifel*) and ultimately despair (*Verzweiflung*) in the determinate object of knowledge, the fixed point of view, and the demand for a correspondence between the two which is free of all contradiction. So Hegel characterizes experience as a "way of doubt" which ultimately proves to be a "way of despair." [128]

The positive side of this way of despair is the development of consciousness to science. With the disintegration of every determinate object of knowledge and every fixed point of view, natural consciousness comes to despair in itself and in nature as the immediate, given, and self-evident. But to despair in the fixed point of view and in the autonomy of nature is to recognize everything particular as a moment in the whole of experience as it unfolds in time, and this is what Hegel understands by "science." So Heidegger comments, "The more completely the portrayal follows the way of despair, the more readily science attains to its own proper appearing." [129]

125. *PG* 89–102 (162–78).
126. *PG* 72–73 (141–43).
127. *PG* 23 (85).
128. *PG* 67 (135–36).
129. "Je vollständiger die Darstellung den Weg der Verzweiflung durchgeht, um so eher vollendet die Wissenschaft ihr eigenes Erscheinen" (*Ho* 139).

Experience is thus a dual process. For natural consciousness it is a way of unfolding doubt—doubt which, in contrast to Descartes' hypothetical and hyperbolic doubt, emerges concretely as successive "truths" are seen to crumble. But for real knowing it is the destruction of fixity and hence the development of a fluid, moving consciousness which recognizes the ground of things in their context and itself in that context. For Hegel these are two sides of the same coin. Heidegger finds them united in Hegel's formula "self-completing skepticism" (*sich vollbringender Skeptizismus*).[130] Skepticism is rooted in *skepsis,* the Greek "insight."

In this way we return to the word *skepsis* its original meaning. *Skepsis* refers to the sort of seeing which . . . observes carefully *what* any being is and *how* it is. *Skepsis* in this sense pursues the being of beings. It has already seen into the being of all beings, and this vision enables it to penetrate the [immediate] situation itself. Every thinker is fundamentally skeptical of beings by virtue of his *skepsis* into being.[131]

The aim of the *Phenomenology* is to demonstrate that there is no fixed truth which can be accepted as indubitably given. "Truth is not a freshly minted coin which can be passed from hand to hand and put into one's pocket." [132] As Hegel portrays the life of consciousness, its motion is circular: the solution to the last difficulty encountered along the way leads back into the difficulty with which the movement originally began, and the circle of consciousness is closed. The circle itself is "simple tranquillity," while all along it there is nothing but "bacchic tumult." The unrest which results from considering any object to be autonomous and insisting on a conception of it which is free of all contradiction keeps consciousness *incessantly* in motion. In the process *all* truths are seen to crumble. The death of the intelligible object is universal. We must take Hegel seriously when he characterizes his own work as "self-completing skepticism."

When every particular object of knowledge has been destroyed and every specific point of view superseded, there remains nothing but the determinate *sequence* in which objects and points of

---

130. *PG* 67 (136).
131. "Dem Wort Skepsis gewinnen wir damit seine ursprüngliche Bedeutung zurück; *skepsis* bedeutet das Sehen, das Zusehen, das Besehen, das nachsieht, was und wie das Seiende als das Seiende ist. Die so verstandene Skepsis geht sehend dem Sein des Seienden nach. Ihr Zusehen hat im vorhinein das Sein des Seienden gesehen. Aus dieser Sicht besieht sie die Sache selbst. Die Denker sind von Hause aus die Skeptiker am Seienden aus der Skepsis in das Sein" (*Ho* 139–40).
132. *PG* 33 (98).

view give way to one another. We have seen one step in this process, in which an atomistic point of view gave way to an organic one. For Hegel this sequence is necessary and cannot be reversed: an atomistic object must always make way for an organic one, not vice versa. Through the destruction of everything which appears there emerges a necessary *order* in which appearance takes place. This is what Hegel understands by truth, calling it the whole or the absolute. Conceived in this way, truth is not distinct from appearance, even though appearance includes error and illusion. It is appearance *seen in its necessary sequence and order*. For this reason Hegel intends his expression "appearing knowledge" to be ambivalent, as the process which begins with the knowledge of mere appearance culminates in the emergence (or appearance) of real knowing. For Hegel real knowing can emerge only out of the destruction of knowledge of appearance, as when, in our example, we became conscious of the quadrangle only by reducing the tree to the status of a part or moment.

The order of destruction is also the order of genesis, since the destruction of one object always gives rise to another.[133] This order, Hegel argues, makes appearance possible. It is the principle of appearing which remains constant throughout all appearances, appearance *as such* (emerging from the application of what appears to be the criterion of knowledge to what knowledge appears to be, the principle of noncontradiction applied to autonomous objects), the *logos* of phenomena. It is an eternal order, but the eternal order *of a temporal process*. "Appearing is the coming to be and passing away which does not itself come to be and pass away but abides in itself and constitutes the reality and movement of the life of truth."[134] For an eternal order beyond appearance Hegel substitutes an eternal order of appearances themselves.

With the disappearance of everything purporting to be a fixed anchor of consciousness, the movement of consciousness reveals itself as the only thing which is fixed. "The secure foothold which a superficial reasoning has in a tranquil and passive subject gives way, and movement itself becomes the object of thought."[135] This movement is a reflection of the *ego*, which Hegel calls the "power of the negative" and describes as "pure reality."[136] So consciousness necessarily leads to self-consciousness. As Heidegger puts it, "[T]he representative thinking [of understanding] presents the

133. *PG* 68–69 (137).
134. *PG* 39 (105).
135. *PG* 50 (119).
136. *PG* 30 (94).

object by representing it to the subject. But in this re-presentation the subject itself is presented as such." [137] Together with the ultimate context of meaning—recalling our example of the tree and the quadrangle—consciousness only becomes explicitly present to itself when all its representations of objects have crumbled, though *implicitly* it was present all along. Thus spirit "attains to its truth only when it finds itself in the midst of being utterly rent apart." [138]

Through the destruction of all objects of knowledge, then, there emerge: (*a*) the necessary *sequence* in which objects appear, (*b*) the *movement* of consciousness which this sequence reflects, and ultimately (*c*) the being of consciousness itself as the *no-thing* which is the principle of movement and which Hegel therefore calls "pure reality." To recognize this is real knowing, and real knowing is nothing more than "the insight of spirit into what knowledge [viz., knowledge of appearance] *is*." [139]

All this, we must remember, is accomplished by understanding alone, and contradiction is essential to its activity. Understanding provides the *material* of consciousness by positing an object distinct from itself. It provides the *impetus* to movement in the unrest which it feels in the face of the contradictions resulting from its hypothesis. And because the movement of consciousness is determined at any given moment by the specific contradiction to be resolved, it even provides the *direction* of conscious development. So Hegel calls understanding "the greatest and most wonderful, indeed the absolute power." [140] Although it clings to the ideal of static equilibrium with its object, understanding is really the source of the movement out of which reason in its fluid character emerges. "So the function of understanding is a process, and as a process it is the function of reason." [141]

The notion of truth which Hegel elaborates in the *Phenomenology* is one which does not stand over and against error and illusion. What is illusory in illusion, according to Hegel, is simply its pretension to be something more than it really is. In this sense he calls all the opinions expressed in the history of philosophy *false*, since they represent the attempt to make of concrete notions like substance, energy, the good, and will the

137. "Das Vorstellen präsentiert das Objekt, indem es dieses dem Subjekt repräsentiert, in welcher Repräsentation das Subjekt selbst sich als solches präsentiert" (*Ho* 121–22).
138. *PG* 30 (93).
139. *PG* 27 (90).
140. *PG* 29 (93).
141. *PG* 47 (115).

bedrock foundation of truth. But every such notion is the resolution of a genuine problem—or impasse of consciousness—and hence a necessary moment in the evolution of the total context from which the meaning of experience derives. Seen in its proper context, every significant opinion expressed in the history of philosophy is *true*.

It is true that individual forms of consciousness and particular thoughts do not stand up before the tribunal of this movement [viz., the evolution of consciousness], but they are just as much its positive and necessary moments as they are negative and vanishing.[142]

Truth is ultimately the recognition of the order underlying error and illusion. It is attained in the dual process of seeing the individual, one-sided thought in its proper context and of drawing the individual, one-sided consciousness into the movement out of which this context necessarily emerges.[143] So truth and untruth, for Hegel, are not "like oil and water": they do not repel each other and they cannot be completely separated.[144]

Knowledge of truth adds to knowledge of appearance only the recognition of the order which makes it possible for anything to appear. In the systems of philosophy evolved throughout history Hegel finds testimony regarding how things appear, and this testimony he simply accepts. But he attempts to show that every system is only possible as a determinate moment in the history of philosophy as it reflects the evolution of consciousness. It is inconceivable that things should appear to Descartes in the same way that they appear to Democritus. And it is the evolution of consciousness since Democritus which allows things to appear to Descartes as they do. Real knowing involves recognizing every expression of knowledge as limited or seeing every particular experience as a moment in the evolution of human experience as a whole. Hegel assumes that these two are one and the same.

The evolution of experience which Hegel portrays not only makes appearance possible but finally leads of necessity to the recognition of its order. In analyzing its object and thus destroying it, understanding invariably "looks away" from the work of destruction: the contradictions which it finds in one object only lead it to posit another. But when there remains no further object toward which it can look away, consciousness is brought inescapably to witness the universal destruction which is its own work, and understanding is transformed into reason. There is nothing for

142. *PG* 39 (105). Compare *PG* 16 (76).
143. *PG* 26–27 (89–90).
144. *PG* 33–34 (98–99).

the philosophical spirit to do but to watch and wait, re-enacting history in a kind of ceremonial celebration which appropriates its truth. Truth is really the work of illusion—even of the illusory aspect of illusion, the one-sidedness which leads to its destruction. If truth is the *logos* of phenomena, it is the phenomena themselves which, in marching to their destruction, lead inexorably to the revelation of their own *logos*. This *logos* Hegel calls "spirit" (*Geist*).[145] Hence the title: *Phenomenology of Spirit.*

This is the notion of truth which emerges from the *Phenomenology,* but it is not the notion which underlies Hegel's later works. Heidegger's commentary in *Holzwege* makes this point forcefully, putting us on our guard against interpretations of Hegel which generalize about his thinking as though it were a simple unity. Applied to the *Phenomenology* such interpretations are almost invariably misleading. A number of examples will make this clear.

In the *Phenomenology* there is no highest stage of development at which all contradiction is finally surmounted, as John Findlay and Kuno Fischer suggest. Findlay says, "Consciousness will thus be made to traverse a series of forms . . . until at length a stage has been reached where the immanent criteria of consciousness have all been satisfied. . . ." [146] Fischer makes substantially the same claim: "Consciousness is forced to go beyond each of its forms or manifestations until it can proceed no further. . . . The point at which consciousness can go no further is the goal in which it finds tranquillity and satisfaction." [147] But the motion of consciousness which Hegel portrays in the *Phenomenology* is literally incessant. A definitive, final stage is never reached: the last stage only leads necessarily back into the first, so that the whole process is eternally circular. In the *Phenomenology* Hegel portrays the absolute as both simple tranquillity and bacchic tumult, and there is no sweeping this tumult under the rug.

If we look upon the goal of conscious development as a fixed

---

145. Baillie's translation of *Geist* as "mind" is unfortunate. The German *Geist* corresponds to the French *esprit* and has the same adjectival mutation as *spirituel* (*geistreich*), "witty." It is dynamic (irrepressible) moving power which runs through things, destroying old forms and giving birth to new—upsetting apple-carts like Till Eulenspiegel. French wit, as is well known, has a sharp cutting edge: it is caustic, ironic, destructive, delighting in nothing more than puncturing pomposity—and the same is true of Hegel's *Geist*. It is significant that in all three languages the word is also applied to alcoholic beverages, our "spirits" (*in vino veritas*). All this is lost in the word "mind."

146. John N. Findlay, *Hegel: A Re-examination,* p. 88.

147. Kuno Fischer, *Hegels Leben, Werke und Lehre,* II, 299.

point or final stage, we cannot help but derogate the role of the negative in the process, as John McTaggart does when he says, "The presence of the negative is not only a mere accident of the dialectic, but an accident whose importance continually decreases as the dialectic progresses. . . ." [148] Such a view stands in opposition to all Hegel's statements in the *Phenomenology:* the designation of the ego as the "power of the negative" or "pure reality," the statement that the realization of any beginning is at the same time a negative attitude toward it, the characterization of the whole process as "self-completing skepticism" and a "way of doubt and despair," and the insistence that spirit wins through to its truth only in being "utterly rent apart."

The sharp distinction which McTaggart and Eduard von Hartmann draw between reason and understanding may apply to the later works, but it has no basis in the *Phenomenology.* McTaggart says, "Reason is not contrary to, but beyond Understanding," [149] while Hartmann speaks of "two powers within the same intellect whose thinking is governed by contrary and conflicting laws." [150] In the *Phenomenology,* however, we confront Hegel's assertion that "the function of understanding is a process, and as a process it is the function of reason." How can reason be beyond understanding, which we have seen Hegel call "the greatest and most wonderful, indeed the absolute power"? Both authors compound the error by suggesting that reason "proves its case" to understanding. McTaggart speaks of the "justification of Reason at the bar of Understanding," [151] while Hartmann sees Hegel "apply himself to the attempt to justify his work before understanding." [152] This would constitute verification in the usual sense, but Hegel warns us not to expect such verification from the *Phenomenology:* "This evolution [is] . . . something other than a proof of science." [153] The truth is rather, as de Waelhens puts it, that in the course of the inquiry understanding forfeits its autonomy, so that in the end there remains no external authority to whom reason must—or even *can*—"prove its case."

Absolute knowledge justifies its claim to being absolute by drawing into its own movement the witness in whose eyes it [supposedly] had to justify itself. In reflecting on its own knowledge, natural consciousness

148. John McTaggart Ellis McTaggart, *Studies in Hegelian Dialectic,* p. 132.
149. McTaggart, *op. cit.,* p. 89.
150. Eduard von Hartmann, *Über die dialektische Methode,* p. 65.
151. McTaggart, *op. cit.,* p. 15.
152. Hartmann, *op. cit.,* p. 66.
153. *PG* 26 (89).

is transcended, left behind, so that the evolution of absolute knowledge no longer has any independent witness to whom it can submit its credentials nor any arbiter to decide whether its credentials are in order.[154]

The fact that Findlay, Fischer, McTaggart, and Hartmann can suggest interpretations of Hegel which are so misleading when applied to the *Phenomenology* leads us to look for a turning in Hegel's thought which parallels the ones we have seen in Plato and Kant. Taking such interpretations for granted, Heidegger stresses in his commentary in *Holzwege* the other side of Hegel's thinking. In order to see the conflict which he finds in Hegel we have to compare this commentary with scattered statements in other works.

Hegel's most significant achievement, in Heidegger's view, is driving home the fundamental distinction between *truth*, the total context of intelligibility, and anything which is *true*, any thing or proposition which, considered in isolation, can equally well be called false. Truth is no longer simply a property which all true statements have in common. In his self-completing skepticism Hegel reduces the claim of understanding to be able to grasp truth and hold it fast in a proposition. Such a reduction entails recognizing knowledge as rooted in existence, of which it is a derivative product and which it can never adequately comprehend, being chained to illusion and contradiction and coming ultimately to confront destruction and despair. As de Waelhens puts it, "The anxiety which seizes human consciousness and pushes it incessantly beyond itself until it is no longer human consciousness . . . is not simply . . . anxiety in the order of knowledge but . . . existential anxiety." [155] This is what Heidegger means when he says, commenting on Hegel, "We do not comprehend the truth of knowledge but only our knowledge of knowledge. For us, being remains the criterion by which we judge the being in itself of knowledge." [156] Hegel sees that knowledge points beyond itself and that, in order to follow its lead, we must recognize the fundamental distinction between anything which is true, meaning true for knowledge, and its truth, which goes beyond knowledge to its roots in human existence.

154. Alphonse de Waelhens, *Chemins et impasses de l'ontologie Heideggerienne*, pp. 22–23.
155. De Waelhens, *Existence et signification*, p. 23. See also pp. 43–48.
156. "Wir fassten nicht die Wahrheit des Wissens, sondern nur unser Wissen von ihm. Das Sein für uns bliebe der Massstab, mit dem wir das Ansichsein des Wissens mässen" (*Ho* 154).

But there is ambiguity concealed in Hegel's thinking, even in the *Phenomenology*. The question is whether the context of intelligibility implied in all conscious experience is a reflection of the movement of consciousness or of a timeless order which makes such movement possible, whether truth is to be seen *in* conflict or *emerging out of* conflict, whether consciousness is to be grounded in itself or to point beyond itself, and whether contradiction is ultimately to prove the limitation of understanding or rather, in being itself taken up into understanding, to testify to its omnipotence. As the ultimate context of intelligibility Hegel's absolute is the counterpart of Heidegger's world. The question is whether there is anything *besides* the world. In the *Phenomenology* the absolute appears in a tenuous equilibrium with incessant unrest, negativity, doubt, despair, and death. But in the later works this equilibrium is lost.

In the beginning Hegel sees human awareness arise out of a breakdown which he describes as negativity, insists that objects of knowledge depend for their intelligibility upon a total context which can never itself become objective, and recognizes an order of knowledge which is unthinkable apart from human finitude, an order of movement which derives its direction from the past and its motive force from a mood—unrest—and has as its goal the recognition of a truth which surpasses understanding. This is Hegel's original insight into the human situation but one from which, like Plato and Kant, he turns away.

We have seen Heidegger's contention that human awareness arises out of a breakdown in practical activity to which man reacts in two ways—either becoming aware of beings or reasserting his control over them—that the two always go hand in hand, and that to each there corresponds a distinctive form of thinking, poetic and technological. Hegel's thinking begins with this breakdown and reflects the duality of motifs which issue from it—in van den Meulen's phrase, the "unity of power and impotence." [157]

Hegel's thinking turns from the poetic to the technological. With the breakdown of the world in which man lives Hegel creates a new world of ideas which is rational and reliable and in which man can once again become preoccupied. Ideas are drawn up into the system as instruments are drawn up into an instrumental complex. Heidegger speaks of Hegel's "flattening difference." [158] Time is taken up into eternity in a complex which

157. Jan van den Meulen, *Hegel und Heidegger*, p. 131.
158. *Ho* 161.

endures through the coming and going of all its replaceable parts. Subject and object tend to merge as they ideally do in a thoroughgoing technological system. Hegel's system of impersonal truth comes about so long as the individual does nothing, but merely identifies himself with the process in its entirety. If Hegel's absolute corresponds to Heidegger's world, his transpersonal spirit reflects the impersonal "one." Heidegger suggests this parallel when he says, " 'Spirit' does not fall *into* time—it is rather factual existence in its fallenness which falls out of its original, authentic temporality." [159]

The crux of this interpretation of Hegel is this: so long as the truth of a thing depends upon its position in the whole, being is approached implicitly as *instrumental* being, or what Heidegger calls being-at-hand. This is why Heidegger interprets Hegel as an expression of *work* and regards the Hegelian metaphysic and modern technology as parallel developments.

The nature of work in the metaphysical significance which it has attained in the modern age is prefigured in Hegel's *Phenomenology of Spirit* as a process in which absolute production comes about of itself, i.e., as the objectification of what is [to be regarded as] real through man conceived as subjectivity.[160]

Hegel turns away from the moment of breakdown in human experience to an illusory world of ideas. But it is not Hegel who has turned, it is Western man. The *Phenomenology* only expresses the truth of this turning as it reveals itself in the course of history, and in this sense even its untruth must be seen as an expression of truth.

Hegel's conception of history as the evolution of "spirit" is not untrue, nor is it partly true and partly false. It is as true as metaphysics, the essence of which, conceived as absolute, first attains expression through Hegel in the system.[161]

159. "Der 'Geist' fällt nicht *in* die Zeit, sondern: die faktische Existenz 'fällt' als verfallende *aus* der ursprünglichen, eigentlichen Zeitlichkeit" (*SZ* 436).
160. "Das neuzeitlich-metaphysische Wesen der Arbeit ist in Hegels 'Phänomenologie des Geistes' vorgedacht als der sich selbst einrichtende Vorgang der unbedingten Herstellung, das ist Vergegenständlichung des Wirklichen durch den als Subjektivität erfahrenen Menschen" (*BH* 88 [287]). Compare *Ho* 137–38, 176–77; *WD* 54–55.
161. "Gleichwohl ist Hegels Bestimmung der Geschichte als der Entwicklung des 'Geistes' nicht unwahr. Sie ist auch nicht teils richtig, teils falsch. Sie ist so wahr, wie die Metaphysik wahr ist, die im System zum ersten Mal durch Hegel ihr absolut gedachtes Wesen zur Sprache bringt" (*BH* 82 [284]). Compare *WD* 145.

The illusion of tradition is an expression of the inauthentic truth of Western man. Being as it was encountered in the breakdown of human design continues to be present at every step in the development of this illusion—only in the mode of absence, as restlessness, dissatisfaction, and alienation. In philosophy there is a constant drive toward new forms of conceptual representation, in life the same drive toward new forms of technological organization.[162] Having turned away from being, man is condemned to incessant turning—just the sort of turning which Hegel portrays—and to experiencing this turning as need. At the point at which it is most "untrue," Hegel's thinking is a profound expression of the truth that inauthenticity leads only to despair.

Heidegger sees Hegel as the end of a tradition characterized by metaphysics.[163] Beginning with the assumption of truth as correspondence—as a particular truth or truths—Hegel shows that, on this assumption, nothing is true, for all particular truths are drawn up into a restless movement without beginning or end. Hegel thus destroys the Western tradition from within, on the basis of its own assumption about truth, and this is one sense in which Heidegger regards the *Phenomenology* as the end of tradition.

But Hegel's thinking is also the consummate expression of metaphysics. For in it the traditional notion of correspondence culminates in a notion of coherence. Heidegger suggests that the notion of truth as correspondence (*adaequatio*) results from regarding beings as instrumental and judging them according to whether they are adequate to the task which they are meant to perform (the twelve "good men and true" of our juries). A notion of truth as coherence only recognizes that the being of any instrument is grounded in the structure of the instrumental totality of which it is a part. Coherence is really the ground and goal of correspondence, and, in destroying the Western tradition from within, Hegel really only draws out its most extreme consequence. "The way in which Hegel's dialectic surmounts the principle of noncontradiction does not in principle undermine the authority of the *logos* but rather represents its *most extreme affirmation*."[164] Hegelian dialectic is the logical outcome of the metaphysical tradition; its untruth "has its hidden ground in the essence of metaphysics rather than in the metaphysical presuppositions which

162. Ho 79–80, 93.
163. EM 144 (189).
164. "Die Aufhebung des Satzes vom Widerspruch in der Dialektik *Hegels* ist daher im Prinzip keine Überwindung der Herrschaft des Logos, sondern nur die *höchste Steigerung*" (EM 143 [187]).

characterize Hegel's philosophy in particular." [165] This is the second sense in which Heidegger regards Hegel as the end of tradition.

Metaphysics as it culminates in Hegel's system and technology as we know it in the twentieth century Heidegger regards as complementary phenomena in the history of being, symptomatic of the decadence of Western man. The organization of that with which (*womit*) we are concerned is reflected in the systematization of that about which (*worüber*) we think.[166] A self-completing metaphysic arises out of a self-completing skepticism with the same necessity with which a thoroughgoing technological system arises out of the reduction of the autonomy of every individual instrument. Heidegger calls this the "decline of the truth of beings."

> The decline of the truth of beings comes about of necessity as the consummation of metaphysics. It is brought about at once by the collapse of the world shaped by metaphysics [Hegel] and through the devastation of the earth which is the consequence of metaphysics [technology].[167]

Heidegger's associating the decline of the truth of beings (which we have seen stands in dialectical opposition to the truth of *being*) with the devastation of the earth points up his doctrine of truth as unhiddenness—insight into the mystery *from error and illusion*—and the impossibility which this implies of finally separating Hegel's positive achievement from his defects and limitations.

Hegel sees that truth is not simply a universal describing what all true propositions have in common. He recognizes a radical distinction between *truth* and *a* truth. He makes truth inseparable from error and illusion, being a consequence of a development of which they are the motive force, and finds it rooted in human finitude, though in such a way that it does not belong to man but man to *it*. This is insight into the mystery. On the other hand, Hegel tacitly identifies being with instrumental being, takes the presupposition *of consciousness* for the presupposition *of human*

165. "Dass Hegel dies alles unterscheidet, aber die Unterschiede doch in ein allgemeines Unterscheiden nivelliert und sie dadurch nicht in ihr Eigenes aufkommen lässt, hat seinen verborgenen Grund im Wesen der Metaphysik, nicht in der metaphysischen Grundstellung der Hegelschen Philosophie" (*Ho* 161).

166. See *SZ* 157–78, 161–62, 360–61.

167. "Der Untergang der Wahrheit des Seienden ereignet sich notwendig und zwar als die Vollendung der Metaphysik. Der Untergang vollzieht sich zumal durch den Einsturz der von der Metaphysik geprägten Welt und durch die aus der Metaphysik stammende Verwüstung der Erde" (*VA* 72).

being as it precedes and transcends consciousness, and evolves an impersonal system of truth which is self-producing so long as the individual makes no decision. Here Hegel falls prey to the perennial illusion of our tradition. And yet he recognizes that the inevitable consequence of this illusion is restlessness, skepticism, and despair and thus wins his way through to the truth of the illusion. Heidegger's claim is that these conflicting motifs cannot be completely disentangled without obscuring the real significance of Hegel's thinking and robbing it of its vitality.

In Hegel the conflict of tradition reaches its climax: insight and illusion have both developed to a point of maximum intensity. Hegel destroys the criterion on which human thinking and being had been securely grounded from the outset of history. He makes truth itself questionable and so precipitates the crisis which Heidegger claims not only justifies the posing of an impossible question but renders it inescapable.

6. Nietzsche: Value and Vengeance

FRIEDRICH NIETZSCHE REVOLTS against the self-producing system of the *Phenomenology of Spirit* and the tradition of which it is the consummate expression.[168] He attacks (*a*) the Western conception of man and the historical man who has evolved under its influence, (*b*) metaphysical thinking as it is characteristic of Western man, and (*c*) the realm of supersensible ideas which provides the foundation of metaphysics. Nietzsche sees Western man as ill, metaphysics as his illness, and supersensible ideas as the disease-carrying bacteria. In *The Joyous Science* we read that Socrates calls life a period of illness

168. No other philosopher has occupied Heidegger's attention as much as Nietzsche, who is the subject of essays in *Holzwege* (pp. 193–247) and *Vorträge und Aufsätze* (pp. 101–28) and of the formidable two-volume study *Nietzsche* (1155 pp.) as well as the "star witness" of *Was heisst Denken?* (175 pp.). This in itself is an index of the inadequacy of the account which I present here. Chiefly I have attempted to integrate the essays of *Holzwege* and *Was heisst Denken?*

This also points up a serious disproportion in the importance which I have assigned to Hegel, whom Heidegger deals with at length in only one essay of *Holzwege* (pp. 105–92). Yet Hegel and Kant are second in importance only to Nietzsche and lend themselves far more to relatively adequate treatment in an introductory study of this kind. Hegel appears prominently at the very end of *Being and Time* (pp. 428–36). The ambivalence of Heidegger's attitude toward Hegel has not, in my opinion, been sufficiently recognized, and this is further justification for emphasizing him here. Finally, I think, Hegel and Nietzsche should be seen, from Heidegger's point of view, as two sides of a single coin; they appear "back to back" in *Holzwege*. See below, pp. 190 and 210–12.

between birth and death. But the man who views life as illness cannot really *live*—it is he who is ill.[169] Nietzsche revolts against what he regards as a morbid tradition, epitomizing his revolt in *Thus Spake Zarathustra* in Zarathustra's cry, "God is dead!" The violence of his attack on traditional values and the atheistic cry which signals it have branded Nietzsche as a nihilist. Heidegger makes Zarathustra's cry the title of his study of Nietzsche in *Holzwege* (1957 [1943]).

In having Zarathustra cry "God is dead!" Nietzsche does not want simply to announce that he is an atheist. God must be understood as Nietzsche's name for the supersensible realm of ideas and ideals—since Plato the only *true* world, the realm of the *really* real. This supersensible world has traditionally provided life with a goal and direction and served as the source of its meaning and significance.[170] But in the course of history, Nietzsche argues, this world has come to lose its moving force and vitality. Zarathustra's cry is thus meant in the first instance to be historical rather than hortatory. "The backlash of 'God is truth'" Nietzsche sees "in the fanatic belief that 'everything is false.'"[171] Nietzsche regards his nihilism not as a reaction against history but as the recognition of its real purport and direction.[172] In effect he holds that we are all nihilists, and if we wish to find a new sense of meaning in life we must begin by facing up to the fact.

Belief in supersensible ideas is not characteristic of Platonism and Christianity alone. One may deny the Platonic idea of the good or the Christian God and still retain the "place" of such an idea—the throne of God—within a hierarchy of value. If so, the place invariably comes to be occupied by another supreme value. Religion may be replaced by reason, divine providence by human progress, personal salvation by social consciousness, but the world dominated by order and based upon a hierarchy of value remains. It is not any particular value but the notion of value itself which Nietzsche attacks, or the demise of which he apprehends. Not only have particular values crumbled in the course of history; if one hears Zarathustra's cry, the place of value itself has disappeared.[173] In Heidegger's interpretation, metaphysics is the sphere in which particular values have arisen one by one to lay claim to the position of supreme value. In crumbling they have rendered it an untenable position.

169. *FW* IV, 340.
170. *Ho* 199–200, 234.
171. *WzM* I, i, 2.
172. *Ho* 196–97, 201, 206; *N* I 35–36; *N* II 33.
173. *Ho* 202–8.

Metaphysics is the historical arena in which destiny has decreed that [Platonic] ideas, God, the moral law, the authority of reason, progress, the greatest happiness of the greatest number, culture, and civilization all lose their formative power and become void.[174]

Nietzsche regards nihilism as the powerful undercurrent of the history of the West—in Heidegger's formula its "inner logic"[175]—and in Zarathustra's cry he calls upon man to recognize what has happened in history. History has made man ill, and the first step toward a cure is diagnosis, recognition of the illness for what it is. "Complete nihilism"—the nihilism which Nietzsche prescribes—is insight into a history which has corrupted our notion of value, and this is something very different from the "incomplete nihilism" which attacks this or that value without realizing that it is the notion of value itself which has contaminated human life like a cancer.[176] There is no curing cancer with Noxema.

Zarathustra's cry echoes the despair of the *Phenomenology of Spirit*. "Complete nihilism" is the counterpart of "self-completing skepticism." Both Hegel and Nietzsche see metaphysics in a historical context, as a process, and in the first instance as a process of destruction. But Hegel is concerned with ideas as ways of conceiving things, Nietzsche with ideals as the source of the value which we attach to things. These are two sides of the same coin, for every idea makes an implicit appeal to an ideal. As Aristotle observes, there is no cognitive difference between a lyre-player and a *good* lyre-player.[177] Our ideas come attached with plus and minus signs which point to a system of value. Whereas Hegel concentrates upon the cognitive aspect of experience, ignoring its plus and minus signs, Nietzsche fastens upon the signs in isolation from the cognitive content to which they may be attached. Hegel's frame of reference is consciousness; Nietzsche insists that the frame of reference be *life*, and here it is values which are decisive, providing life with the motivation and direction which it requires.

Nietzsche sees value in inseparable conjunction with life:

174. "Die Metaphysik ist der Geschichtsraum, worin zum Geschick wird, dass die übersinnliche Welt, die Ideen, Gott, das Sittengesetz, die Vernunftsauthorität, der Fortschritt, das Glück der Meisten, die Kultur, die Zivilisation ihre bauende Kraft einbüssen und nichtig werden" (*Ho* 204).

175. *Ho* 206.

176. Nietzsche uses the expressions "complete nihilist" (*der vollkommene Nihilist* [*WzM* I, 21]) and "incomplete nihilism" (*der unvollständige Nihilismus* [*WzM* I, 28]). On the necessity of exorcising the traditional notion of value see *N* I 442–43; *N* II 35–36, 280–82.

177. *Nic. Eth.* 1098a8–11.

only a living being can encounter things as valuable, and life in Nietzsche's sense is not possible without value. What life is must remain an open question, but it occurs only within the realm of becoming, the transition *from* something *to* something. The notion of value arises when this transition is represented in quantitative or comparative terms, as progress, increase, fulfillment, or the like. Nietzsche comes closest to a definition of value when he writes in *The Will to Power:*

> The point of view of "value" is the point of view specifying the conditions of conservation and intensification applicable to a complex structure of relative duration of life within [the realm of] becoming.[178]

Supersensible ideas—or ideals—are projections beyond life of the values encountered within life and without which life would not be possible. Values seem to point toward, or depend upon, the existence of such ideals. But this is an assumption which Nietzsche challenges. For supersensible ideas degrade life and the realm of becoming: if true being is found only in the realm of the supersensible—if only the eternal is *really* real—then all that is earthly and living, coming to be and passing away, has only a relative degree of reality and can only be said "to be" *in a sense.*[179] Nietzsche wants to clear away such ideals in order to make room for values which enhance rather than degrade life. When he speaks of the "devaluation of supreme values" (*dass die obersten Werte sich entwerten*)[180] he means values which represent ideals in this sense. This is to be followed by a "transvaluation" (*Umwertung*) which derives new values from the principle of life itself.[181]

The principle of life which is the source of all values—including ideals—Nietzsche calls the will to power (*Wille zur Macht*), the urge to expand and express. Power is essentially unstable and dynamic, the negation of fixity. There can be no eternal values, for values are relative to the conservation and intensification of expanding power, and, as power expands, the conditions of its conservation and intensification are constantly changing. Conservation implies a certain stability, but only the relative stability of a stage which is subsequently to be left behind. Conservation is oriented toward intensification, as capital is to

178. *WzM* III, 715. Quoted by Heidegger, *Ho* 210.
179. *N I* 87, 489–90; *N II* 67–68, 86–87.
180. *WzM* I, 2.
181. *Ho* 206–9; *N I* 186; *N II* 276–77.

investment, but the reverse is also true: intensification depends upon conservation, as investment requires capital. Values reflect the conditions which the will to power posits for itself: conditions of conservation which are to be transcended and conditions of intensification which are to be realized. Since life is expanding power, eternal values, though at first stimulating, must ultimately prove to be antithetical to it.

Metaphysics represents the attempt to confer on values a validity which transcends life and its temporal conditions. It would make a set of values which are conducive to the conservation and intensification of life at one time or under certain conditions valid for all time and under any conditions. Though such values arise out of life and the will to power, they become antithetical to life when they are accorded a supersensible basis beyond time and rigidify as ideals. Nietzsche's transvaluation of values is therefore an effort to overcome metaphysics.[182]

What is this "will to power" which is the principle of life and value? The expression "will *to* power" might lead us to believe that will is one thing and power quite another. Yet will *is* power—for Nietzsche the only genuine power. What the will seeks in willing power is *itself*: the will to power wills the power of willing. In contrast to the wish or whim, *will* involves a reference to command: it is the power of commanding the self and thereby overcoming it. The will to power, then, is the drive to become oneself by overcoming oneself through command. It is essentially *self-control*.[183] Nietzsche's nihilism is not meant to open the door to chaos; his will to power is anything but unbridled passion.

But because the will to power is the principle of life it does not follow that life necessarily exhibits the will to power, at least not in its pure form. Nietzsche portrays life and will as the result of a struggle which he casts in the figure of Zarathustra. Zarathustra is a "convalescent" (*der Genesende*),[184] one who is under way to becoming what he is. Man is at the point of assuming total dominion over the earth—Nietzsche trembles at the prospect—and in order to be equal to his new role he must go beyond himself. Zarathustra points the way with the question, "Indeed *do* I yet live?"[185] Since life is a striving toward will, Heidegger translates

182. *Ho* 214.
183. *Ho* 215–17; *VA* 105–6; *WD* 24–26.
184. *ASZ* III, 13.
185. *ASZ* Preface 10. This is an unusual reading of 'Wahrlich, lebe ich noch?" But it makes better sense than "Am I still alive?" Compare: "Gibt es noch Eis?"

the question: Does my will answer to the will to power which lies at the heart of all things? [186]

Heidegger entitles his essay on Nietzsche in *Vorträge und Aufsätze* (1953) "Who Is Nietzsche's Zarathustra?" In Nietzsche's own words, he is the teacher of the "eternal recurrence" (*ewige Wiederkunft*) and of the "superman" (*Übermensch*).[187] Heidegger finds Zarathustra's identity in the "inner identity" of these two notions. Both represent, in different ways, the goal toward which Zarathustra strives, the object of Nietzsche's "supreme hope." Nietzsche tells us what this is: *"That man may be saved from vengeance: for me this is the bridge to the supreme hope. . . ."* [188]

Nietzsche's vengeance (*Rache*) should not be understood in a moral or psychological sense; his supreme hope is not to separate the Montagues and the Capulets. Nietzsche regards vengeance as the principle of reflection underlying the entire Western metaphysical tradition and Western history: where there is injury there must also be punishment, and where there is deficiency there must be correction. Platonic ideas correct the deficiencies of nature, and so does modern technology. Such correction, Heidegger suggests, goes hand in hand with the notion of truth as correctness or correspondence.[189] To have seen this is Nietzsche's signal achievement: vengeance describes the way in which Western man has related to things throughout history. In hoping to save man from vengeance, Nietzsche wants to rescue him from a history and tradition dominated by the vengeance of metaphysics.

Vengeance is the supreme assertion of the self, the will to depose, dispossess, put at a disadvantage. Vengeance deposes the other in order to exalt the self; it is power which knows itself only *through another*.[190] The question is: against what "other" is the vengeance characteristic of the Western tradition directed? Nietzsche answers: against *time*. Vengeance is "the will's defiance of time and its 'once was.' " [191] The will cannot tolerate time and must wreak its vengeance on it.

In describing vengeance, Nietzsche emphasizes the transient and fleeting character of time, time as the medium in which things pass away. Ignoring present and future, he identifies time with the past, its "once was." The will has ample reason for

186. VA 104.
187. ASZ III, 13; Preface 3.
188. ASZ II, 7.
189. See Ho 225–58.
190. VA 112–13; WD 33.
191. ASZ II, 20.

wanting to depose the past, for that which has passed away—
"fallen prey to time" as we say—is no longer under its control. It is
the stone which the will cannot roll out of the way, the arrow
which it cannot tear from out its wound. The past is the intransi-
gent and inimical under which the will *suffers*. In willing that this
suffering pass away, the will wills its own passing away, avenging
itself by willing *everything* as fit to pass away, as unworthy to
survive. Things do not survive because they are *unworthy* to survive. In its defiance of time the will degrades the temporal: all
that is earthly and temporal is not possessed of *true* being. Plato
calls it the *mē on,* relative nonbeing. Eternity—independence of
time—becomes the mark of true being, and the world of supersensible ideas is born. Metaphysics is thus the visible mark of the
vengeance which Western man has wreaked upon time.[192]

This is the diagnosis of Western man's illness. And
Nietzsche's prescription? How can man be saved from his vengeance? Salvation is to be found in a reversal of the act of will. In its
defiance the will negates time as past and passing. But passing
away is the destiny of *becoming,* and becoming entails not only a
constant passing away but a constant renewal as well. Passing
away is itself abiding—it is eternal. The past and passing are thus
preserved in an eternal recurrence, and the negation of time past
can become the affirmation of time future, the defiance of time's
perpetual passing a dedication to its continual coming.[193]

The salvation of man lies in the transition from the defiance
of time in a supersensible world of eternal values to the affirmation of time in the eternal recurrence of the fleeting and temporal.
Zarathustra is "the spokesman for life [will], for suffering [time
past], and for the circle [eternal recurrence]." [194] When being manifests itself to man as an eternal recurrence rather than as a perpetual passing away, man will become superman. The doctrines of
eternal recurrence and the superman are two moments of the
same movement of thought by which Nietzsche seeks to transcend
tradition, or, in Heidegger's terms, to overcome metaphysics.

The will to power is the essential characteristic of any being as
such (*Sein des Seienden*); eternal recurrence is being itself (*Sein
selbst*),[195] the *telos* of (convalescent) human life. Human
being—Zarathustra—is the transition from one to the other. In
Heidegger's interpretation this is Nietzsche's way of expressing

192. *VA* 115–17; *WD* 36–39, 77–78.
193. *VA* 117–18; *WD* 43–47.
194. *ASZ* III, 13. See *VA* 102, 119.
195. *N I* 33; *VA* 124; *Ho* 233.

the essential relation between *being* and *human being,* a relation such that "being" is not simply a human projection on the one hand nor man simply a particular instance of being on the other. Both man (whether the invalid of the past or the superman of the future) and being (both as eternal recurrence and as illness or vengeance) are essentially related to *time.*[196] This is Nietzsche's original insight into the mystery and the means by which he seeks to overcome metaphysics. But it is an insight which never finds complete expression in his thinking.

Nietzsche ultimately identifies being (*Sein*) and a being (*Seiendes*). The index of this identification is the fact that there is a determinate aspect of things (the will to power) with which it is possible for man's will to correspond (as eternal recurrence). Like traditional metaphysics Nietzsche's thinking culminates in the notion of a supreme being and in an ideal of human being which confers meaning and significance on human life. In the end we are left with a distinction between being and "*true* being," the traditional distinction between "higher" and "lower" orders of reality. For Heidegger this, rather than the distinction between the sensible and the supersensible, is the hallmark of metaphysical thinking. For an eternal *Jenseits* Nietzsche substitutes an eternal *Diesseits,* but he does not give up the notion that it is the eternal which is really real, and his own thinking therefore remains metaphysical. Nietzsche has not overcome but only *reversed* traditional thinking, and Heidegger comments, "The reversal of a metaphysical proposition remains a metaphysical proposition."[197] That Nietzsche's own thinking is ultimately metaphysical can be seen in the notion of eternal recurrence: "The predicate 'eternity' belongs, according to [traditional] metaphysical doctrine, to the being of any being."[198] Like Hegel, Nietzsche gives us the notion of eternity in time, or takes time itself up into eternity.

The traditional notion of truth as correspondence remains intact as the necessary complement of the notion of true being, only now it is no longer the intellect which must correspond with its true object but the will which must correspond with its true objective: man's will must correspond with the will to power which lies at the heart of all things. Eternal recurrence is the form

196. *VA* 122.
197. "Aber die Umkehrung eines metaphysischen Satzes bleibt ein metaphysischer Satz" (*BH* 72 [280]). See also *BH* 85 (286); *Ho* 32 (670), 200, 214; *N I* 469, 605, 617.
198. "Das Prädikat 'Ewigkeit' gehört nach der Lehre der Metaphysik zum Sein des Seienden" (*VA* 118).

which this correspondence takes. The superman is the will which, by corresponding to the being of things, realizes the true being of things.[199] Similarly, by submitting to the randomness of things, technology is able to realize a constancy nowhere given in nature.

In the end Nietzsche himself elaborates a doctrine of vengeance. Becoming is stamped with the mark of being in the traditional metaphysical sense: the passing is transformed into the abiding, the transient into the eternal. "To stamp becoming with the mark of being," Nietzsche says, "that is the supreme will to power."[200] Our thinking thus takes becoming under its protection. Heidegger asks if this is not the most unbridled form of vengeance. "There is *vengeance*," Nietzsche says, "vengeance upon life itself, when the tragic sufferer *takes life under his protection*."[201]

Nietzsche does not escape ideals; he idealizes life. His transvaluation of values is to make of nihilism (the absence of any transcendent goal of life) "the ideal . . . of superabundant life."[202] And like the ideals which he criticizes, Nietzsche's new ideal is to correct a deficiency; it too is relative to man and to the self, to the historical man who is to be surpassed and the projection of a new self which is to be realized—it is an ideal of self-control. But for Heidegger the "self" and "control" have been dominant— though concealed—motifs of the history of the notion of truth from the beginning. Because both find their extreme expression in Nietzsche, Heidegger calls him "the most unbridled Platonist in the history of Western metaphysics,"[203] seeing in him as well as in Hegel the consummation of metaphysics. If we remember how Heidegger understands *ratio*—as calculation and control—we can see why he regards Nietzsche's superman as the ultimate expression of *animal rationale*.[204]

The eternal recurrence justifies being (life), but the need for justification assumes that there is deficiency and that where there is deficiency there must be correction. "Being has become value . . . but in being honored as value it is [really] degraded to [the status of] a condition posited by the will to power."[205] Heidegger

199. *Ho* 232; *VA* 124.
200. *WzM* III, 617.
201. *Die Unschuld des Werdens*, I, 1310.
202. *WzM* I, 14.
203. ". . . der zugelloseste Platoniker innerhalb der Geschichte der abendlandischen Metaphysik" (*PL* 37 [263]).
204. *N II* 23. See *Ho* 224–27.
205. "Das Sein ist zum Wert geworden. . . . Allein indem das Sein als ein Wert gewürdigt wird, ist es schon zu einer vom Willen zur Macht selbst gesetzen Bedingung herabgesetzt" (*Ho* 238).

calls this "blasphemy." "In relation to *being*, thinking in values is . . . the supreme blasphemy." [206]

Nietzsche has not succeeded in transcending tradition, but he has recognized its hidden purport and direction, seeing in Western history and thinking, as they culminate in modern science and technology, the restless drive of a will to power. Beneath scientific-technological objectivity he recognizes the self-aggrandizement of man as subject. He sees the inner connection of the dichotomy of subject and object, knowledge as re-presentation, and man's will to power. He understands that man's increasing domination of the earth leads to ever greater demands of self-control, and at the prospect of man's assuming total dominion over the earth he experiences an anxiety which we may well call existential.

Hegel has shown that, on the traditional assumption about truth, nothing is true. Nietzsche shows that, on the traditional assumption about value, nothing is valuable. "The desert is spreading!" [207] Man, the source of all worth, he portrays in a worthless world. What is this but the world of modern technology? And what is modern technology, Heidegger asks, but the vehicle of eternal recurrence? [208]

7. Science and Technology: Mathematics and Manipulation

THE WESTERN TRADITION, rooted in metaphysics, finally culminates in twentieth-century science and technology. Heidegger regards science and technology as parallel developments expressing the inner meaning and direction of the Western tradition from its inception. They reveal what Western man has come to understand what it means for things "to be" and for himself "to be there."

Science and technology are not generally thought to have the "inner unity" which Heidegger claims. Technology may utilize the discoveries of science, while science, in turn, may depend upon technology for the precision equipment which it requires for its research. Science may even arise in the seventeenth century under pressure created by demands for technological progress to keep pace with the rapidly expanding scope of human activity. But science is a form of knowing, technology a form of doing or

206. "Das Denken in Werten ist . . . die grösste Blasphemie, die sich dem Sein gegenüber denken lässt" (*BH* 99 [293]). (Italics added in translation.)
207. *Poems*, IV, i.
208. *VA* 126; *WD* 47.

making, and these have been regarded as mutually exclusive categories from Aristotle to Kant. Heidegger, however, challenges this distinction, drawing science and technology together in a triumvirate with modern metaphysics. On the one hand he identifies the essence of modern technology with the essence of modern metaphysics; [209] on the other hand he calls contemporary science the "true heir of metaphysics" [210] and insists that it "belongs within the realm of the essence of modern technology and nowhere else." [211]

Science and technology are one, for Heidegger, in their drive toward *control*. Science is the controlled observation of nature, technology its controlled exploitation; science is exact, technology exacting. Heidegger calls them both *herausfordernd,* "provocative." [212] Of the two he regards technology as the more fundamental. [213]

Science arises out of the mathematical representation of nature. Such representation makes possible the interpretation of nature according to laws expressing exact quantitative relationships, and these laws are worked out in accordance with rules which are universally accepted but which no one in particular has laid down. Scientific research then arises as a coordinated effort which becomes more and more specialized as it proceeds. Mathematics, laws and rules, and specialization are, for Heidegger, the three essential prerequisites of science. [214]

The essence of the mathematical is not the numerical or quantitative. It is the a priori, the basis on which cognitive demands can be made of nature. [215] If the scientist goes to nature, in Kant's metaphor, as a judge to a witness, compelling it to give answers to questions of his own devising, mathematics gives him this authority, providing the means with which to compel the witness to answer. The numerical character of mathematics is only a consequence of its original a priori nature.

Because numbers are the most conspicuous case of what is familiar in advance and in this sense the most familiar of everything mathematical, the term "mathematical" immediately came to be reserved to

---

209. *Ho* 69; *VA* 80, 99; *ID* 48 (44); *BH* 88 (287–88).
210. ". . . die zur eigenen Nachkommenschaft der Metaphysik gehören" (*Ho* 195).
211. "[D]ie heutigen Wissenschaften gehören in den Bereich des Wesens der modernen Technik und nur dahin" (*WD* 49).
212. *VA* 22, 29. See also *Ho* 265–68; *SG* 98–100.
213. *Ho* 195, 267; *SG* 201.
214. Heidegger's terms are "project" (*Entwurf* [*Ho* 71–73]), "rules" (*Regel* [*Ho* 73–77]), and "coordinated activity" (*Betrieb* [*Ho* 77–80]).
215. *Ho* 71–73, 80; *VA* 58–59; *SZ* 362–63; *FD* 53–59, 71–74.

the numerical. But the essence of the mathematical is in no way determined by the numerical.[216]

The essence of mathematics is its "exactness" in the sense of making it possible to "exact" knowledge from nature, and numbers are supremely "exact" in this sense. So Heidegger says, "The binding character of the mathematical science of nature is its exactness." [217] It is no defect of the humane discipline that it is not exact, and this is not because it is based on words instead of numbers—it is really the other way around.

Mathematics provides the basis for rules of scientific procedure, and from the mathematical hypothesis springs the discovery of scientific law. Scientific laws organize human experience in such a way as to make it regular and reliable—"familiar" in the sense in which Heidegger uses the word in the above passage. Scientific method makes regularity and reliability possible, and the scientific temperament will accept nothing less.

Because of the regularity and reliability of its method, scientific research can be organized into a complex of interrelated special sciences. With its drive toward the exact knowledge which results from controlled experiment, science necessarily becomes specialized, fragmented into an ever increasing number of quasi-autonomous areas of research. "As research," Heidegger says, "science is necessarily special science." [218] Science thus becomes a "team effort." The individual scientist in isolation from his colleagues is as unthinkable as an individual instrument divested of all relation to other instruments.[219] Yet the special sciences do not stand in need of any explicit coordination—their relations are self-adjusting. From a Heideggerian point of view it is impossible not to suspect, behind such self-adjusting cooperative activity, the presence of the impersonal one.

The world becomes a suitable subject of scientific inquiry when it is reduced to the single dimension of extension and number, when its differences have been reduced as nearly as possible to quantitative differences, so that things become appropriate

216. "Nur weil die Zahlen das gleichsam aufdringlichste Immer-schon-Bekannte und somit das Bekannteste unter dem Mathematischen darstellen, deshalb wurde alsbald das Mathematische als Benennung dem Zahlenmässigen vorbehalten. Keineswegs aber wird das Wesen des Mathematischen durch das Zahlenhafte bestimmt" (Ho 72).

217. "Die Strenge der mathematischen Naturwissenschaft ist die Exaktheit" (Ho 73).

218. "Jede Wissenschaft ist als Forschung . . . notwendig Einzelwissenschaft" (Ho 76). Compare VA 59.

219. See Ho 77–80.

material for calculation. This is the process of objectification in which things are reduced to the status of objects.[220] If, as Walter Biemel puts it, "it is the pro-ject which renders possible the ob-ject,"[221] it is the scientific project which renders possible the object par excellence, the "mere object."

While the world is objectified in order to become the proper object of scientific inquiry, man is called upon to be objective in order properly to conduct such inquiry. In order to pursue scientific research we must reduce ourselves to the transparent medium in which the quantitative structure of the world can manifest itself. This demand goes hand in hand with the objectification of the world, for in becoming objective we remove ourselves from the world, ridding ourselves of the mood and concern which characterize our immediate relation to things. We can then proceed in accordance with rules which are universally accepted but which no one in particular has laid down. Such impersonality is essential to scientific research.

Any contribution to science is judged primarily in relation to the context of scientific knowledge as a whole. It is the context and not the individual discovery which counts; the discovery derives its significance from the contribution which it makes to the context. This context has constantly to be reorganized and renewed. If we search for it, we cannot find it, for it is constantly expanding, shifting, being modified. The source of the significance of individual discoveries and the basis of their validity, it nevertheless always eludes our grasp. Yet it is a context with which every working scientist is familiar; among scientists it is what "everybody knows."

Finally, scientific knowledge aims at being definitive. The scientific object is gradually to be reduced, in successive stages, to complete explanation in scientific terms. The unknown remains only as the "surd" of such explanation, the residue providing material for further research, a sign that science is always "under way." Heidegger speaks of science "using up" or consuming (*verbrauchen*) the material of its research. But since nature is inexhaustible, scientific research is in principle interminable, a process which is essentially without end.[222]

All of the characteristics which Heidegger attributes to science—impersonality, flattening, self-coordinating teamwork, and the vanishing source of meaning—we have already encountered

220. *Ho* 79, 236; *VA* 55–63; *WD* 56–58; *SZ* 156–59, 360–64.
221. Walter Biemel, *Le concept de monde chez Heidegger*, p. 150.
222. *WM* 48 (388); *SG* 201–2.

in one form or other in our discussion of decadence. There can be little doubt that Heidegger regards science primarily—almost exclusively—as an expression of decadence.[223] Such a view hardly does justice to the aspect of science which we call humanistic. It does not account for the feeling which the scientist often displays for his subject matter—the botanist for his specimens, for example—or for the personal dedication which he brings to his research. Strictly speaking, Heidegger's view of science does not seem compatible even with his own principles. Decadence is an existential characteristic which belongs to the preparatory analysis of Dasein; science is a phenomenon which belongs to the history of being. Though decadence may be the source of history and inauthenticity a constant factor in history—the ground of its continuity—neither can properly be said to *have* a history, as science does. If we are to understand science in conjunction with metaphysics, we require a duality of motifs, and this is for the most part lacking in Heidegger's interpretation.

It is clear that the work of epoch-making scientists like Newton and Einstein is not the result of self-coordinating teamwork. Scientists of this stature bring about a new way of looking at the world and, by challenging the old foundations of science, elicit a form of reflection which goes beyond mere calculation and problem-solving. Heidegger admits that such scientists discover beings and therefore manifest truth directly, but for this reason he includes them in the history of philosophy. "To the extent that any science goes beyond accuracy to truth and thereby to an essential disclosure of beings as such, it is philosophy." [224] Such a statement, as Jan van den Meulen observes, puts undue strain on the verb "to be." [225] It would be easier—and more in keeping with Heidegger's own principles—to recognize science as a complex phenomenon manifesting both authentic and inauthentic motifs. That we find it difficult to say the same of technology, which Heidegger sees as wedded to science, points up a further difficulty of interpretation.

Technology is generally regarded as an organized form of making or as a systematic process of adapting means to ends. Both definitions are correct, in Heidegger's view, but neither pene-

223. *SG* 58–61; *VA* 55–61; *Ho* 79; *WD* 57–58; *WM* 43 (381), 48 (387–88).
224. "Wenn und sofern eine Wissenschaft über das Richtige hinaus zu einer Wahrheit und d.h. zur wesentlichen Enthüllung des Seienden als solchen kommt, ist sie Philosophie" (*Ho* 50 [685]). Compare *N I,* 372, 521.
225. Jan van den Meulen, *Hegel und Heidegger,* p. 175.

trates to the essence of technology.[226] The essence of technology, he says, is not itself technological.[227] Technology may describe man's attitude toward machines, but its essence is not to be found in the nature of the machine. It is rather the spirit of technology which requires the machine and so produces it. Machinery is the consequence, not the ground, of technology.[228]

Our word "technology" comes from the Greek *technē*, which signifies the skill involved in any making or production. But Heidegger sees a fundamental distinction between technological production and every other form of making. He suggests that there is a radical difference between the traditional farm and the hydroponic farm, between raising animals and force-feeding them, between the windmill and the hydroelectric dam.

"Making" Heidegger understands as "bringing forth" (*Hervor-bringen*) and hence as a form of revelatory activity. In this sense the cobbler reveals leather, the plow reveals the richness or barrenness of the soil, and the windmill reveals the relation of the elements of earth, wind, and water between which it is situated. The artifact, the product of *technē*, reveals the conflict of the world and the earth, of human design and the fertile, opaque, inexhaustible source from which human life arises and on which it depends. "*Technē* is a form of 'bringing forth,' of *poiēsis*; it is [essentially] poetic." [229]

The simple artifact reveals nature by inserting itself into nature. But technology does not so much insert itself into nature as absorb nature into itself. The windmill inserts itself between the elements, revealing them, but the hydroelectric dam appropriates and consumes them. The handiwork submits, while the technological work exacts and exploits.

The hydroelectric dam is not built into the Rhine in the same way as the wooden bridge which for centuries has joined its banks. Rather the river is built into the dam, from which it now derives its significance as a river: a source of hydroelectric power.[230]

226. *VA* 14.
227. *VA* 13; *WD* 53.
228. *Ho* 268; *ID* 26 (25); *WD* 53–54.
229. "Die *technē* gehört zum Her-vor-bringen, zur *poiēsis;* sie ist etwas Poietisches" (*VA* 20). See also *Ho* 47–48 (682–83); *EM* 122 (159); *VA* 42, 160.
230. "Das Wasserkraftwerk ist nicht in den Rheinstrom gebaut wie die alte Holzbrücke, die seit Jahrhunderten Ufer mit Ufer verbindet. Vielmehr ist der Strom in das Kraftwerk verbaut. Er ist, was er jetzt als Strom ist, nämlich Wasserdrucklieferant, aus dem Wesen des Kraftwerkes" (*VA* 23). Compare *VA* 150–54.

Technology is a form of bringing forth which proceeds by forcing. Nature is approached exclusively as material to further human design, and to this end it must be reduced to maximum pliability so that it can be rebuilt into a complex which is regular and reliable. The individual thing becomes a replaceable part of a complex which is indeterminate in scope; it is sucked up into fluid process in which it loses its distinctive character and its autonomy. The same is true of man, who is called upon to fit in and do things "as they are done," for technology regards all things—man included—as material of human design.[231]

The more advanced any system of technology becomes, the more difficult it is to trace decisions—for Heidegger the source of openness in human experience—to their origin. Like science, technological organization is a form of coordinated activity without explicit coordination. If we ask who determines the course of technological development, we must answer: no one. (This is not, and cannot be, the case with art.)

Science and technology thus emerge in Heidegger's interpretation as correlative phenomena of the Western metaphysical tradition. Both absorb men and things into a total structure, the *raison d'être* of which is regularity and reliability. Both tend toward increasing diversification and specialization on the one hand and toward impersonal coordination on the other. Both are concerned primarily with the determinate *as determinable*, and for this reason they are essentially endless pursuits, incessantly organizing and reorganizing, repairing and replacing, improving and innovating. Both propose as the highest mode of "being there" an ideal of impersonality and objectivity in which Heidegger sees the manifestation of the impersonal one. Together they produce *power*. "Presence no longer reigns; it is the *assault* which prevails." [232]

Heidegger regards science and technology as part of a concerted attack on nature which begins in the seventeenth century. Both are essentially *modern* phenomena. The Greek would have been incapable of technological organization, but he was also incapable of science in the strict (i.e., modern) sense. His attitude toward nature would not allow him to pursue scientific research; controlled experiment he would have regarded as a kind of blasphemy. This is not because the Greek is *primitive* in this respect. Heidegger is not willing to explain the modern emergence of

231. VA 22–24, 28–29; Ho 265–68; ID 27–33 (25–31). See also SZ 239–40.
232. "Nicht das Anwesende waltet, sondern der Angriff herrscht" (Ho 100). (Italics added in translation.)

science and technology by an appeal to a historical development in which precision lenses, blast furnaces, and chemical retorts are gradually evolved. He sees them rather as symptomatic of man's changing *attitude*—which we have called conduct and mood—in the midst of the totality of beings. This attitude is expressed in the notion of truth which characterizes any particular historical epoch and is fundamental to the way in which things manifest themselves by being allotted their respective places in the openness of the human project. The clearest expression of the attitude of the modern age is Descartes' notion of truth as the certainty of controlled representation, the precursor of Nietzsche's will to power. Technology is the supreme form of controlled representation.[233] "The perfection of technology is only the echo of the claim of verification to be definitive, i.e., perfect."[234]

Yet Heidegger's interpretation of science and technology does not simply repeat Nietzsche's claim that impersonal, dispassionate contemplation conceals the most radical aggrandizement of the self. The rationale of a metaphysical tradition which culminates in science and technology, according to Heidegger, is not Nietzsche's will to power but the turning away from the mystery toward control, the effort to insure that being does not manifest itself in the breakdown of human design. "The insistent turning toward the practicable and the ex-istent turning away from the mystery belong together. They are one and the same."[235] As we saw in Chapter 2, this is the moment of truth out of which beings first emerge in their determinate character and, with them, the human self as we know it. The rationale of tradition is revelation issuing from this dual movement, with science and technology as its principal manifestations and Descartes and Nietzsche its most significant spokesmen. Science and technology have tremendous significance for Heidegger because they belong together at the very heart of the human situation.

Science and technology do not simply *happen*. They are the product of a long tradition which comes to fruition only in the modern era, when Francis Bacon proclaims that knowledge is power, Descartes expresses the hope of replacing the old theoretical philosophy with a new and practical one which will make us "lords and masters of creation," and Marx concludes that the

233. See *Ho* 80, 91–92; *N II* 24, 148–58, 165–66.
234. "Die Perfektion der Technik ist nur das Echo des Anspruches auf die perfectio, d.h. die Vollständigkeit der Begründung" (*SG* 198).
235. "Jene insistente Zuwendung zum Gangbaren und diese ek-sistente Wegwendung vom Geheimnis gehören zusammen. Sie sind eines und dasselbe" (*WW* 22 [344]).

proper task of philosophy is not to *interpret* the world but to *change* it.[236] Marx in particular, Heidegger suggests, recognizes the inner technological direction of Western history. When he proposes a materialistic interpretation of history, we should not understand by "matter" any crude, corporeal world-stuff. Such matter, as has often been observed against Marx, does not move and develop dialectically. All things—that is to say, all laws, all *truths*—are "matter" for Marx in the sense that crime is a matter for the police or rural electrification a matter for county government: they are essentially material for human design.[237]

For Heidegger science and technology are the expressions of metaphysics in somewhat the way the United States Supreme Court is an expression of the Constitution. They reflect—and in turn contribute to—the divorce between Dasein and its world, which they attempt to organize, understand, and control (corresponding to the traditional division of philosophy into logic, ethics, and physics), approaching beings primarily insofar as they are (or threaten to become) "on hand" with the covert aim of rendering them ultimately "at hand," an aim which is first explicitly recognized, perhaps, when Kant proclaims that the law of causality is grounded in the law of freedom.[238] They are much like Goethe's Mephistopheles: they increase the impersonality of human existence by reducing the necessity of personal decision, and yet ultimately they contribute to human awareness by increasing human power. The history of science from the simple mechanical model to statistical correlation and probability calculus and the history of technology from rudimentary mechanization and industrialization to electronics and automation Heidegger sees prefigured in the history of metaphysics from Plato to Hegel.

The result of the triumph of the scientific-technological spirit in Western history is "the flight of the gods, the destruction of the earth, mass culture, and the primacy of the mediocre." [239] But we should not conclude from this that science and technology *falsify* nature or even twist or distort it in any way. (This is a bias of nineteenth-century Romanticism.) The scientific a priori and technological organization are not imposed on the world *ab extra*, any more than Kant's categories are imposed on the objects which

236. This point is made by Josef Pieper, *Was heisst Philosophieren?* pp. 32–33.

237. *BH* 87–88 (287).

238. *GMS* 110–11 (453–54).

239. ". . . die Flucht der Götter, die Zerstörung der Erde, die Vermassung des Menschen, der Vorrang des Mittelmässigen" (*EM* 34 [45]). Compare *Ho* 87–88; *VA* 90–96.

they unify and organize. On the contrary, it is as though they came about of themselves. They must therefore reveal a permanent possibility of being human and of the being which man is not.[240]

In the first instance science and technology reveal human being in its inauthentic mode. In this sense they manifest what Western man has chosen to be and the instrumental possibilities of the beings which share in his destiny. Innerworldly beings really *are* suitable material for human design—otherwise the scientific-technological spirit could not have achieved such success. But in the end science and technology reveal more than this: they reveal the futility of willing. The earth, as we have said, is infinitely pliable and eternally adamant. The more insistent man's effort to subject it to his will and thereby to transcend the finitude of the human situation, the more clearly he is brought to realize that all such effort is doomed to failure and so to confront his own essential finitude as the source from which things spring.

The earth allows every calculative intrusion to shatter on her [density], every attempt at appropriation to deteriorate into destruction. These may give the appearance of mastery and progress in the form of the scientific-technological objectification of nature, but such "mastery" really remains [the touchstone of] the futility of willing.[241]

Thus ultimately science and technology reveal not only a mode of Dasein but Dasein itself as a thrown project. They reveal the finitude of human being in a way which is only possible if man makes the supreme effort to transcend it. And they thereby reveal untruth in its twofold sense: as the error out of which truth emerges and as the mystery which lies at its heart.

When the world is reduced by science and technology to the single dimension of extension and number, it becomes like a mirror in which nothing is reflected. Through them man can thus be brought to a confrontation with nothingness, which we have called the moment of truth.

[In the first half of the nineteenth century] Dasein began to slide into a world lacking the depth out of which the essential arises to confront human being. All things were reduced to the same level, a surface

240. VA 39–40; ID 26–27 (25–26); WD 142.
241. "Die Erde lässt so jedes Eindringen in sie an ihr selbst zerschellen. Sie lässt jede nur rechnerische Zudringlichkeit in eine Zerstörung umschlagen. Mag diese den Schein einer Herrschaft und des Fortschrittes vor sich hertragen in der Gestalt der technisch-wissenschaftlichen Vergegenständlichung der Natur, diese Herrschaft bleibt doch eine Ohnmacht des Wollens" (*Ho* 36 [673]). Compare *SG* 60.

resembling a blank mirror, one in which nothing is any longer reflected, which mirrors nothing.[242]

However pejorative Heidegger's doctrine of science and technology may be, it is important to insist that he does not *oppose* them. Spirited affirmation and adamant rejection both fall short of the mark. Science and technology are the consummation of a tradition of which we are a part and product. We cannot escape them; we can only strive to *understand* them.[243]

8. Conclusion: Justification of the Starting Point

HEIDEGGER BEGINS HIS analysis of truth with an examination of the traditional notion of truth as correspondence (Chapter 1). Such a notion applies only to knowledge—even in this respect Heidegger finds it unsatisfactory—and so tacitly identifies the truth *of knowledge* with truth *as such*. Heidegger attempts to show that it presupposes another notion which is not cognitive at all, the notion of truth as unhiddenness, which I have called the phenomenological notion (Chapter 3). The two notions are based on different and opposed presuppositions. The traditional notion identifies being (*Sein*) with some particular manifestation of being (*Seiendes*), makes knowledge primary in human experience, and assumes a fundamental distinction between subject and object, intellect and thing, Dasein and its world. The phenomenological notion, on the other hand, draws a radical distinction between being and beings, regards knowledge as derivative in human experience, and assumes that the world belongs to the being of Dasein (Chapter 2). The two notions are thus necessarily in conflict. The history of philosophy, in Heidegger's analysis, is the history of this conflict.

Because he regards knowledge as derivative in human experience, Heidegger sees the conflict in the history of philosophy as symptomatic of a deeper conflict in the being of Western man as he has evolved through history, a conflict between what he calls the authentic and inauthentic modes of "being there." This conflict, which becomes more acute as it proceeds, eventually becomes intolerable, theoretically as well as existentially, so that we are

242. "Das Dasein begann in eine Welt hineinzugleiten, die ohne jene Tiefe war, aus der jeweils das Wesentliche auf den Menschen zu- und zurückkommt. . . . Alle Dinge gerieten auf dieselbe Ebene, auf eine Fläche, die einem blinden Spiegel gleicht, der nicht mehr spiegelt, nichts mehr zurückwirft" (*EM* 35 [46]).
243. *Ho* 88–89; *VA* 13, 33, 42; *WD* 13, 49, 57–58; *ID* 33 (31); *BH* 112–13 (298–99); *N II* 28; *Gel* 24.

driven to pose an impossible question, the question of what truth is. This is Heidegger's justification of his new problematic: not only posing the question of truth but approaching experience and explanation in a way which challenges the traditional foundations of logic.

If we go to history, we find that the phenomenological notion of truth, which is presupposed by the traditional notion in the order of analysis, also precedes it in the order of time: the Greeks originally named truth unhiddenness, *alētheia*. So Heidegger claims that his notion of truth is original in a historical as well as an ontological sense. In the course of time—specifically in Book VII of the *Republic*—the traditional notion of truth comes to replace the original notion. Henceforth the history of philosophy is the history of an illusion, but of an illusion from which truth is never wholly absent, of which, in fact, it is the vital moving force. This is what Heidegger calls "the reigning presence of the mystery in illusion," and it is the working of this reigning presence which he seeks to uncover in his studies in the history of philosophy.

In the analogy of the cave we find Plato's thinking oscillating between two notions of truth: truth as unhiddenness, grounded in the being of man as the truth of his experience as a whole, and truth as eternal intelligibility standing over against and above man, the truth of knowledge. In the one case truth is portrayed by the analogy as a whole, with its four stages: the breaking of the chains, the ascent within the cave, the emergence into openness, and the redescent into the cave. In the other case truth is identified with the third stage of the process by itself, the order which man confronts outside the cave. The original notion is ultimately submerged in its derivative counterpart—human experience, as Heidegger puts it, "comes under the yoke of the idea"—and with this event begins the history of metaphysics. The being of man is sundered into higher and lower parts, corresponding to which are higher and lower orders of reality, and man is sundered from his world. Being is identified with *a* being, the idea of the good as the principle of fitness or function, and truth is attained when man answers to this being. Knowledge, as man's response to ideas, is decisive in the process by which this comes about.

Kant's thought reveals the same duality. Truth is grounded, on the one hand, in the experience of the finite human being in time and, on the other hand, in the structure of human reason as it transcends time. Eventually the notion of truth as the projection of transcendental imagination in a being characterized by finitude and dependence gives way, as in Plato, to a notion of truth as eternal order. Once again being is identified with *a* being, the pure spontaneity of reason as the highest element in man's being—all else is "mere appearance"—and man attains to truth to the extent that he answers to this being, primarily through moral (i.e., impersonal) action. Moral action approaches more closely to the source of truth than theoretical knowledge, but action is understood according to categories derived from knowledge, categories worked out in the *Critique of Pure Reason:* sensibility, understanding and reason, form and content, the universality and necessity of moral principles analogous to that of apodictic propositions. Knowledge thus retains its primacy. Truth is no longer grounded in an order standing over against man but in an order in which man participates, in the a priori order of reason. The references "subjective" and "objective" are now reversed: the objectivity of human experience (space, time, categories) springs from the structure of the human mind, while everything subjective (*sensa*) is ascribed to the object independent of the human mind.

The history of metaphysics, in Heidegger's analysis, is the history of emergent human subjectivity and objectivity,[244] beginning with Plato's bringing unhiddenness under the yoke of the idea, bifurcating subject and object. Subjectivity finds its culminating expression in Marx, for whom scientific laws are objective insofar as they can be turned to human purpose, and in Nietzsche, who judges things according to their contribution to the augmentation of life.

Nietzsche also identifies being with *a* being, the will to power as the urge to expand and express—all else represents only the relative nonbeing of illness. The notion of truth which eventually comes to dominate his writings is the health of a will which answers to this supreme being, as Platonic man answers to the form of the good. This is really an extension of the notion of correspondence (*adaequatio*), the traditional ideal of man's cognitive relation to things—or what I have called the truth of knowledge.

Nietzsche seems to challenge the supremacy of knowledge—and does in fact challenge the supremacy of a certain sort of knowledge—which, in seeking to fix its object and hold it fast, eventually provides an obstacle to willing (expansion and expression). But when he calls truth "a kind of error without which a certain kind of living being could not live" [245] (i.e., without which

244. *Ho* 81, 102–3.
245. *WzM* III, 493.

a certain kind of willing being could not will), it is clear that he still understands truth as the truth of knowledge, now cast in the role of an obstacle which all "true willing" presupposes. But the traditional notion of truth as the truth of knowledge does not survive in Nietzsche only as an obstacle; the truth which is beyond the "truth" which can be called error is cast in terms appropriate to the error which it surpasses (and presupposes). For the notion of "true (or genuine) willing" implicitly identifies being with *a* being (the will to power), the being with which willing must correspond if it is to be true or genuine. And this is the being of health, which is the criterion of illness, the "truth of things" to which we make implicit appeal when we refer to our jurymen as "good men and true." [246]

There is certainly a reversal of tradition implied in this extension of the traditional notion of truth. The fixed object of knowledge which had traditionally provided the ground of objective judgment is now seen in relation to the being of the subject as *will*, so that objectivity comes to be recognized only as a condition of subjectivity. But this is a reversal of tradition which occurs *within* the traditional framework, and one which is clearly prefigured in Kant.

In Hegel this development is reversed, and the subjective dimension of human experience is taken up into an objective order of history and knowledge in which the identity of subject and object is realized. Being is identified with the circle of consciousness which manifests itself in history, a total context of intelligibility which Hegel calls the absolute, and anything is "true" insofar as it relates explicitly to this absolute. In such a relation there is no longer any room for will. Jean Hyppolite comments, "It is true that, in this case, one can ask what the distinction between a 'subjective logic' and an 'objective logic' any longer means." [247]

With the identity of subject and object, as it is portrayed in the *Phenomenology of Spirit*, the notion of truth as correspondence, the ground of metaphysics, is negated. Passing the history of metaphysics in review and allowing all its truths to prove their inadequacy, Hegel destroys from within the tradition of which Plato is the father. It only remains to effect the same destruction from without, from the ground of knowledge in the radically finite being of Dasein—a project which Nietzsche begins. So Heidegger's aim in rethinking the history of metaphysics is to show its

246. See above, pp. 11–12.
247. Jean Hyppolite, *Genèse et structure de la phénoménologie de l'esprit de Hegel*, I, 67.

origin in human experience as it precedes and transcends knowledge (Plato) and to recognize its illusion as a reflection of the experience of Western man (Hegel).

As the Western metaphysical tradition reaches its fruition, its inner conflict becomes progressively more acute and irreconcilable. Hegel seeks to destroy tradition with his self-completing skepticism, but tradition endures in the form of a self-completing metaphysic. Nietzsche longs to save man from the vengeance of ideals, but ultimately, in the will to power, an ideal of life reasserts itself with a vengeance. Modern technology, of which Marx is the prophet, is directed at the unlimited extension of human power and control, but in the end man is subjected to the tyranny of the impersonal one.

At the center of this tradition, and as the key to its meaning, Heidegger sees the notion of truth as correspondence (*adaequatio*). Such a notion implicitly approaches beings insofar as they are instrumental, as beings "at hand." It is the instrumental being which must "correspond to" the function which it is meant to perform and which we tend to regard as "true" insofar as it is adequate to its function—the "good men and true" whom we swear into our juries. Viewed in this way, the pragmatic and coherence theories of truth do not stand in opposition to the doctrine of correspondence but are its legitimate heirs. The pragmatic theory, of which we may regard Nietzsche as one of the most extreme exponents, recognizes the true purport of correspondence; the coherence theory, as it is represented in Hegel, draws out its most extreme consequence.

Because its view of truth is grounded in the being of the instrument, the history of metaphysics proves to be a drive toward *control*. Schelling sums this up most effectively when he writes:

> In the final analysis and in the deepest sense there is no other being but willing. Willing is primal being (*Urseyn*) and on it alone all the predicates of being depend: absence of cause or reason (*Grundlosigkeit*), eternity, independence of time, self-affirmation. All philosophy strives toward the single goal of finding this supreme expression.[248]

But the history of metaphysics and technology shows the futility of this drive to control, revealing human being as a "thrown project" and its radical finitude as a "projection into nothing."

The history of metaphysics is a "turning into need." The greater the gulf between subject and object—the more irreconcil-

248. F. W. J. Schelling, *Werke*, VII, 350. Quoted by Heidegger, *WD* 35; *VA* 113.

able the inner conflict of metaphysical thinking—the more inescap- ably the effort to transcend finitude reveals the futility of all such effort, bringing Dasein to the confrontation with nothingness which is the first moment of truth. This need provides Heidegger with the sense of eschatological direction in history and serves as his justification for posing the question of truth in its most radical form: history renders the question inescapable. As the doctrine of the determinate, intelligible, and controllable—which Heidegger groups together under the heading "essence"—the history of met- aphysics is thus a necessary preliminary of the confrontation of truth. Truth is revelation, not correspondence, but it can best be seen—or can *only* be seen—in the revelation which the history of the doctrine of correspondence entails. This is the sense of Hei- degger's formula, "The essence of truth [revelation] is the truth of essence [correspondence]." [249]

Like Socrates in the *Meno* and Aristotle surveying the *apo- riae* of Book III of the *Metaphysics,* Heidegger does not know the solution which he is after, but he knows that it is the solution *of this difficulty.* His eschatology of history is not one of knowl- edge—his approach to truth, after all, subverts the absolute claims of knowledge—but one of hope. Modern technology threat- ens the existence of Dasein as the tension between authenticity and inauthenticity which we find reflected in the writings of great philosophers throughout history. The danger has never been greater. But Heidegger shares the faith of the poet Hölderlin: "Where there is danger . . . there is also hope of salvation. . . ."

Wo aber Gefahr ist, wächst
Das Rettende auch.[250]

249. "[D]*as Wesen der Wahrheit ist die Wahrheit des Wesens*" (WW 26 [350]). See above, p. 136.
250. Friedrich Hölderlin, "Patmos" (Hellingrath ed.), IV, 227. Quoted by Heidegger VA 36, 43.

Bibliography

I. Works by Heidegger

(The following list appears in roughly chronological order. Most of Heidegger's writings were initially presented as lectures, to be published, in some cases, years later. My chronology follows the order of presentation rather than publication, as indicated in parentheses immediately following the titles. Series of lectures and collections of essays often embrace a considerable span of time.)

Sein und Zeit (1927). Tübingen: M. Niemeyer, 1953. 437 pp. (First published in *Jahrbuch für Philosophie und phänomenologische Forschung,* Vol. VIII, and as offprint, 1927.)

Vom Wesen des Grundes (1928). Frankfurt a.M.: V. Klostermann, 1955. 54 pp. (Foreword added to 3d ed., 1949.)

Was ist Metaphysik? (1929). Frankfurt a.M.: V. Klostermann, 1955. 51 pp. (Postscript added to 4th ed., 1943; Introduction added to 5th ed., 1949.)

Kant und das Problem der Metaphysik (1929). Frankfurt a.M.: V. Klostermann, 1951. 222 pp.

Einführung in die Metaphysik (1935). Tübingen: M. Niemeyer, 1953. 157 pp.

Die Frage nach dem Ding (1935–36). Tübingen: M. Niemeyer, 1962. 189 pp.

Platons Lehre von der Wahrheit (1942). Berne: Francke, 1947. 52 pp.

Vom Wesen der Wahrheit (1930–43). Frankfurt a.M.: V. Klostermann, 1954. 27 pp.

Erläuterungen zu Hölderlins Dichtung (1936–44). Frankfurt a.M.: V. Klostermann, 1951. 144 pp.

Holzwege (1936–46). Frankfurt a.M.: V. Klostermann, 1957. 345 pp.

Nietzsche I, II (I: 1936–39; II: 1939–46). Pfullingen: Neske, 1961. I: 662 pp. II: 493 pp.

Brief über den "Humanismus" (1946). Published together with *Platons Lehre von der Wahrheit*: pp. 53–119.

Was heisst Denken? (1951–52). Tübingen: M. Niemeyer, 1954. 175 pp.

Vorträge und Aufsätze (1936–53). Pfullingen: Neske, 1954. 284 pp.

Gelassenheit (1944–55). Pfullingen: Neske, 1959. 74 pp.

Zur Seinsfrage (1955). Frankfurt am Main: V. Klostermann, 1959. 44 pp.

Was ist das—die Philosophie? (1955). Pfullingen: Neske, 1956. 46 pp.

Der Satz vom Grund (1955–56). Pfullingen: Neske, 1957. 211 pp.

Identität und Differenz (1957). Pfullingen: Neske, 1957. 76 pp.

Hebel—der Hausfreund (1957). Pfullingen: Neske, 1957. 38 pp.

Unterwegs zur Sprache (1950–59). Pfullingen: Neske, 1959. 270 pp.

Kants These über das Sein (1962). Frankfurt a.M.: V. Klostermann, 1962. 36 pp.

II. ENGLISH TRANSLATIONS

Being and Time [*Sein und Zeit*]. JOHN MACQUARRIE and EDWARD ROBINSON, trans. With marginal pagination of the German edition, Glossary of German Expressions, and Index of English Expressions. London: SCM Press, 1962. 589 pp.

Essays in Metaphysics: Identity and Difference [*Identität und Differenz*]. KURT F. LEIDECKER, trans. New York: Philosophical Library, 1960.

"On the Essence of Truth" [*Vom Wesen der Wahrheit*]. R. F. C. HULL and ALAN CRICK, trans. In WERNER BROCK, *Existence and Being*, pp. 317–51.

Introduction to Metaphysics [*Einführung in die Metaphysik*].

RALPH MANHEIM, trans. New Haven: Yale University Press, 1959. 214 pp.

The Question of Being [Zur Seinsfrage]. WILLIAM KLUBECK and JEAN T. WILDE, trans. With German text *verso.* New York: Twayne, 1958. 109 pp.

"The Way Back into the Ground of Metaphysics" [Introduction to *Was ist Metaphysik?*]. WALTER KAUFMANN, trans. In WALTER KAUFMANN, *Existentialism from Dostoyevsky to Sartre,* pp. 206–21. New York: Meridian Books, 1957.

"What Is Metaphysics?" [Lecture and Postscript to *Was ist Metaphysik?*]. R. F. C. HULL and ALAN CRICK, trans. In WERNER BROCK, *Existence and Being,* pp. 355–92. London: Vision Press, 1949.

III. BOOKS ON HEIDEGGER

(I have indicated books which I would especially recommend with an asterisk. For a definitive bibliography of literature on Heidegger until 1955 see Herman Lübbe, "Bibliographie der Heidegger-Literatur 1917–55," *Zeitschrift für Philosophische Forschung,* XI (1957), 401–52.)

BARRETT, WILLIAM. *Irrational Man.* New York: Doubleday, 1958. Pp. 184–212.

*BIEMEL, WALTER. *Le concept de monde chez Heidegger.* Louvain: E. Nauwelaerts; Paris: J. Vrin, 1950. 184 pp.

BOLLNOW, OTTO F. *Existenzphilosophie.* Stuttgart: Kohlhammer, 1955. 137 pp.

BRECHT, F. J. *Bewusstsein und Existenz: Wesen und Weg der Phänomenologie.* Bremen, 1948. Pp. 114–60, *passim.*

BRÉHIER, E. *Histoire de la philosophie allemande.* Paris, 1954. Pp. 239–58, *passim.*

BROCK, WERNER. *Existence and Being.* London: Vision Press, 1949. 309 pp.

BUDDEBERG, ELSE (RIEMANN). *Denken und Dichten des Seins: Heidegger-Rilke.* Stuttgart: Motaler, 1956. 210 pp.

CORVES, MAURICE. *La philosophie de Heidegger.* Paris: Presses universitaires de France, 1961. 136 pp.

DELP, A. *Tragische Existenz: Zur Philosophie Martin Heideggers.* Freiburg i.Br., 1935.

FISCHER, ALOIS. *Die Existenzphilosophie Martin Heideggers.* Leipzig: F. Meiner, 1935. 134 pp.

FÜRSTENAU, PETER. *Heidegger, das Gefüge seines Denkens.* Frankfurt a.M.: V. Klostermann, 1958. 185 pp.

GABRIEL, LEO. *Existenzphilosophie von Kierkegaard bis Sartre.* Wien: Harold, 1951. Pp. 113–66.

GRENE, MARJORIE (GLICKSMANN). *Introduction to Existentialism.* Chicago: University of Chicago Press, 1959. 149 pp. (First published in 1948 under title: *Dreadful Freedom: A Critique of Existentialism.*)

———. *Martin Heidegger.* London: Bowes & Bowes, 1957. 128 pp.

HEINEMANN, F. H. *Existentialism and the Modern Predicament.* New York: Harper Torchbooks, 1958. Pp. 84–108.

HOBERG, CLEMENS A. *Das Dasein des Menschen, die Grundfrage der Heideggerschen Philosophie.* Zeulenrode: B. Sporn, 1937. 159 pp.

JOLIVET, R. *Le problème de la mort chez M. Heidegger et J.-P. Sartre.* Abbaye S. Wandrille, 1950.

KANTHACK, KATHARINA. *Das Denken Martin Heideggers, die Grosse Wende der Philosophie.* Berlin: W. de Gruyter, 1959. 94 pp.

KERÉNYI, K. *Geistiger Weg Europas: Fünf Vorträge über Freud, Jung, Heidegger, Thomas Mann, Hofmannsthal, Rilke, Homer und Hölderlin.* Zürich, 1955. *Passim.*

KING, MAGDA. *Heidegger's Philosophy: A Guide to His Basic Thought.* Oxford: B. Blackwell, 1964.

KNITTERMEYER, H. *Die Philosophie der Existenz.* Wien-Stuttgart, 1952. Pp. 207–322.

KOCKELMANS, JOSEPH J. *Martin Heidegger: A First Introduction to His Philosophy.* Pittsburgh: Duquesne University Press, 1965. 181 pp.

KROCKOW, CHRISTIAN. *Die Entscheidung: Eine Untersuchung über Ernst Jünger, Carl Schmitt, Martin Heidegger.* Stuttgart: F. Enke, 1958. 184 pp.

KUHN, H. *Encounter with Nothingness: An Essay on Existentialism.* Hinsdale (Ill.), 1949. *Passim.*

LANDGREBE, L. *Philosophie der Gegenwart.* Bonn, 1952. *Passim.*

LANGAN, THOMAS. *The Meaning of Heidegger: A Critical Study of an Existentialist Phenomenology.* London: Routledge & Kegan Paul, 1959. 247 pp.

LÖWITH, KARL. *Heidegger, Denker in dürftiger Zeit.* Frankfurt a.M.: Fischer, 1953. 110 pp.

LUKÁCS, G. *Die Zerstörung der Vernunft.* Berlin, 1954. Pp. 389–412.

MACQUARRIE, JOHN. *An Existentialist Theology: A Comparison* of Heidegger and Bultmann. London: SCM Press, 1955. 252 pp.

MARCIC, R. Martin Heidegger und die Existentialphilosophie. Bad Ischl, 1948.

*MARX, WERNER. Heidegger und die Tradition: Eine problemgeschichtliche Einführung in die Grundbestimmung des Seins. Stuttgart: W. Kohlhammer, 1961. 268 pp.

*MAY, ROLLO (ed.). Existence. [A symposium.] New York: Basic Books, 1958. 445 pp.

MEULEN, JAN VAN DEN. Hegel und Heidegger oder Widerstreit und Widerspruch. Meisenheim/Glan: A. Hain, 1953. 216 pp.

MULLER, MAX. Die Existenzphilosophie im Geistigen Leben der Gegenwart. Heidelberg: Kerle, 1949. 159 pp.

MULLER-LAUTER, WOLFGANG. Möglichkeit und Wirklichkeit bei Martin Heidegger. Berlin: De Gruyter, 1960. 107 pp.

NESKE, GÜNTHER. Martin Heidegger zum siebigsten Geburtstag; Festschrift. Pfullingen: Neske, 1959. 347 pp., illus.

OTT, H. Denken und Sein: Der Weg Martin Heideggers und der Weg der Theologie. Zollikon, 1959.

PFEIFFER, J. Existenzphilosophie: Eine Einführung in Heidegger und Jaspers. Leipzig: F. Meiner, 1933. 64 pp.

*PÖGGELER, OTTO. Der Denkweg Martin Heideggers. Pfullingen: Neske, 1963. 318 pp.

RICHARDSON, WILLIAM. Heidegger: Through Phenomenology to Thought. Preface by MARTIN HEIDEGGER. The Hague: M. Nijhoff, 1963. 764 pp.

ROBINSON, JAMES MCCONKEY. The Later Heidegger and Theology. Ed. JAMES M. ROBINSON and JOHN B. COBB, JR. New York: Harper & Row, 1963. 212 pp.

SCHÖFER, ERASMUS. Die Sprache Heideggers. Pfullingen: Neske, 1962.

SEIDEL, GEORGE J. Martin Heidegger and the Pre-Socratics: An Introduction to His Thought. Lincoln: University of Nebraska Press, 1964. 169 pp.

SPIEGELBERG, HERBERT. The Phenomenological Movement: A Historical Introduction. 2 vols. The Hague: Nijhoff, 1960.

SYMPOSIUM. Martin Heideggers Einfluss auf die Wissenschaften. Bern: Francke, 1949. 174 pp.

USSHER, ARLAND. Journey through Dread. [A study of Kierkegaard, Heidegger, and Sartre.] New York: Devin-Adair, 1955. 160 pp.

*VERSÉNYI, LASLO. Heidegger, Being and Truth. New Haven: Yale University Press, 1965. 201 pp.

VYCINAS, VINCENT. *Earth and Gods: An Introduction to the Philosophy of Martin Heidegger.* The Hague: Nijhoff, 1961. 326 pp.

*WAELHENS, ALPHONSE MARIE ADOLPHE DE. *La Philosophie de Martin Heidegger.* Louvain: Publications universitaires, 1942. 379 pp.

———. *Phénoménologie et vérité, essai sur l'évolution de l'idee de vérité chez Husserl et Heidegger.* Paris: Presses universitaires de France, 1953. 167 pp. See esp. pp. 63–166.

———. *Chemins et impasses de l'ontologie Heideggerienne, à propos des Holzwege.* Louvain: E. Nauwelaerts; Paris: Desclee de Brouwer, 1953. 52 pp.

———. *Existence et signification.* Louvain: E. Nauwelaerts; Paris: Beatrice-Nauwelaerts, 1958. 289 pp.

———, and BIEMEL, WALTER. *De l'essence de la vérité.* [French translation of *Vom Wesen der Wahrheit.*] Louvain: E. Nauwelaerts; Paris: J. Vrin, 1948. 106 pp. See Introduction, pp. 7–64.

WAHL, J. *L'idée d'être chez Heidegger.* Paris, 1951.

———. *La Philosophie de Heidegger.* Paris, 1952.

WYSCHOGROD, M. *Kierkegaard and Heidegger: The Ontology of Existence.* London, 1954.

IV. ARTICLES ON HEIDEGGER

ALLERS, RUDOLPH. "Heidegger on the Principle of Sufficient Reason," *Philosophy and Phenomenological Research,* XX (1959–60), 365–73.

ANONYMOUS. "Being, World and Understanding," *Review of Metaphysics,* V (1951–52), 157–72.

AZAVEDO, JUAN LLAMBIAS DE. "Der Alte und der Neue Heidegger," *Philosophisches Jahrbuch,* LX (1950), 161–74.

BARTH, T. "Identität und Differenz: Eine Begegnung mit M. Heidegger," *Wissenschaft und Weisheit,* XXII (1959), 81–92.

BIEMEL, W. "Heideggers Begriff des Daseins," *Studia Catholica,* XXIV (1949), 113–28.

BOER, WOLFGANG DE. "Heideggers Missverständnis der Metaphysik," *Zeitschrift für philosophische Forschung,* IX (1955), 500–545.

BOLLNOW, O. F. "Heideggers neue Kehre," *Zeitschrift für Religions- und Geistesgeschichte,* II (1949), 113–28.

CASSIRER, ERNST. "Kant und das Problem der Metaphysik:

Bemerkungen zu Heideggers Kant-Interpretation," *Kant-Studien*, XXXVI (1931), 1–26.

CERF, WALTER F. "An Approach to Heidegger's Ontology," *Philosophy and Phenomenological Research*, I (1940–41), 177–90.

DELFGAAUW, BERNARD. "La phénoménologie chez Martin Heidegger," *Les études philosophiques*, IX (1954), 50–56.

DONDYNE, ALBERT. "La différence ontologique chez M. Heidegger," *Revue philosophique de Louvain*, LVI (1958), 35–62, 251–93.

DUFRENNE, MIKEL. "La mentalité primitive et Heidegger," *Les études philosophiques*, IX (1954), 284–306.

———. "Heidegger et Kant," *Revue de métaphysique et de morale*, LIV (1949), 1–28.

FARBER, MARTIN. "Heidegger on the Essence of Truth," *Philosophy and Phenomenological Research*, XVIII (1958), 523–32.

GLICKSMANN, M. "A Note on the Philosophy of Heidegger," *Journal of Philosophy*, XXXV (1938), 93–104.

GRAY, J. GLENN. "Heidegger 'Evaluates' Nietzsche," *Journal of the History of Ideas*, XIV (1953), 304–9.

———. "The Idea of Death in Existentialism," *Journal of Philosophy*, XLVIII (1951), 113–27, *passim*.

HYPPOLITE, JEAN. "Ontologie et phénoménologie chez Martin Heidegger," *Les études philosophiques*, IX (1954), 307–14.

KRAFT, JULIUS. "The Philosophy of Existence, Its Structure and Significance," *Philosophy and Phenomenological Research*, I (1940–41), 339–65.

KRÜGER, GERHARDT. "Martin Heidegger und der Humanismus," *Studia philosophica*, IX (1949), 93–129.

LEVY, H. "Heideggers Kant-Interpretation," *Logos*, XXI (1932), 1–43.

LOTZ, J. "Denken und Sein nach den jüngsten Veröffentlichungen von M. Heidegger," *Scholastik*, XXXIII (1958), 81–97.

LÖWITH, KARL. "Heidegger: Problem and Background of Existentialism," *Social Research*, XV (1948), 345–69.

MARX, W. "Heidegger's New Conception of Philosophy: The Second Phase of 'Existentialism,'" *Social Research*, XXII (1955), 451–74.

MEINERTZ, JOSEPH. "Das Sein und das Nichts," *Zeitschrift für Philosophische Forschung*, IX (1955), 32–55, 461–89.

NINK, C. "Grundbegriffe der Philosophie Heideggers," *Philosophisches Jahrbuch*, XLV (1932), 129–58.

RICHEY, CLARENCE W. "On the Intentional Ambiguity of Heidegger's Metaphysics," *Journal of Philosophy*, LX (1958), 1144–48.

RYFFEL, HANS. "Zu den neuen Veröffentlichungen von Martin Heidegger" [viz., *EM, WD*], *Studia Philosophica*, IX (1949), 93–129.

SCHAEFFLER, RICHARD. "Martin Heidegger und die Frage nach der Technik," *Zeitschrift für Philosophische Forschung*, IX (1955), 116–28.

SCHILLING, K. "Heideggers Interpretation der Philosophiegeschichte: Bemerkungen anlässlich des Erscheinens der 'Einführung in die Metaphysik,'" *Archive für Rechts- und Sozialphilosophie*, XLI (1955), 399–421.

SCHRADER, GEORGE A. "Heidegger's Ontology of Human Existence," *Review of Metaphysics*, X (1956–57), 35–56.

SCHRAG, CALVIN O. "Phenomenology, Ontology and History in the Philosophy of Martin Heidegger," *Revue internationale de philosophie*, XII (1958), 117–32.

SEYPPEL, J. H. "A Comparative Study of Truth in Existentialism and Pragmatism," *Journal of Philosophy*, L (1953), 229–41, esp. 232–36.

STRASSNER, S. "The Concept of Dread in the Philosophy of Heidegger," *Modern Schoolman*, XXXV (1957–58), 1–20.

STURM, F. G. "Authenticity and Other Persons," *Christian Century*, LXXX (1963), 340–42.

THÉVÉNAZ, P. "Qu'est-ce que la phénoménologie? II. La phénoménologie de Heidegger," *Revue de théologie et de philosophie*, II (1952), 126–40.

THYSSEN, J. "A priori, Unbewusstes und Heideggers Weltbegriff," *Archiv für Philosophie*, III (1949), 115–43.

TRIVERS, H. "Heidegger's Misinterpretation of Hegel's Views on Spirit and Time," *Philosophy and Phenomenological Research*, III (1942–43), 162–68.

TURNBULL, R. G. "Heidegger on the Nature of Truth," *Journal of Philosophy*, LIV (1957), 559–65.

VIETTA, E. "Being, World and Understanding," *Review of Metaphysics*, V (1951–52), 157–72.

WAEHLENS, A. DE. "Heidegger et le problème de la métaphysique," *Revue philosophique de Louvain*, LII (1954), 110–99.

WAHL, JEAN. "L'Introduction à la métaphysique de Martin Heidegger," *Revue de métaphysique et de morale*, LXI (1956), 113–30.

WERKMEISTER, W. H. "An Introduction to Heidegger's

'Existential-Philosophy,' " *Philosophy and Phenomenological Research*, II (1941), 78–87.

WIENPAHL, PAUL D. "Philosophy and Nothing," *Chicago Review*, XIII (1959), 59–74.

V. OTHER WORKS CITED IN FOOTNOTES

BUBER, MARTIN. *Schriften zur Philosophie* in *Werke*. Munich: Kosel-Verlag, 1962. 3 vols.

FINDLAY, JOHN N. *Hegel: A Re-examination*. London: George Allen & Unwin, 1958.

FISCHER, KUNO. *Hegels Leben, Werke, und Lehre*. Heidelberg: C. Winter, 1901. 2 vols.

HARTMANN, EDUARD VON. *Über die dialektische Methode*. Bad Sachsa: H. Haache, 1910.

HYPPOLITE, JEAN. *Genèse et structure de la phénoménologie de l'esprit de Hegel*. Paris: Aubier, Editions Montaigne, 1946. 2 vols.

McTAGGART, JOHN McT. E. *Studies in Hegelian Dialectic*. Cambridge: Cambridge University Press, 1922.

PIEPER, JOSEF. *Was heisst Philosophieren?* Munich: Kösel-Verlag, 1949.

Index

185; of meaning, 172 ff.; total, 175 ff.

Contradiction, 50, 127, 133–34, 181. *See also* Law

Control, 200, 205, 212

Correspondence, doctrine of, 3–27, 90, 93, 114, 123–24, 134, 181; and coherence, 189; and freedom, 98; and mood, 80, 119; source of, 152; and truth of knowledge, 142–43

Crisis in thinking, 8–9, 65–66, 133, 140, 145–46; as moment of truth, 83

Dasein ("being there"), 28–29, 62–72, 97; as being-in-the-world, 30–33; emergence of, 133; and freedom, 98–99, 102; ontological characteristics of, 122; and truth, 25, 95–102, 125

Death, 56; and anxiety, 58; birth and, 190; and destruction, 174

Decadence (*Verfallensein*), 75, 81, 85, 87, 91, 154; existential derivation of, 84, 88; in science, 162

Deception, 104, 131, 144

Decision, 66, 78, 139; and context, 26; and intelligibility, 132; and project, 64, 83; and thrownness (*Geworfenheit*), 78. *See also* Judgment

Democritus, 181

Descartes, 4, 18, 54, 74, 105, 109, 123, 137, 181, 205

Despair, 139–40, 184, 187–88; and doubt, 177

Destruction, 138–39, 184

Dialectic: Hegelian, 8, 187; Platonic, 8

Discovery, activity of: and knowledge, 28, 34; and openness, 29, 96; and truth, 17–18, 24–25

Distraction, and immediate experience, 43

Earth (*Erde*). *See* World

Ego, 32; reflection of, 179

Einstein, Albert, 202

Eliot, T. S., 80

Encounter, 93–94

Environment (*Umwelt*). *See* World

Existence, 32–33, 76, 81; authentic (*eigentlich*), 87, 89, 133, 143; inauthentic (*uneigentlich*), 87, 89–90, 100, 144–46; truth grounded in, 122

Existentiality, 75

Experience: cycle of, 146, 148; immediate, 7–8, 74, 81 ff., 147, 176; as process, 174 ff.

Facticity, 65, 75, 78, 80, 101, 115

Familiarity, 66, 77, 174

Faulkner, William, 48

Fear (*Furcht*), 54–55

Fichte, 172–73

Findlay, John, 182

Finitude, 107, 121, 126; and transcendence, 154–68, 213

Fischer, Kuno, 182

Flattening (*Einebnung*), 85

Form, 86, 90. *See also* Matter

Freedom, 93, 99–102, 147–48; and truth, 98. *See also* Obligation

Freud, Sigmund, and illusion, 14, 26, 112, 131, 135, 140

Fürstenau, Peter, 137

God, 76, 123, 161, 190

Hartmann, Eduard von, 183

Hegel, 8–9, 13, 25, 68, 131, 134, 138–39; and conflict in Western philosophical tradition, 168–69; and presuppositions of experience, 21–24

Hiddenness, 90, 108, 110, 126–27

History: and conflict, 141–213; continuity of Western, 102; human, 113–15; and illusion, 135–36, 209; inauthentic, 144–45; and knowledge, 127; and mood, 121; and openness, 132; source of, 130–31; and truth, 131 ff.

Hobbes, 59, 86

Homelessness (*Unheimlichkeit*), 84

Hume, 61, 85, 144

Husserl, 61

Hyppolite, Jean, 211

Idealism, 59

Illusion (*Irren*), 25–26, 90, 104–6, 111–12, 134–35, 180–82, 184; of tradition, 139–40; as untruth, 129 ff. *See also* Freud

Imagination, 155–68

Inauthenticity. *See* Existence, History

Insistence (*insistieren*), 109, 119

Instrument, 36 ff., 84, 133, 143, 147; being as, 187–89, 212; broken, 44 ff., 83, 149